T0313714

THE CYBERNETIC BORDER

THE CYBERNETIC BORDER

DRONES, TECHNOLOGY, AND INTRUSION

Iván Chaar López

Duke University Press *Durham and London* 2024

Printed and bound by CPI Group (UK) Ltd, Croydon, CR0 4YY
Project Editor: Melody Negron
Typeset in Minion Pro by Westchester Publishing Services

Library of Congress Cataloging-in-Publication Data
Names: Chaar López, Iván, [date] author.
Title: The cybernetic border : drones, technology, and intrusion /
Iván Chaar López.
Description: Durham : Duke University Press, 2024. | Includes
bibliographical references and index.
Identifiers: LCCN 2023027205 (print)
LCCN 2023027206 (ebook)
ISBN 9781478030034 (paperback)
ISBN 9781478024859 (hardcover)
ISBN 9781478059035 (ebook)
Subjects: LCSH: Immigration enforcement—Technological innova-
tions—United States—History. | Border security—Technological
innovations—United States. | Cyberinfrastructure—United States.
| Electronic surveillance—United States. | Borderlands—United
States—History. | United States—Emigration and immigration. |
United States—Boundaries. | BISAC: HISTORY / United States /
20th Century | SOCIAL SCIENCE / Technology Studies
Classification: LCC JV6483 .L717 2024 (print) | LCC JV6483 (ebook) |
DDC 325.73—dc23/eng/20230927
LC record available at https://lccn.loc.gov/2023027205
LC ebook record available at https://lccn.loc.gov/2023027206

Cover art: Images from "Best of Luck with the Wall" (Josh Begley,
2016). Courtesy of the artist and Field of Vision.

For Francheska

Contents

Contents

Acknowledgments

Books are strange artifacts. Often subscribed by a single individual, books are received as if the product of a lone actor: a subject who stands apart from yet in relation to the text. Their words stand as little more than ink stains on a page but are received as traces of an imaginary authorial voice. The author is conceived *as if* operating in isolation even when they are inevitably entangled with webs of relations, ideas, and practices. Books are among their many creations; they are mirages cast over these webs. The following pages are my attempt to undo the blurred contours of this mirage by recognizing those who have made this book a reality.

Across the ten years since I began work on this project, many people shared ideas, provided intellectual support, offered words of guidance, and granted solace and care. I would not have been able to start, continue, and finish without them. And even though I am responsible for the ideas put forth here, I would be remiss if I did not recognize their contributions. Friends, colleagues, family, and acquaintances gave their time, minds, and hearts so that you hold this book in your hands or have it flash across your screen.

The Cybernetic Border saw its first light in work that I undertook in American Culture at the University of Michigan, under the guidance of Lisa Nakamura and Alex Stern. Lisa's creativity and expansive knowledge about digital media theory and history informed how I came to understand racial formation and technology. More fundamentally, she was always a model of generous and bold scholarship. Alex joined the project without hesitation as I began putting together my initial proposal. Her thinking about nation making, borders, race, and infrastructures was critical in my intellectual formation. Both Lisa and Alex managed the insurmountable challenge of reining in my curiosity without stifling it. Their attentive and demanding feedback challenged me to tighten my ideas and justify my analytical maneuvers. This book is a humble homage to their teaching.

John Cheney-Lippold was a constant mentor and companion. He always pushed me to think about the politics of code and systems and how cultural practices embodied computational routines. Paul Edwards's ideas about cybernetics, computing, discourse, and the Cold War accompanied me as well. He challenged me to carefully trace the construction of categories and to account for the relation between subjectivity and political systems. Others at the University of Michigan—Amy Sara Carroll, William Calvo-Quirós, Maria Cotera, Jesse Hoffnung-Garskof, Larry LaFountain-Stokes, Matthew Lassiter, and Anthony Mora—contributed to my thinking about art, borders, cultural history, and governmentality. And I made it through the end of my program relatively unscathed thanks to the steadfast caring and resourceful support of Marlene Moore, our department's graduate administrator.

My time at the Universidad de Puerto Rico, Río Piedras, obtaining my undergraduate and master's degrees in history was essential in my intellectual development. Mayra Rosario Urrutia's teachings on transgressions, power, crime, and media as well as Manuel Rodríguez's discussions on war, the social construction of soldiers, and nation making were formative in my thinking. Carlos Pabón's work on the writing of history and the fictions upon which nations are made created new pathways for me to understand the discipline, especially because these fictions have material repercussions. María del Carmen Baerga taught me to critically examine the making of archives and to interrogate the stories archives made possible. I will forever be indebted to them.

Many people contributed to the stages of developing this book. As a postdoctoral fellow in the Department of Science and Technology Studies and the Latina/o Studies Program (LSP) at Cornell University, I benefited from participating in weekly SSRG meetings. I learned much from conversations with Luisa Cortesi, Stephen Hilgartner, Steven Jackson, Ronald Kline, Christine Leuenberger, Bruce Lewenstein, Michael Lynch, Owen Marshall, Kim Overby, Trevor Pinch, Alison Power, Rachel Prentice, Sara Pritchard, Jessica Ratcliff, Juddith Reppy, Margaret Rossiter, Phoebe Sengers, Suman Seth, Rebecca Slayton, and Malte Ziewitz. My colleagues within American studies (AMS) and beyond at the University of Texas at Austin have been a permanent source of optimism and inspiration: Amelia Acker, CJ Alvarez, Jossianna Arroyo, Alex Beasley, Simone Browne, Iokepa Casumbal-Salazar, Karma Chávez, Lina Chhun, Tanya Clement, Cary Cordova, Maria Cotera, Janet Davis, Celina Davidson de Sá, Yoav Di-Capua, Edgar Gómez Cruz, Lauren Gutterman, Chantal Hailey, Steven Hoelscher, Joe Izaguirre, Randolph Lewis, Stephen Marshall, Erin McElroy, Jeffrey Meikle,

Julia Mickenberg, Karla Peña, Samantha Pinto, Megan Raby, Carlos Ramos Sharron, Cherise Smith, Shirley Thompson, and everyone in the Critical Digital Studies Group and the initiative on Gender, Race, Indigeneity, Disability, and Sexuality.

Many of the ideas in this book benefited from critical feedback through conference papers, talks, workshops, and other venues. To all their participants, my deepest gratitude, although especially I wish to thank Richard Rottenburg and the African Technoscapes Cluster at the Wits Institute for Social and Economic Research at University of the Witwatersrand; Michelle Moyd and Vanessa Cruz at the Center for Research on Race and Ethnicity in Society at Indiana University; Sydney Skybetter at the Conference for Research on Choreographic Interfaces at Brown University; and Judith Reppy and the Institute for Peace and Conflict Studies at Cornell. Suman Seth read a version of the manuscript and, early on, championed the notion that the book was about information regimes instead of drones. Megan Raby read an early version of the revised introduction to the book and helped me think about audience and the politics of classifications. Trevor Pinch and Stephen Hilgartner helped me come up with the title of the book as they got me to think more about epistemological regimes. Sara Pritchard was always a voice of encouragement for the project and its potential as well as a dynamic interlocutor around the politics of infrastructures. CJ Alvarez's insightful and reflexive commentary on border environments and infrastructures was a source of motivation. Ricardo Dominguez's tactical media and conceptual work deeply informed my thinking about computing, politics, and life within the machine. Alex Rivera's audiovisual work inspired me to write about and document practices of refusal and speculation in the borderlands. My distributed web of interlocutors around questions of critical ethnic studies and science and technology studies (STS) included Cassius Adair, Michael Aguirre, Héctor Beltrán, Casidy Campbell, Kate Chandler, Sony Corañez-Bolton, Edgar Gómez-Cruz, Meryem Kamil, Jenny Kelly, Marisol LeBron, Kyle Lindsey, Silvia Lindtner, Cindy Lin, Erin McElroy, Megan Rim, Cengiz Salman, Hanah Stiverson, and Kalindi Vora. I'll never tire of thanking Lucy Suchman for her insightful, challenging, and smart review of my work. Courtney Berger at Duke University Press was not only a strong advocate for this book, but she was also a sharp reader, questioning some of my writing decisions and calling me to refine my ideas further. I cannot ask for a better editor. Cathy Hannabach and Emma Warnken Johnson at Ideas on Fire worked with me in revising the overall structure of the manuscript.

Deborah Castillo, our fearless leader in LSP, was among the strongest sources of support and care in Cornell. I learned so much from her and my colleagues in LSP (Mary Pat Brady, Maria Cristina Garcia, Sergio Garcia Rios, Shannon Gleeson, Héctor Vélez Guadalupe, Sofia Villenas) about how conducting research is better done building community and solidarity. Marti Dense helped me make the transition to life as a postdoc in LSP, and Stephanie Kaufman supported me when I joined AMS as an assistant professor in the early days of the COVID-19 pandemic. They always found answers to the most difficult questions. Their vital assistance made possible the creation of my research collective, the Border Tech Lab (BTL), at Cornell and the University of Texas at Austin (UT). BTL alumni and current members at Cornell and UT (Odalis Garcia Gorra, Alexandra Gutiérrez, Emma Li, Isaiah Murray, Anahí Ponce, Victoria Sánchez, Carolina Vela) got me to think carefully about my abstract divagations and to elaborate them into clear and manageable concepts. Our weekly meetings were always a source of comfort and intellectual excitement for me.

From 2015 to 2018, I also received diverse material support from the Rackham Merit Fellowship, the Rackham Graduate School, the Department of American Culture, and Lisa Nakamura. The Digital Studies Fellowship from the John W. Kluge Center at the Library of Congress gave me the opportunity to conduct research at the library and in Washington, DC. Work on the book was further supported by a Mellon Postdoctoral Diversity Fellowship from Cornell and a summer research award from the College of Liberal Arts at UT. Archivists and librarians at the Library of Congress, US Citizenship and Immigration Services History Library, the San Diego Air and Space Museum, and the Seattle Public Library were instrumental to this project. They shared their extensive knowledge of the research collections that I examined, and they proposed unexpected avenues of inquiry. At the University of Michigan Library, I benefited from conversations with Catherine Morse and Alexa Pearce, who identified primary source sites to explore for the project.

We make lifeworlds with many people over the years, those with whom we build relations of reciprocity and care and of camaraderie and comfort. Without them, we are but transient figures. I wish to acknowledge the familial companionship of Abuelo, los Alers, Amanda, Amy, Charlie y Carmen, Enrique, Gabi, Grace, Ian Carlo, Issack, Jared, Jaydee, Jayren, Kianna, Kiko, Mariana, Mickey, Maiki, mi Vieja, mi Viejo y Yolanda, Padrino y Carmen, Rafi, Raúl, Shiara, Tati, tío David, titi Ivette, titi Ixa, titi Khalila, titi Rosita y Juan, titi Silvia, titi Violeta, and Yiyi. There are those who once accompanied me but have now joined my ancestors: I thank Aba, Abo, Beba, Madrina, Mami Otra, and titi Enid. The complicity and insider jokes of Andrés, Brenda, David, Frania, Gabe, Genevieve, Pablo, Sarita, Tara, Verónica, and Viviana. The Itharican crew: Christian, Enrique y Pamela, Eva, Karel y Koen, Fernando, Frances, Héctor y Josie, JJ, and Julia. Our Austinite oasis amid dread: Edgar, Leila, Bryce, and Lindsay. The spontaneous parties with Antonio, Carlos, Danny, Jossianna, KeKe, Mónica, Odalis, Piero, and Wilfredo. Game nights with Joe and Liz, and my comedic routines with Ella and Rebecca. Travel, wine, and foodie adventures with Carola, Joan, and Josep. Itinerant encounters at restaurants, farmers markets, and home with Erin, Candace, and Lily "The Slayer of Chickens, First of Her Name." Happy hours and food with Jordan and Sharon. Fútbol (un)winding with the BarçaWave *corillo*, the FC Barcelona Penya Austin, and the folks at Fuller Park (Ann Arbor, Michigan), Cass Park (Ithaca, New York), and Mueller and Zilker Parks (Austin, Texas).

My partner and lifelong accomplice, Francheska, heard and read every iteration of this book, from mere conjecture all the way to manuscript. And throughout all of it, she always approached the project with fresh eyes and a generative spirit. Her keen interpretation of the book's ideas challenged me to render them coherent and relevant. Her love, cheers, and passion motivated me to get this book over the line. I am eternally grateful for her.

INTRODUCTION

Toward a Theory of the Border Technopolitical Regime

Longtime computer and tech enthusiast Steven Levy was impressed when a Samsung virtual reality headset immersed him in a digital world that simulated the exact view he enjoyed in real life. The headset was part of a surveillance system called Lattice, an artificial intelligence, sensor fusion platform with networked sensor towers and small unmanned aerial systems collecting, processing, and communicating data. The Texas desert valley appeared in virtual form, transcoded into data processed by the platform. Three dark gray rectangles called attention to a "Person 88%," another "Person 93%," and a "Car 91%" (see figure I.1).[1] The real-life "exact view" was enhanced, reconfigured by statistical processes assessing the humanity of entities in the desert landscape. Information processing parsed out the barrage of environmental data, separating human from nonhuman and making the human a target for potential removal from US territory. The demonstration set up by Anduril Industries was meant to highlight how the solution to the perennial problem of border control came down to data and information technologies. A haunting threat in the borderlands continued to be addressed through new infrastructural foundations that never quite stop the danger or deliver on their promise. Trust in technological solutions persists as an unsatiated fantasy in the will to power.

The matter of "the border" is as much a technological question as it is a cultural one. Stories give shape to the kinds of material arrangements

FIGURE I.1. Lattice system identifies people, vehicles, animals, and other nonhuman phenomena. Source: Anduril Industries.

through which borders are made, just as material arrangements embody and pursue political objectives and make possible the performance of distinct stories. Anduril Industries takes its name from Aragorn's enchanted blade in the fantasy novel series *The Lord of the Rings*. Anduril is a sword that defends the world from darkness, from the evil forces of Lord Sauron, from orcs and trolls—recurrent literary tropes of a racial worldview. Technologies developed by Anduril are meant to protect "the world of men"—a world where humanity is narrowly coded through the alabaster imagination of J. R. R. Tolkien.[2] According to CEO Brian Schimpf, Anduril Industries developed the Lattice system to be a "smart wall" to "get information in the hands of [US Border Patrol] agents."[3] Even though borders as walls and fences take precedence in most debates, Border Patrol officials and their corporate allies know they are not the end-all-be-all of border enforcement. They believe that agents need "situational awareness," understanding borderland conditions in time and place to better respond to them. Just like Anduril, the "Flame of the West," stood between "the world of men" and the racialized dangers from the East, the networked platform also produces geopolitical borders. And it does so through data. It is an information regime drawing boundaries around bodies classified as threats to the US nation and making possible practices of immobilization like apprehension, incarceration, and deportation in the name of security.

Anduril Industries' attempt to deploy information technology to "fix" the problem of control of the border is but the latest attempt to update an infrastructure that has been in operation for almost half a century. Smart walls, virtual walls, and smart fences are emblematic of what I call the "cybernetic border": a regime centered on data capture, processing, and circulation in the production and control of the boundaries of the nation. In the 1970s, the Border Patrol installed an electronic fence that combined ground sensors, computers, and radio communications. And just like Lattice, statistical analysis processed sensor data to determine the nature of its trigger. Known as an intruder detection system, the electronic fence labeled "unauthorized border crossers" as "intruders" and menaces to the nation. Apprehending and removing intruders were some of the political objectives coded into the electronic fence.[4] Anduril's Lattice system, on the other hand, avoids judging its target by recognizing it as a "Person," even if their full humanity is reduced to a statistical probability.[5]

The Cybernetic Border offers a sustained examination of unmanned aerial systems (UAS), ground sensors, and other information technologies deployed in border enforcement during the second half of the twentieth century. These artifacts, like walls and fences, not only help maintain the demarcation of national boundaries, but they also create them through their relation to operations. Information technologies are operational because they play key roles in organizing on-the-ground efforts by actors. They allow border enforcement operations to be multisited, concerted, dynamic, and interconnected.[6] Operational technologies speak to the "datafication" of border enforcement. Inasmuch as they funnel unauthorized border crossers into more remote desert landscapes monitored by the information infrastructure of the Department of Homeland Security (DHS), walls and fences can be said to be a part of the cybernetic border. But border barriers have their own distinct histories and complexities—as both material and symbolic artifacts.[7] By investigating operational technologies, this book interrogates the epistemological and procedural relations of the cybernetic border and their investments in information.[8] The cybernetic border is made through and makes possible relations between information and racial formation; information is fundamentally a boundary-making enterprise without which geopolitical borders could not exist. By opening the cybernetic black box, the book shows the border politics of the empire-nation, of industry, and of the academy.

One of the entry points to the operations of the cybernetic border is the category of "the intruder"—the target of Lattice and its antecedent the "electronic fence." The intruder embodies military logics and is used by actors in government, the press, and the technical community. Intruders are irrevocably entangled with "enemies." They are surreptitious, interceding subjects that cross the boundaries of self-determination and undermine the capacity of an Other to exercise their sovereignty. The intruder hails a defensive subject, a figure struggling to preserve and maintain their existence. It is this struggle that philosopher Achille Mbembe finds at the heart of what he calls "the society of enmity." For Mbembe, contemporary life is characterized by the ceaseless pursuit of forms of exclusion and hostility and by a fight against an enemy. This ceaseless pursuit is built on a drive, an energy, a desire directed toward one or several objects. "Since in reality this object has never existed—does not and will never exist—desire must continually invent it."[9] Enmity is traversed by the principle of race, creating distinctions attached to a body and a group of bodies. It solidifies human difference as oppositional relations that stigmatize, exclude, eliminate, or physically destroy a human group.[10] This movement to invent enemies is at its core a mode of assembling relationships within imperial formations. These are relationships that can be described by following the robust materialities that underpin them.

Both the Lattice system and the electronic fence are part of a long history of technological fixes that don't quite deliver on their promise to control the border. But they do succeed in recording unauthorized border crossers as threats to the nation. They are effective in embedding these populations as targets of systems designed to apprehend and remove them—systems that prescribe their exclusion on the basis that they are transgressors of order and dangers to the rule of law. They are enemies to be eliminated. And just like the enchanted sword's namesake, Anduril works to protect "the world of men."

The use of sensors, computers, and drones for border enforcement reveals how US government officials, Border Patrol agents, and technicians rely on data as keys to rein in the persistent problem of governing the border—which is to say, to exert control over the mobility of racialized populations. This book asks: What kind of political project animates infrastructures of information? And conversely, how do informational infrastructures shape political projects? Against whom is this project leveraged? Who or what is protected when informational logics of differentiation are entangled with imperial practices of exception?

The Cybernetic Border tracks two main and interrelated processes. The first deals with how border enforcement in the United States, itself a central practice in the making of the nation, relies on identifying a threat against which a range of techniques and devices must be leveraged. I show how US government officials, politicians, technicians, and the technologies they create have targeted ethnic Mexicans, both as individual subjects and as a category, since the mid-twentieth century by treating them as intruders and enemies. As the end of the Cold War slowly metamorphosed into the War on Terror, ethnic Mexicans were joined by new targets from the homogenized spaces of Latin America and the Muslim world. The making of the US nation requires the production and targeting of a racialized enemy against whom to construct the imagined community. This has led to the creation, maintenance, and proliferation of complex infrastructures around those deemed to constitute an existential threat to the nation.

Second, I show how the construction of a "cybernetic border" became central to US immigration and border enforcement since the mid-twentieth century. US government officials and technicians reimagined and reorganized border and immigration enforcement through the language and techniques of the science of cybernetics, which privileged the role of information in the existence of complex systems. These actors made data control and communication integral to surveilling the national border. Border Patrol agents have used devices like ground seismic sensors, computers, cathode-ray tubes, and drones to transform unauthorized and surreptitious border crossings into sensible data. These data shape the behaviors of agents by organizing their day-to-day operations; they inform where, when, and how agents will intervene. Data-centered entities then produce the nation as a bounded, territorial space, and they demarcate the nation's boundaries by policing bodies prescribed for exclusion.

In tracing out these two processes, this book tells the history of how ideas about communication and control shape the practices of and build out border enforcement and settler colonial structures of feeling informed by the US frontier and its racial politics. The first three chapters of the book grapple with how people in government, the military, and defense employed technologies to institute a semblance of control on and over the borderlands. These chapters track historical associations between actors, ideas, and technologies across corporate and government records, promotional documents and films, technical reports, news reporting, and surveillance footage. The range of materials assembled to constitute the border and its populations and to subject them to control highlights a technoaesthetic dimension to the cybernetic border. The fourth chapter is devoted to studying how activists and artists have sought to challenge these efforts to arrange and order human sensory experience of the border. By expressing their dissent through aesthetic projects, they create an opening to reimagine the US-Mexico borderlands with and against the racial politics of national boundaries.

Borders as Technoscientific Struggles

The territory of the US-Mexico border is not a fixed area with neatly defined boundaries; rather, it is a never-ending process, made and remade, shaped and shaping the history of US empire. *The Cybernetic Border* builds on a robust, interdisciplinary scholarship studying the southern geopolitical boundary to argue that the border needs to be understood as both a site of struggle and a sociotechnical assemblage. The border is a space as well as an amalgam of artifacts; it is a field of networked materialities constituted by relations, devices, institutions, humans, practices, ideas, flora, fauna, and topographies mediating flows, blockages, and encounters. Approaching the border in this manner creates room to theorize the relation between borders, technology, and imperial formations. Since the nineteenth century, US empire has wrestled with the frictions inherent in its practices of inclusion and exclusion. Imperial desire to establish and patrol territorial and identity boundaries was tested through expansion and the differential treatments of racialized populations.[11] Perhaps no other discourse encapsulates these frictions so poignantly than Manifest Destiny, a kind of preordained justification for continental expansion. "Americans," border historian Rachel St. John holds, "embraced the notion that their national boundaries would continue to expand to incorporate ever more land and people under the umbrella of republican government."[12] Manifest Destiny expressed a political, civilizational drive to bring lands and people, especially those in the US Southwest, into the fold of the US government. Science and technology offered US actors the ideas, tools, and methods through which borders could be expanded, constructed, and policed. Yet this assemblage also highlights the tenuous and unstable existence of "the border." There is no evident boundary to which actors can point to; instead, the border beckons iterative actions, operations, knowledges, and instruments to produce it. Technoscience is integral to the making and enforcement of borders as much as to governing who can be included and excluded from the nation.

The Cybernetic Border studies the moments when US government officials imagine data, interpreted through the framework provided by cybernetics and information theory, as the technoscientific production of the nation's boundaries on people's bodies and on land. Border Patrol agents—armed with seismic sensors, computers, and radio communications—record the surreptitious entry of unauthorized border crossers. Operational technologies transform border crossers into knowable entities, data subjects to be apprehended and processed by the border regime. They also make land into territory, as technologies actualize sovereign claims over the southern landscape. A focus on data goes beyond visual control. Data, a legacy of "the avalanche of printed numbers," are the things to be collected and circulated to make sense of the world just as much as to govern it. Actors throughout the twentieth century practiced border and immigration enforcement by using psychology, blood quanta, and other biometrics that sought to determine and fix essentialized racial characteristics of subjects—and, by extension, their admissibility to the nation.[13] The visual field was but one field among various sensory systems and modes of knowing, of "objectively" bringing the Other under the command and control of the knowing subject.[14] Since the 1970s, government and nongovernmental actors restructured the production of the border through the design and use of information technologies. Immigration officials back then spoke of the need for computing and automated technologies to govern a "flood of immigrants" and help the immigration system avoid from "'drowning' in paper."[15] Migrants as data-producing subjects and as subjects of data, respectively, could only be controlled by an information technoscientific regime. This ongoing regime organizes and materializes border enforcement through routines and feedback loops; it is an abstract and abstracting regime where sovereignty and information technologies are mutually contingent.

BORDERS AND GOVERNMENTALITY

By studying enforcement, the actors, artifacts, practices, institutions, and ideas that sustain the border become scrutable. Just as well do its gaps, frictions, and failures—all of which are integral to the history of the border. Competing sovereignties in the border zone continue to call into question the US and Mexican governments' claims over land and people. Persistent Indigenous refusals over the centuries have produced what Indigenous studies scholar Audra Simpson calls "settler precariousness," or the lingering sense that assumptions about the permanence of national boundaries are on shifting grounds.[16] Border and immigration enforcement highlights the contingency of the border and that it is a political technology in the making of empire and the nation—that is, the making of its people and its social space for rule.

The border is concomitant to the deployment of technological devices and scientific knowledge meant to bring it forth into the world. Ideas about race, citizenship, and the nation shaped the formation of an increasingly restrictive immigration regime since the turn of the nineteenth century.[17] Along the southern border, this regime targeted racialized populations such as Chinese, Mexicans, and Native Americans in its pursuit to control the border.[18] In her work on medicalization and nation building along the US-Mexico border, historian of science Alexandra Stern shows how passage of the 1893 National Quarantine Act and subsequent immigration acts standardized medical inspection into law.[19] Physicians at sea and land ports of entry examined the bodies of immigrant and nonimmigrant aliens. They also performed cursory psychological profiles of them, gauging any possible reasons to enforce their exclusion. Along the US-Mexico border in the 1910s and 1920s, government officials incorporated medicalization directly into the entry process by turning land port buildings into assembly lines. Migrant bodies moved from one kind of inspection to another as they navigated their way through the building: delousing, bathing, vaccination, clothing and baggage disinfection, medical evaluation. In the process, human bodies were turned into excludable or includable subjects, into categories to be managed and processed. "Boundaries, at this edge of the empire-nation," Stern contends, "moved reversibly from the epidermis or body itself, to the landscape of rivers and deserts, and onto bodies *en masse*, or 'races,' as classified by censuses and other indexical strategies."[20] And still, the medicalization of inspection struggled to make sense of how Mexicans troubled US racial logics predicated on the binary white and Black. It was the focus of eugenic discourses on blood that allowed for the production "of a new racialized group at once non-white and non-black, while helping to delimit Mexico as a totally foreign land."[21] Immigration officials made Mexicans into excludable subjects by racializing Mexicans as "non-white and non-black." They did not fit the narrow scope of the existing racial order in the United States. In the early twentieth century, the aim of actors was to sever the shared histories of the US Southwest by racializing Mexicans as subjects and population.

Racial difference informs how border officials have governed the degrees of inclusion/exclusion by which subjects, especially Latina/o/es, can participate and belong or not to the US imagined community.[22] Practices of identification and differentiation highlight how the border is the product of calculated and systematic ways of thinking and acting. Such practices seek to shape, regulate, and manage the conduct of individuals and populations with distinct ends. Chief among these, Latina/o studies scholar Jonathan Xavier Inda tells us, are "immigrants" as targets—unwillingly enrolled in their subjection. US governmentality operates through an epistemological regime that defines fields and terms of engagement whereby unauthorized migration is constituted as an object to know, calculate, and manage as much as an entity that material implements and inscriptions make visible.[23] Practices of differentiation not only create boundaries of expulsion from the nation but an evacuation of the possibility to have rights in the first place. This is what American studies scholar Lisa Marie Cacho points to as a foundational friction within immigration law. "Illegal aliens" are "anti-citizens" because they do not have the option to abide by the law; they are the limits of the law, "people ineligible for personhood."[24] In its impetus to target Latina/o/es in the borderlands and to police their inclusion/exclusion from the nation, border enforcement is associated with the racial management of populations, and such management depends on technoscientific practices that structure and make sense of the world.

This book studies government approaches to the border through networks of material inscriptions—imaginaries and practices such as Immigration and Naturalization Service (INS)/DHS policy documents, reports to Congress, journalistic reports, enforcement techniques, and operational footage. These networks of inscriptions are constitutive and representative of enumerative practices that sort, group, and divide people into classified quantities.[25] Intrusion detection sensors and drones, as subsequent chapters demonstrate, detect and record border incursions. These incursions are translated into data and, as such, are automatically processed and sorted through predetermined classificatory schema that privilege the policing of some racialized bodies over others. Networks of material inscriptions are meant to render these bodies legible to intervention. Enumerative practices are not just articulations of an "avalanche of printed numbers," a phenomenon Ian Hacking argues emerged in the nineteenth century.[26] Instead, I argue, they are the result of a shift toward information communication and control. This shift makes new sense of biopower and governmentality on the border through the calculation and automation of the political.

THE TECHNOPOLITICS OF IMPERIAL FORMATIONS

Border technopolitical regimes comprise the historical entities involved in governing the material boundaries of imperial and national formations. Regimes are enrolled by human actors to prescribe the kinds of subjects and objects—such as people, knowledge, artifacts—to be included or excluded from them. Border technopolitical regimes are, building on the work of science studies scholar Gabrielle Hecht, those associated peoples, ideas, institutions, ways of acting, technological devices, and political goals that promote a certain style of organization and participation.[27] Border technopolitical regimes are made of people who govern, the ideas that guide their behavior in the world, and the artifacts and organizations they create to act on the world.[28] The INS/DHS and its vast range of corporate and higher education partners form one of those regimes, which I return to throughout the book. Within it, technologies are designed to provide the basis and mechanisms for political power, which is to say for (mis)recognition, for (im)mobility, and for inclusion/exclusion. Entities are *brought together by* just as much as *they spring forth from* a regime of truth—the range of practices and orderings that govern the boundary between the true and the false, the admissible and inadmissible.[29] In this sense, border technopolitical regimes are, according to Black studies scholar Alexander Weheliye, "racializing assemblages": a sociotechnical agglomeration of entities, forces, velocities, intensities, interests, ideologies, and desires that produce relations of control as much as relations of fugitivity.[30] These regimes work to classify, differentiate, and govern land, people, goods, and rights; however, in doing so, they inevitably leave room open and create outsides where desires of liberation can escape.

The southern US border, as a space and an amalgam of artifacts, is integral to US imperial and national formations because of its role in the making of sovereignty. In the early twentieth century, as chapter 1 argues, air power represented the possibility to institute a regime whereby racialized Others (Asian, Mexican, and Indigenous) could be managed and administered from the air through the deployment of aviation. Air power emerged, then, as a spatial as much as a racial technique to limit the kinds of bodies that could enter and be a part of the "American" nation. People's mobility was governed through their classification, just as land was partitioned into parceled and enclosed spaces that responded to the demands of a sovereign. The fabrication of sovereignty, then, included determining who could move and where, when, and under what conditions. These dynamics are what make imperial formations into generative machines—they produce practices of exception meant to differentiate people and places while making them manageable.[31] Discriminatory practices, as science and technology studies (STS) scholar Ruha Benjamin suggests, are not only coded into laws and policies but also in everyday objects, tools, and infrastructures.[32] The analytical move is to ask who and what are fixed in place in the matter of sovereignty. Practices of exception reveal the distinct style of border technopolitical regimes; they are the genres through which border regimes fabricate the bounded spaces where sovereignty is enacted, contested, and negotiated. Genres of border technopolitical regimes tackled in this book include air power and the cybernetic border itself (more on this soon). To think about border regimes in relation to imperial and national formations is to open the black box of their techniques of rule. Techniques such as race and territorialization are among the practices of most consequence because they operationalize the grounds (literal and metaphorical matter) for domination.[33]

Throughout this book, I understand race as a technology of distinction. Race is often an unmentioned heuristic artifact to make meaning of peoples and the performance of devices. To classify and to sort means to produce and harness sentiments of similarity and difference. Since its inception as a categorization technology, digital studies scholar Wendy Chun shows us, race has been wielded "as an invaluable mapping tool, a means by which origins and boundaries are simultaneously traced and constructed and through which the visible traces of the body are tied to allegedly innate invisible characteristics."[34] Paradoxically, racial ideas differentiate between peoples by constructing certain attributes as essential or bound to the body so that they cannot be undone. But racial ideas must be permanently enforced so that their structuring of relations endures.[35] This is what Chun describes through the notion of "race and/as technology." A focus on "race *as* technology," she argues, building on ideas from digital studies scholar Beth Coleman, "shifts the focus from the *what* of race to the *how* of race, from *knowing* race to *doing* race by emphasizing the similarities between race and technology."[36] This book deploys the framework of "race and/as technology" to understand how actors entangled racial ideas with techniques of control. Through drone operations and intrusion detection systems, Indigenous folks and Mexicans in the mid-twentieth century were, for example, prescribed to play roles of enmity. These technological systems were shaped by racializing settler colonial narratives as much as by creating new material inscriptions of them.[37] While concerned with a different context, digital studies scholar Lisa Nakamura has similarly argued that racial images are integral to the articulation of digital communication, which is the case with systems like Anduril's Lattice and the electronic fence—operational technologies that record, store, process, and communicate racialized behaviors.[38] By examining digital racial formations, I show that historical narrative tropes of the frontier help frame how technical artifacts are imagined once they enter the borderlands and that artifacts also recode how social relations in the "wild" frontier take place.

Imperial formations are not clearly bordered or bounded polities, and so they are incessantly drawing and erasing their boundaries of rule. And yet, they are dependent on the fabrication of durabilities, of enduring relations of power that safeguard the perpetuation of empire and the nation. The process of making land into territory, or what sociologist Nandita Sharma calls the abstraction of land into "state space," is not some natural process. It requires deliberate effort in forging both the sense of some "natural" separation between an enclosed space and what exceeds it and a "natural" identification between a group of people and this newly enclosed space.[39] Without durabilities, imperial formations dissolve into thin air. This is where border technopolitical regimes are of fundamental importance to them. These regimes, often visible in the built environment, produce boundaries that demarcate and trace the spatial arrangements within and through which actors act and subjects are made. Normative citizens are safely enfolded by the embrace of such regimes, even as second-class citizens and noncitizens, especially those deemed intruders or illegal, are differently situated within and without the spectrum of belonging.[40] Border technopolitical regimes manage the boundaries of inclusion/exclusion, which is to say the boundaries of participation in the body politic.

To describe a regime's subjects and objects of knowledge is to grasp the political commitments of its actors and the techniques designed to materialize said commitments. The border technopolitical regime examined here comes together through operations of governance executed by a range of actors entangled with sovereignty—such as Border Patrol agents, engineers at computing and military manufacturers, and journalists. In other words, the notion of border technopolitical regimes does not presume the existence or legitimacy of imperial and national sovereignty. It stresses that sovereignty is constructed and permanently performed and under duress.[41] Border technopolitical regimes are also organized around the promotion of a specific style of technical development. In today's case, it is the central role assigned to data as the vector through which the national border is produced. The regime of the cybernetic border leverages data and information as the means to govern—that is, to manage and order entities in relation to the nation. By privileging data, the regime favors specific kinds of sociotechnical arrangements associated with feedback loops of data capture, processing, and communication that shape operations.

The cybernetic border, the ongoing hegemonic genre of the border technopolitical regime analyzed in this book, is the product of sovereign practices just as much as it is the producer of sovereign practices. Data are simultaneously the objects and vectors of the cybernetic border.[42] Bodies of data and data bodies structure relations of nation making. The cybernetic border is part of what international relations scholar Antoine Bousquet calls "the logistics of perception," or the organization of the perceptual field in modern warfare through the systematic collection, storage, and transmission of information.[43] The logistics of perception operates through technoaesthetics by arranging the sensible and the epistemological grounds for engaging the world. Human-machine configurations of the cybernetic border striate land and bind subjects through quantification, computation, and probability. It is an epistemological order of things and beings. It designates the legal categories of rule and their exceptions. Unauthorized border crossers and Border Patrol agents are differently subjected to the flows of the cybernetic border. Some resist it, others maintain it, and even others seek to avoid being brought into its modular fold.

How should readers interpret the relation between the cybernetic border and sovereignty? Drawing inspiration from the work of visual arts scholar Benjamin H. Bratton, I suggest that the point is not that sovereignty is a timeless constant that is now articulated through a cybernetic border regime. Rather, since the mid-twentieth century, the cybernetic border and sovereignty are mutually contingent. "The systems that mediate governance bind them to it just as it is bound by them."[44] The management and administration of borderlands, its people and territory, is co-constructed by how and what its technical infrastructures allow it to sense, measure, and organize.[45] By working with a technopolitical framework, I propose we pry open the technological black box. The framework of border technopolitical regimes requires the tracing of relations across entities (peoples, ideas, institutions, practices, technical devices) to reassemble its machinations. As this book shows, operational technologies are all part of a broader arrangement that treats the borderlands as a data-generating space where racialized populations are prescribed the role of intruders to control. They are the matter of the cybernetic border.

Uses of technoscience in border enforcement stress that the border is not some line in the sand or some transparently enforced policy prescription. Borders are the infrastructural media matter of sovereign practices. They are the products as much as the producers of distinct lifeworlds. And as such, they require material, interpretive, critical, and interdisciplinary approaches for inquiry.

Militarization and Enmity

Throughout this book, I study a range of military technologies that spanned foreign battlefields and the war fields of domestic space. This, in addition to the participation of military actors themselves and the use of military logics, is what many border studies scholars often describe as the militarization of border enforcement. Some scholars date the militarization of border and immigration enforcement to the 1970s with the federal government's increased interest in controlling drug smuggling.[46] Others see militarization as occurring well before the war on drugs or even policing efforts like Operation Wetback in 1955. They refer to aerial surveillance by US federal troops during General Pershing's expedition against Pancho Villa and his rebels in the period of the Mexican Revolution, or longer than that, examining the appropriation of Indigenous knowledge practices for border enforcement since the nineteenth century.[47] The creation of the Border Patrol in 1924 and its existence is often the point of consensus for scholars who support the thesis on the militarization of the border.[48]

I am skeptical of this framing for two reasons. First, it treats military logics as the effects of technology or the mere presence of military actors. Technologies such as intrusion detection systems and drones were most certainly developed for US military engagements, often overseas. But to say these technologies are military and that they, therefore, militarize a given space or practice does not explain them. This kind of argument keeps the lid closed on the perpetual technological black box by taking for granted the kinds of relations it enacts. What makes a technology embody a martial logic? Often this has to do with the exercise of the monopoly of violence and the "enemy-friend" distinction. Border historian Miguel Antonio Levario elaborates this point by claiming that the presence and activity of US police forces in the early twentieth century, including paramilitary organizations, agitated racial frictions between whites and Mexicans in the southern borderlands. These processes led to the treatment of Mexicans as enemies of the nation.[49] Technologies, however, have their own logics, and these should not be disregarded as if they were epiphenomenal or only socially determined. Scrutinizing technology, including military technologies, requires understanding the relations that produce them (and that they produce) just as much as the meanings that these relations hold for actors.

My second reason to be skeptical of the thesis of the militarization of the border is that it assumes there was a time when it was not militarized. This is a common argument in debates about policing as well because it helps separate police power from war power—the notion that the former keeps the internal peace of the nation while the latter defends it from external threats. The institutions associated with each of these modalities of power, however, are historically entangled in the fabrication and preservation of a sovereign social order.[50] When it comes to US borders, police and war power are historically linked to the settler colonial project, of producing territory and policing citizenship through racial dispossession and violence. Throughout the nineteenth century, for example, US soldiers, sometimes with allies and other times by themselves, conducted wars of expansion and "pacification" so that US sovereignty was established, recognized, and maintained over land, goods, and people.[51] To produce the territory of the nation and its boundaries of separation from other territorialized sovereignties meant to exercise both police and war power in the engagement of an unruly, transgressive enemy.[52]

The persistent presence of science and technology in border making and border enforcement suggests a pressing need to understand their roles. One such role is the creation, maintenance, and reproduction of relations of enmity. Examining these roles requires tracing the coproductions between the military logics embedded in imperial and national sovereignties as much as the distinct human-machine configurations that make them and that they make possible.

Cybernetics and Drones

Cybernetics shapes the technologies discussed in this book. This knowledge formation has been integral to research and development in computing and information systems since the mid-twentieth century. Cybernetics posits that all complex systems depend on the management and processing of information to function and to maintain themselves. Focus on information allows cyberneticians to abstract and thereby blur the boundaries between entities. They use the same terms that name mental faculties and processes (e.g., memory, intelligence, learning) to describe computer hardware and computational processes (e.g., storage, software, pattern recognition).[53] Drones, intrusion detection systems, and computer networks owe much to the interdisciplinary science of communication and control processes in living organisms and machines. Operational technologies function through information as much as they contribute to information infrastructures guiding Border Patrol performance in the borderlands. Often discussed in relation to military ventures outside of US territory, this book situates cybernetics and drones as imperial formations at home, with special attention given to their roles in the production of enmity. By approaching drones through cybernetics, this book treats them as part of a changing information infrastructure made by and making the US empire-nation.

Immigration and border enforcement in the mid-twentieth century were imagined through the language of cybernetics as constituted by and governed through information. As I show in chapter 2, officials believed that effective operation of the immigration system required new techniques for information recording, processing, and communication at ports of entry, immigration offices, and the remote areas of the borderlands. Controlling data inputs and outputs was a central concern for immigration administrators—part of a long history in the control revolution of the information society.[54] This is what cybernetics portrayed through the metaphor of "steering," or how living organisms and machines sustained themselves by governing information flows. Drawn from the realm of cybernetics, steering became a structuring practice guiding human activity and human-nonhuman relations.[55]

Since its emergence in the 1940s, cybernetics has been a part of an imperial technopolitical regime designed around enmity. The focus on an enemy is what led STS scholar Peter Galison to describe cybernetics as part of the Manichean sciences, which also included operations research and game theory. The Manichean sciences were the product of a growing "iron triangle" that enrolled academic institutions during World War II for the development of new military technologies.[56] Following the work of mathematicians Norbert Wiener and John von Neumann, Galison shows how the Manichean drive emerged through "the continuing struggle against an active oppositional intelligence."[57] The purposeful monitoring and forecasting of human behaviors led to the development of an "Enemy Other" that was generated, he argues, not out of the racial discourses commonly latched onto bodies, but from the laboratories associated with war making at the Massachusetts Institute of Technology (MIT) and other universities in the United States and Great Britain. This enemy operated in a "world of strategy, tactics, and maneuver, all the while thoroughly inaccessible to us, separated by a gulf of distance, speed, and metal."[58] The merging of pilot with machine helped blur the human-nonhuman boundary as pilots and their airplanes were abstracted into statistical plots. The enemy in this construct was not a moral/immoral model against which to be measured. Instead, it was like one of von Neumann's game players, "perfectly intelligent, perfectly ruthless operators" producing moves and countermoves in an opposing relationship to fundamentally different but like forces.[59] Cybernetics in this sense is the product and producer of a border technopolitical regime that submits the world—its human bodies and nonhuman entities—to the abstract language of engineering and the drawing of exceptions that prescribe some to play the role of enemies of the nation. Cybernetics is more than a military-academic-industrial project. It is a knowledge formation affecting the differential management and administration of life and death.

This book makes plain that the laboratory production of an Enemy Other cannot be disentangled with the more messy and insidious creation of the racial Other. The "monstruous, racialized images of hate," which Galison talks about as distinct from the anonymous enemy, were not an addendum or supplement to the Enemy Other.[60] The racial enemy and the Enemy Other are entangled, coproducing each other. The supposed inhumanity of the former buttresses the abstracted "nonhuman-ness" of the latter. Celebratory narratives about the liberatory potential of the cyborg, the posthuman, and of cybernetics must never forget that these are artifacts of a military technopolitical regime geared toward the fabrication of exceptions.[61] In the case of the intruder monitored, tracked, and anticipated by the electronic fence, it emerged out of the articulation of a war-making milieu that imagined Vietcong fighters as "dirty," less-than-human targets to eliminate. Such milieu was also informed by a discourse positioning Mexican migrants as invaders from the "Third World." Without such racial imaginaries devaluing the humanity of these targets, the technical Enemy Other cannot emerge. In a sense, one might say that Enemy Others are paradigmatic of the posthuman subject position—not tightly bounded and overdetermined but never far from the regime excluding them from humanity. Targets and Enemy Others are one and the same boundary objects through which the technopolitical regime of the US empire-nation actualizes itself.

To examine operational technologies in relation to cybernetics is to connect them to computing. Scholars in the history of computing contend that this technology was the product of intricate relations between military, industrial, and academic actors.[62] Narratives often emphasize that actors shifted the use of the computer from being a military and scientific instrument into a business machine in the 1950s and 1960s and a personal device in the 1970s. Other scholarship shows how cybernetics and computing were deployed in urban planning during the 1960s, in the social sciences and art and design in the United States, and in the making of socialist governance in Chile during the Salvador Allende presidency.[63] This book builds on such work by making sense of the encounter between cybernetics and INS/DHS, one of the largest federal agencies in the United States. Immigration and border enforcement are also part of the history of computing. These practices expanded the reach of computers to new areas beyond strict military, scientific, business, and personal uses. Computers used in drones, intrusion detection systems, and smart borders were and continue to be important in the process of constructing and administrating the boundaries of enmity and in territorializing the nation.

Technicians increased the autonomy of drones through the use of electronics and, later, computers. The UAS became capable of deciding and executing actions without the intervention of a human actor. Historically, the term "drone" was used to refer to a remotely piloted vehicle (RPV), the focus of chapter 1. Though unmanned, RPVs required the active control of a human through radio waves emitted from a controlling device on the ground or mounted on a different vehicle and sent to another device that, equipped on the "unmanned" vehicle itself, actuated its different mechanisms, such as motor speed and steering.[64] Increases in autonomy led to changes in nomenclature as these vehicles began autonomously executing a plethora of actions. Hence, there was a turn away from RPV to a cybernetics-informed and more nuanced conception of drones as unmanned systems. This move acknowledges the layering of technologies of remote control and tactical operations (e.g., cameras, sensors, lethal weaponry). It also demonstrates how drones are not stable and unified wholes but assemblages of humans, machine, ideas, practices, and media.[65] Throughout this book, "drone" and "unmanned aerial system" are treated as synonymous terms. The focus is on large military UASs rather than the growing small UASs used by hobbyists and industry.[66] Chapter 3 is devoted to UASs used for border enforcement today that do not carry weapons and that are operated by the Customs and Border Protection (CBP) Office of Air and Marine for patrol, investigations, and disaster relief.[67] UASs feed data into a wider information infrastructure that includes ground sensors, CCTV cameras, and radio and satellite communications. All information or "raw data" gathered in their operations is processed, exploited, and disseminated by the Office of Intelligence and Investigative Liaison. Drone data, either delivered in real time or used retroactively, inform enforcement operations designed to control unauthorized border crossers—either as a "show of force" that dissuades them from venturing into dangerous border landscape or by aiding Border Patrol agents to apprehend them. UASs discussed in this book do not shoot at unauthorized border crossers, but they are tactical instruments in an enforcement approach that drives crossers father into remote areas of the borderlands, where hundreds lose their lives every year.[68]

While having an international history, drones are also the embodiment of political formations and logics at the heart of US empire. Some scholars have shown that drone-hunters and target-prey are animated by the production of enemies in state making. Of greatest concern is the fact that drones propel a "warfare without risk," a mode of military engagement that removes or minimizes the human calculus from those remotely operating them.[69] Other scholars, equally interested in questions of sovereignty and biopolitics, examine UASs as part of the US empire-nation's commitment to expand the reach of actors by reconfiguring space and territory.[70] Drone warfare, in other words, materializes a regime designed to safeguard the security of the US nation by segmenting populations into those made to live and those allowed to die. Enemies and territory are (re)drawn through the politics of drone operations.[71] What some of these scholars construe as a drone empire, this book studies within the framework of cybernetics. In doing so, I situate UASs as part of a larger information infrastructure animated by and animating the bounds of sovereignty.[72] This is the cybernetic border.

The cybernetic border transcodes physical space and all kinds of entities within it into electrical or digital signals that are then stored on databases, processed by algorithms, or displayed on a screen. Such representation of objects in the borderlands is not an isolated, technical process but one shaped as well by relations and imaginaries. Data are filtered through relations of enmity and segmentations of land into territory. Interrogating the processes of recognition and data capture reveals the ways that border and immigration enforcement depend on human-machine configurations of mediation to identify, name, and sort. Enforcement practices require information infrastructures, and consequently, said practices are transformed by them. As part and parcel of the cybernetic border, drones and intrusion detection systems distribute the labor involved in producing and enforcing the border, though more importantly, they operationalize the law.

The datafication of humans, human behaviors, and land as well as their integration into the recursive loops of cybernetics begs the question of agency. Border Patrol agents are trained to internalize cybernetic routines of enforcement in reading out ground sensor data, using drone video streams to guide operations on the ground, and recording enforcement data to measure its purported efficiencies. Agency is distributed across shifting and iterative networks of operations. But what about the agency of unauthorized border crossers and intruders within this system? The former is a fugitive figure. They transgress the order of the border technopolitical regime and, in doing so, undermine the sense of stability of the sovereign project of national formations. Their agency is premised on their capacity to escape the territorialization of the bordered space and avoid capture. The figure of the intruder, on the other hand, is the integration of the unauthorized border crosser into the machinations or operations of the cybernetic border. Within this system, their agency is tightly determined by this regime, which embeds it in its routines. The agency of the intruder reifies and justifies the regime itself. Even if the intruder avoids capture, the transgression is read as a technical or systemic failure in need of reprogramming or upgrade. In this sense, it might seem as if the agency of the intruder is unthinkable because it is an object of the cybernetic border. But the intruder is a data assemblage, an amalgam of data sources as much as a political project of the empire-nation. Even when human-machine configurations of the cybernetic border succeed in shaping some intruder behavior, they are incapable of fully apprehending their targets—unauthorized border crossers cannot be contained by the category of intruder, nor can their lifeworlds and their complexities. These are some of the data haunts of the cybernetic border, the excesses or shadows that activists and artists identify as generative dynamics to disassemble this regime.

The Cybernetic Border grapples with the making of sociotechnical arrangements around racialized intruders to shed light on the role of information and computing in the US empire-nation. What happens if we consider cybernetics and computing through the lenses of racial and imperial formations? And, conversely, what happens when we examine racial and imperial formations through the framework of technopolitical regimes? This book answers these questions.

Mapping the Cybernetic Border

Border crossing has long been understood through processes of empire and settler colonialism concerned with intrusion. In making sense of intrusion, actors often drew from frontier imaginaries and a settler colonial structure of feeling. White settlers imagined the edges of the empire-nation as naturally belonging to them because it was there they would pioneer a new and stronger nation. When the contest between the United States and the Soviet Union mushroomed into the Cold War, chapter 1 argues, the border technopoliti-

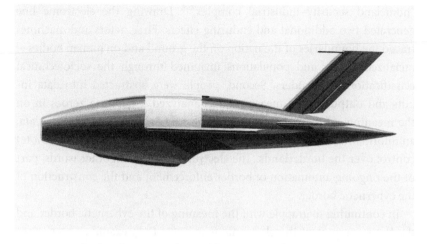

FIGURE I.2. Firebee drone manufactured by San Diego–based Ryan Aeronautical. Source: San Diego Air and Space Museum.

cal regime enrolled unmanned aerial vehicles like Ryan Aeronautical's Firebee (see figure I.2) to be the perfect intruder target to test the technological frontiers of the nation. Like cowboys hunting after "intransigent" Indigenous peoples, human pilots and their "trusty mounts" were imagined aiming their metaphorical pistols on drone targets. Chapter 1 demonstrates that the regime combined the technopolitics of air power and unmanning in the reproduction of settler colonial and imperial logics of differentiation. To police the national border and defend the nation was to treat the nonhuman, racialized intruder as expendable.

Government officials, technicians, and journalists translated the idea of drones as intruders of the borderlands onto the bodies of Mexican migrants by 1970. Chapter 2 probes the moment when INS worked in the articulation of, and the supposed solution to, an "illegal alien" problem. Construed as illegal and "deportable aliens," Mexicans were the targets of a growing experimental and infrastructural arrangement.[73] Cybernetic ideas and intrusion detection systems were adopted to draw an electronic "line in the sand" in the management and administration of the US-Mexico border.[74] The system, originally developed for military use in Vietnam, established the conditions of possibility for future collaborations between the US military, the electronics industry, academia, and the INS. These collaborations are at the core of what I have termed the "border technopolitical regime"; two decades after the attacks of September 11, 2001, others often call it the "homeland security–industrial complex."[75] Drawing the electronic line generated two additional and enduring effects. First, actors and machines traced the boundaries of the nation on the ground and on human bodies— racialized bodies and populations imagined through the sociotechnical classification of intruders. Second, people were abstracted into data inputs and outputs to be measured and analyzed. Chapter 2 zeroes in on the meanings of these data technopolitics. By ordering and sensing data, an information infrastructure was made responsible in executing (remote) control over the borderlands. The electronic fence is, in other words, part of the ongoing automation of border enforcement and the construction of the cybernetic border.

In continuing to grapple with the meaning of the cybernetic border and the lasting impact of the electronic fence, chapter 3 examines DHS plans for "operational control" through a strategic commitment to smart borders. Nativist, anti-immigrant, and populist discourses successfully pressed the federal government throughout the 1990s and after 9/11 to adopt more aggressive approaches to immigration. Combining the logics of war and security, the technopolitical regime that came out of the War on Terror is tasked with managing the clash of civilizations against Latina/o/es, Arabs, and Muslims. This is a regime devoted to operational control and "smart borders." While the electronic fence of the 1970s was an isolated sociotechnical arrangement, the smart borders of the twenty-first century are supposed to be interconnected, integrated into a wider network of technologies of change detection—also known as a system of systems (figure I.3). For DHS, change detection is part of the strategic commitment to smart borders, an arrangement measured through border metrics and the capacity to influence the behavior of actors in the borderlands—unauthorized border crossers as much as Border Patrol agents. The pursuit of smart borders treated the border as a networked platform that prescribes how border crossers within its datafied field are engaged, as risk objects of the nation.

The final chapter shifts gears by flipping the scripts of the cybernetic border. Chapters 1 to 3 trace how a range of government and corporate actors entangled ideas about the frontier, the nation, and race with the human-machine configurations at the heart of the cybernetic border. These technologies and their deployment often evoke a totalizing aura of absolute knowledge and mastery over its targets. Their failures and incapacities are many, some of which are discussed in this trio of chapters. Yet, the aim of chapter 4 is to explore the limitations of the technoaesthetics of the cybernetic border, or how the sensible and the epistemological grounds for engaging the world

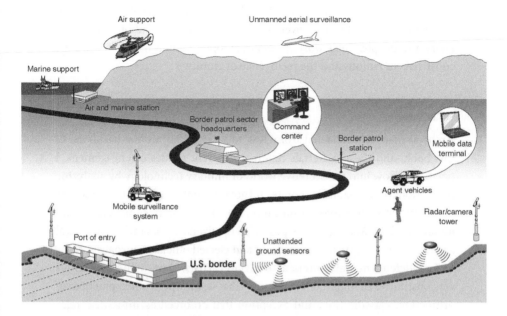

FIGURE I.3. Diagram explosion of the "system of systems." Source: Government Accountability Office, "Secure Border Initiative: DHS Needs to Address Significant Risks in Delivering Key Technology Investment," GAO-08-1086 (Washington, DC: Government Accountability Office, 2008).

are arranged. Technoaesthetics is about reconfiguring human sensory experience. Activists and artists disturb these configurations through disassembly and data haunts.[76] The interventions of Alex Rivera, Humane Borders, Ricardo Dominguez, Ian Alan Paul, Jane Stevens, and Josh Begley subjected the regime's technoaesthetics to inquiry and critique. Their work scrutinizes the cybernetic border's privileging of data and their limits—the haunting shadows that escape capture in processes of datafication. Chapter 4 offers thick descriptions of their works as technoscientific scenes to draw out the relations constituting the cybernetic border. I also conducted oral history interviews with Dominguez and Paul, and listened to and read interviews with the other activists and artists to learn more about the kinds of associations they make between the border and infrastructures. Their interventions and the language they produce challenge the ways the cybernetic border operates at the intersection of life, death, and data in the fabrication of intruder targets. For these activists and artists, drones, computers, and databases are machines to think with and against as actors seek to reorient their functioning. In recognizing and inhabiting the assembling work of the cybernetic border, activists and artists disassemble it. They use operational technologies to contest the sovereign project of borders and of making territory and people. Their work generates an opening that moves beyond the constructs of nations and the recurrence of enmity.

On Methodology

Archival materials collected from 2015 to 2022 constitute the backbone of this book, and these materials required different modes of engagement. I open a window into the secretive world of military technology by analyzing promotional documents, corporate and government memoranda, transcripts of congressional hearings, technical reports, newspapers, film, surveillance footage, and art. Materials were produced by diverse actors including federal agencies (e.g., INS, DHS), government and elected officials, journalists, technicians, defense manufacturers, activists, and artists. Many of these materials are constitutive of imperial formations—that is, they performed practices of distinction, classification, and exception that enforced asymmetrical relations. As a result, they require a reflexive disposition to identify their logics and politics as well as to avoid reproducing them. Drawing together the heterogeneous materials of imperial formations and telling stories about them renders these materials more solid and steady than they are. This book seeks then to reveal their fractional coherence, or how entities are imagined coming together, to exist and to relate with other entities.[77] Operational technologies and the sociotechnical relations they embody are differently produced by a range of materials and actors that, in working to stabilize them, inevitably recognize their mutability.

This book analyzes materials from INS and DHS that sought to define the contours of alienage, the methods for differentially subjecting those populations identified through alienage, and the techniques for drawing up the shifting geographic zones for the exercise of US sovereignty. Engaging bureaucratic thought-work creates an opportunity to scrutinize the routine production of "orders that bind differentiated wholes together."[78] This thought-work is embedded in and enacted through iterative human-machine relations. The practices examined in this book, such as treating the borderlands and its bodies through cybernetic concepts and technologies, shape the conditions of knowing—the kinds of bodies, identities, and imaginaries that can be made perceptible. These practices also set the conditions for the materiality of the contemporary archive of the US empire-nation: papers, .PDF files, wires, computer screens, manned and unmanned airplanes, film, B-roll footage, streaming platforms, and webmaps. "Systems of written accountability," anthropologist Ann Laura Stoler concludes, call "for elaborate infrastructures. Paper trails of weekly reports to superiors, summaries of reports, and recommendations based on reports all [call] for systematic coding systems by which they [can] be tracked."[79] Control emerges, or at least actors hope, through categorical and technological sorting, through networks of inscriptions.

INS/DHS materials as well as materials produced by other actors in industry and the wider public create networked inscriptions dependent on, as much as generative of, protocols of control. When I decided to write about military drones on the US-Mexico border, I found myself with the challenge of writing about an object cordoned off by what Galison calls the "closed world" of military research and military technology.[80] The design, technical elements, and people involved in the development of military technology, among other things, are kept secret through the use of government classification schemes. Even when documents might be released through Freedom of Information Act requests, chunks of information might still be redacted, and to all extent removed, to prevent others from knowing and, at times, to protect the people involved. And materials made for public consumption such as INS and DHS reports are deliberately vague to preserve the secrecy of security practices and arrangements. The classification regime of the closed world is part of the border technopolitical regime's archival logic.

This book navigates the fragmented logic of the archive by engaging its materials as technoscientific scenes. While incompleteness is integral to archives themselves, in the archive at the heart of this book it was intensified by the classification regime of modern state making. When it came to the artifacts of the cybernetic border like drones, intrusion detection systems, computing, and smart borders, I was challenged to figure out how to do research with a ruptured and dispersed archive whose materials speak not of a singular object but different versions of the same one. Archival materials are both the products and producers of gaps, omissions, and fissures in public knowledge about (military) technoscience.[81] In this sense, these materials constitute scenes or subdivisions in technoscientific acts, units of action in larger stories. But they are also the stage settings and the stage itself. They are disassembled wholes, the matter on which partial relations are inscribed and executed by discrete actors. This is where roles are given and performed. I had to track what actors in different sectors and constituencies discussed and, in doing so, recompose the stories they had for a particular sociotechnical arrangement. Archival materials generated by different institutions, companies, and people all strove to coordinate the multiple objects they create and make them into stable and legible unities.[82] These materials worked to reconfigure space and people into neatly ordered entities folded into the world made by technological objects and by the materials themselves.

The cybernetic border becomes a legible entity by drawing ideas, practices, and devices together. I trace associations and describe their meanings—the kinds of political imaginaries they sought to enact. Materials produced by the US government and its military, by the popular and trade press, and by engineers and technicians document what data and drones do and how they are imagined and engaged. These materials help us retrieve the scripts that assign entities their different roles in the cybernetic border. Scripts are the scenes or scenarios played by human and nonhuman actors. They are retrieved through descriptions contained in the likes of technical reports, system diagrams, demonstrations, and footage of operations.[83] Actors design the cybernetic border with specific roles in mind for entities—some perform the role of hunters or predators, and others are the prey or target. Design of the system is the kind of upstream work that prescribes positions well before any scripts are performed.[84] Prescriptions expose the actions they validate and their intended goals, which is to say their technopolitics. Chapters 1 through 3 scrutinize the prescriptions performed during Air Force military exercises, the operation of the intrusion detection system, and the experimental deployment of UASs in border enforcement. These scripts, like those in the demonstration of Anduril's Lattice system, reveal the biopolitical project of the US empire-nation in its treatment of Mexican migrants and unauthorized border crossers as enemies of the nation. Treated as enemies, these populations were pushed toward a mode of social existence that made them into expendable lives. They mattered only to the extent that they justified the construction and operations of the cybernetic border. Their lives, on the other hand, did not matter, and as a result, they were driven toward the lethal border landscape.

The operations of scripts throughout this book reveal how actors in the network are differently situated and engaged. Unauthorized border crossers are not just one more actor in the network of the cybernetic border. They are the targets of racializing assemblages that police the bounds of modern selfhood, of who is legible and liable for rights under the law. Of greater concern here is the fact that not all humans equally participate in the network. Racializing assemblages, Weheliye argues, "discipline humanity into full humans, not-quite-humans, and nonhumans."[85] To a large degree, this is the result of a Western philosophical tradition that cannot evacuate its provincializing boundaries. The Manichean sciences such as cybernetics and computer science cannot evade their entanglement with the abstraction and calculation of humanity and the targeting of enmity that are central to the machinations of border technopolitical regimes.

Imperial formations operate through archival logics that gather, draw together, connect, and disconnect entities by treating them as information.[86] The cybernetic border, as an imperial and settler colonial apparatus, is equally concerned with records, storage, and informational flows that simultaneously document, afford, and execute control. As I reconstituted the fragmented archive of the cybernetic border, I often found documents discussing, debating, and describing how bodies are identified, recognized, and policed during their attempts to cross the border without authorization. In making sense of the practices of these bodies, the actors made them intelligible and manageable. These are some of the organizing principles and the raison d'être for the archives of imperial formations. In the case of INS/DHS, their archival logics revolved around surveillance, social control, and expanding or negotiating the boundaries of US sovereign power. Engaging the materials of imperial formations means there is an ongoing potential of reifying their logics.[87]

Relying mostly on government archives calls for a reflexive approach that is attuned to each agency's archival logic while reading "along the archival grain." Doing so is not to assume a seamless texture in the ways that actions unfold. Instead, it is to acknowledge the fact that the archive is a rough "field of force and will to power."[88] Human actors, especially the most vulnerable people, might seem to be missing from this story. I propose, however, that they are at the core of the operations of the border technopolitical regime—in how it construed the boundaries of humanity and the nation, and in its networked inscription of human actions and their categorical sorting. Analysis of the operations of this regime brings to the fore its frictions. People are central to the stories told in this book. They are figures of speech and the sources of said discourse. They are entities that challenge the imperial desire to make and govern populations and territories. They are the bodies pushed into the desert environment of the southern borderlands as well as those who jam the border machine's incessant politics of death. Human actors haunt the border technopolitical regime. "To write ghost stories," as sociologist Avery Gordon holds, "implies that ghosts are real, that is to say, that they produce material effects. To impute a kind of objectivity to ghosts implies that, from certain standpoints, the dialectics of visibility and invisibility involve a constant negotiation between what can be seen and what is in the shadows."[89] This book is an effort to open the archival logics of the border technopolitical regime to understand its material effects. This pursuit inevitably demands attention be paid to the haunting (in)visibility of human actors and how bodies drop in and out of networked inscriptions.

The struggle of US actors to shape and engage an adversarial Other requires robust human-machine configurations. Government agents often describe these configurations in terms of platforms. *The Cybernetic Border* shows that the articulation of platforms of enmity is anchored to the fabrication of the empire-nation and the boundaries of its territorialized sovereignties and imagined community. Investments in border and immigration enforcement have not dwindled after the events discussed in this book. Elected and government officials continue to embrace the promise of technological mastery that companies like Anduril Industries profess. The budget for DHS has grown steadily since its first appropriation: from about $27 billion in fiscal year 2004 in net discretionary funds to about $54 billion in fiscal year 2021.[90] The deaths of unauthorized border crossers in the Sonoran Desert persist, despite claims by DHS officials that drones and other new technology are crucial to save lives. The politics of enmity undergirding the cybernetic border, part of a centenary project in imperial nation making, perhaps became only more pronounced during the Donald Trump presidency. The overall approach to border and immigration enforcement, however, has not changed in the last five decades—it is even more enmeshed with information technologies centered on data capture, processing, and communication. Technological failures accumulate even while the narratives of technological progress and the politics of enmity that feed the machines of US empire grow ever more deadly.

1. SCRIPTING THE FRONTIER

Drone Intruders and the Racial Politics of Unmanning

He rode his "trusty mount" just like any other cowboy confronting a "villain" would. One hand firmly grabbed the reins while, with the other, he held his long barrel revolver. Something about this, however, was uncanny. Perhaps it was his helmet with retractable lens, his facial expression of sheer delight while facing an enemy, or the fact that he was riding his trusty mount miles high in the air. For the artist designing the cover of *Naval Aviation News* (see figure 1.1), aircraft pilots were nothing else than "cowboys in the sky." Their enemy, in this instance, was not another fighter pilot but Ryan Aeronautical's jet-powered Firebee drone. The scene depicted on the cover drew from popular narratives imagining aviation as a new frontier. Just like in the past, this frontier required techniques for instituting lawful order.

The cover of *Naval Aviation News* was a creative representation of the US Navy's Fourth Annual "Operation Top Gun," a competitive aerial weapons training exercise with teams of sailors and pilots from Atlantic and Pacific Fleet squadrons. A press release from the Department of Defense's Office of Public Affairs stated that the objective of the event, celebrated from November 30 to December 4, 1959, was to evaluate aviation and weapons systems and supporting equipment as well as training and operating techniques. Ryan's Firebee was tasked with simulating real-world combat conditions and allowing the military to institute and test its plans for air defense.[1]

This chapter wrestles with the meanings and relations performed by drone operations on the borderlands in the mid-twentieth century. Drones,

FIGURE 1.1. Tom Gregory, "Cowboy in the Sky." Source: *Naval Aviation News*, November 1959, cover.

as science and technology studies (STS) scholar Kate Chandler contends, are an assemblage of human, machine, and media.[2] And as an assemblage, they draw together human operators, metal structures, cables, radio spectra, knowledge practices, and imaginaries apprehending the world. The first part of this chapter offers a situated backdrop to drones by examining the racial politics of air power in the settler colonial context of San Diego. Among the companies responsible in this process was Ryan Aeronautical. The second part shows the role of the company and the US military in imagining their drones as instituting a new unmanned aerial technopolitical regime in the borderlands—a regime that disavowed human intervention through remote control and push-button warfare. Unmanned technopolitics were interpreted by military and company officials through technoscientific scenes, or scripts through which humans, science, and technology were written to play clear roles. As technoscientific scenes, Operation Top Gun and Project William Tell deployed Ryan's Firebee to embody the racial politics of enmity and the US empire-nation. These scenes drew from frontier fantasies that rehearsed and prescribed how foreign intruder entities in the borderlands should be engaged.

Drones, I argue, were delegates that prescribed human behavior within spatial relationships. They were both a material infrastructure and a signifier.[3] Based on normalizing ideas about foreign bodies, they demonstrated how US citizens ought to (re)act when faced with the presence of intruders in national territory. Military officials and technicians thought target drones, in use since the 1930s, offered a way to train anti-aircraft gunners and airplane pilots to take down enemies without the danger of unnecessarily hurting pilots or damaging aircraft. By unmanning the target using remote control, military officials, engineers, industry, and government subscribed to a desire that detached the human and the political.[4] Yet imagined as foreign or enemy, remotely piloted vehicles articulated the place of alien bodies threatening the existence of the US nation. Drones were a technology of rule through which actors negotiated territorial ambiguity and attempted to exclude external and internal enemies. Air Force and Navy pilots as well as corporate actors were trained to eliminate them through the enactment of frontier biopolitical scripts. These are the scenes, either figurative or nonfigurative, played by human and nonhuman actors in the administration of populations.[5] Biopolitical scripts verge on the governance of peoples organized around and through a series of categories like Indian, intruder, alien, or Mexican. These scripts set the stage for how actors relate to one another and how they ought to behave. They encode racial imaginaries into plans—prescribed actions, ideas, and relations to be performed and executed when situations arise.[6] Plans, as feminist STS scholar Lucy Suchman demonstrates, are not rigid sequences of action but structured and structuring artifacts through which situations are engaged.[7] Actors translated settler tropes of civilizing the frontier into the operations of drones and the military's theater of war.

Military exercises are technoscientific scenes through which to describe the politics and technological styles of the border technopolitical regime. Expanding the work of postcolonial studies scholar Rey Chow, Chandler argues that military officials and technicians involved in air power—and consequently drone development and use—came "to conceive of the world as a target."[8] The "view from above" simultaneously created a view from below whereby a civilizational struggle unfolded between these two subject positions—an imperial dialectics of air power. Chandler notes that this aerial order of things was not merely an exercise of war power but was part and parcel of the exercise of domestic control—one could say it was one with police power. The enemy was not merely an externalized subject but figured as an internal one, an "enemy-as-criminal" to police.[9] Operation Top Gun and Project William Tell were part of a range of exercises developed by a border technopolitical regime making and unmaking the boundaries of the nation on people's bodies and on land. Participating in these technoscientific scenes, drones enacted a theater of war—the projection of threats and self-fashioning that was necessary in the making of the nation, its territory, its peoples, and its foes.[10] These entities were conscripted as much as they were prescribed by a view from above that flattened the field of possibility through its desire for domination. Among the politics embedded in US air power and unmanning was the racial project of enmity, a cornerstone of imperial and national formations.

The Politics of Air Power and the "Air Capital of the West"

Air power is a genre of border technopolitical regimes and its imperial desire stretching across a vast global expanse, folding time and space in practices of wonder and domination. The fantasy of mastering air and gravity enamored public discourse in the United States just as much as it did in Europe. A 1906 *New York Times* article concluded that aviation was imagined to open "the porches and gateways of the air, hitherto the birds' privilege and franchise, to the generation of the sons of men."[11] That men—in clearly gendered connotations—could elevate themselves over land through skill and artifice was a story worthy of epic poetry. It was also a story of empire making, of policing non-white bodies through force and technique. Aviation materialized centuries of desire to attain a "cosmic view" from above, a view that actors construed as yielding clarity and garnering empowerment over that and those subjected to its swift movements.[12]

Drones are first and foremost aircraft, and thus they must be understood in relation to air power and its racial politics.[13] The ideas of military theorists like Giulio Douhet and William Mitchell demonstrate air power was marked by racial anxieties at the heart of imperial and national formations. These anxieties are examined in the context of San Diego, California, a critical site for the development of air power through the establishment of military settlements and bases, experimental sites, and aircraft manufacturers. Focusing on air power in San Diego shows how its pursuit produced a border technopolitical regime.

Historically, air power has relied on a fabulous logic that operates on a future anterior, a future possibility justifying "command of the air" in the present. In *Il dominio dell'aria* (1921), Italian air power theorist Giulio Douhet argued that "to have command of the air means to be in a position to wield offensive power so great it defies human imagination. It means to be able to cut an enemy's army and navy off from their bases of operation and nullify their chances of winning the war. It means complete protection of one's own country, the efficient operation of one's army and navy, and peace of mind to live and work in safety."[14] Air power went beyond human imagination for it promised absolute aggression and protection. Total superiority over an enemy rose from the soil of a speculative fiction. Air power grew from a preventive logic that, like the radioactive nation building discussed by anthropologist Joseph Masco, created a virtual world to disarm the Other before they could disrupt a nation's "peace of mind."[15] It was an offensive mode of relating to an Other who constituted a prospective threat; it was a desire for self-protection and self-perpetuation. Following this fabulous logic, to have command of the air meant that an air force, made up of devices and actors dedicated to acting from the air, sought to dictate and constrain the behavior of enemies in the present to guarantee national survival in the future.

An imperial logic can be found in the discourse of air power. The features of this imperial logic were territorial expansion, the redrawing of boundaries, and population displacement and dispossession.[16] The whole planet and, for that matter, every country was imagined now to be within the reach of whoever exploited aviation's potential. During the 1920s and early 1930s, William Mitchell, a veteran pilot during World War I, was among the most outspoken and forceful proponents of air power in the United States. He saw aircraft as "set[ting] aside all ideas of frontiers. The whole country," he argued, "now becomes the frontier and, in case of war, one place is just as exposed to attack as another place."[17] The frontier here, as in much popular culture, was a space where racial differences were enforced through law, policy, and technology. Though he seemed to contend that air power got rid of the frontier, Mitchell quickly reasoned that it dispersed the frontier to the point of making "the whole country" and the globe into a "frontier." More troubling, since World War I, "the trend in war [was] to treat combatant and non-combatant alike, if to do so [realized] any substantial military gain."[18] While combatants had been generally construed as the members of state armed forces, noncombatants were the unarmed and nonbelligerent citizens of the same state. The expansive, imperial logic of air power, once reserved for the frontiers of colonial conquest, now blurred the boundaries of so-called civilized countries and also those between combatants and noncombatants. All human actors and the whole planet were now treated as participants and sites in the social fabrication of war. Yet not everyone was equally subjected to air power.

Mitchell's theorization in 1934 offered a vision imbuing air power with an imperialist framework that split the world into civilizing and uncivilized forces, Western and non-Western nations.[19] It was the task of "the white races of western Europe and America," he reasoned, to fully exploit air power's defensive qualities to protect themselves from the aggressions of non-Western, Asian "yellow races."[20] Mitchell feared that the growing "friction . . . between the white [the West] and yellow races [Asia]" stemmed from the latter's attempts to take their share of the wealth that the former had amassed— through the sheer violence of dispossession and exploitation of labor and land. His focus on the yellow races stemmed from his immersion in a wider public discourse regarding Asians in the United States. Since the turn of United States the twentieth century, the US public produced, circulated, and consumed ideas about "health" and "cleanliness" that Chinese men and women were perceived not to fulfill. Chinese bodies were deemed "unhygienic" and "unhealthy"; they were considered to be dangerous and inadmissible to the US nation.[21] Their exclusion from the nation, made official since 1882, was soon shared by Japanese, Indians, and other Asians identified as racially ineligible for citizenship by the Johnson-Reed Act of 1924.[22] Their inadmissibility pushed them into the margins of legal personhood to the point of being imagined as representative of the "illegal" subject, a "foreign" menace against which the resources of the empire-nation had to be mobilized.[23] Alluding to the danger posed by the "yellow races," Mitchell saw the United States as the sole "great white power whose shores touch the Pacific Ocean." And in his plea to "[give] America airplanes," he positioned air power as a strategic technology to prevent Asians from entering the nation, all the while preserving the capacity to expand its territory and police the boundaries of its imagined community. Air power would keep Asians at bay, firmly under control at "the outer barriers of the white's dominions" so as to secure "the future preservation of the independence of [the United States]."[24] National preservation, which implied a racial ordering of local and global spaces, was guaranteed by the development and exercise of air power by "white" or so-called Western societies.

Air power, then, should be understood as enacting a racial politics in the configuration of space. Airplanes offered actors novel techniques to organize and intervene in land from the air. Pilots, aerial photographers, artists, and other air power advocates argued that the view from above afforded the separation of the human body from its environment and, in doing so, instituted a standpoint from which to objectively construe subjects and objects on the ground.[25] Aviation and its "cosmic view" were critical interventions in the making of social space, especially in the vein of the concrete abstraction and political monumentality that sociologist Henri Lefebvre demonstrated comprises the intense circulation of information, representations, and knowledge bound with power.[26] Air power was entangled with ways of knowing and making sense of those down below.

During the Mexican Revolution, the US military mobilized air power in an attempt to enforce and govern the territorial boundaries of the nation. To that end, the military organized an expedition in March 1916 led by Brigadier General John J. Pershing. According to the US State Department, the expedition would "simply [be] a necessary punitive measure, aimed solely at the elimination of marauders who raided Columbus [New Mexico] and who infest an unprotected district near the border, which they use as a base in making attacks upon the lives and property of our citizens within our own territory."[27] Aircraft used in the Pershing expedition gathered and transmitted information on the movements of people in the border zone.[28] The "marauders" alluded to by the State Department were Pancho Villa and his men who had embarked on cross-border "raids." These "marauders" were identified as subjects who "infest." Their presence was not just disruptive because they plundered the private property of (white) US citizens but also perilous for the health of the nation. Implicit in the statement was the idea that they were racially undesirable, a public nuisance to US citizens. By treating Mexicans as vectors of infection, the State Department participated in the wider production of racialized medical discourses designed to justify the exclusion of Mexicans by policing their presence.[29]

Air power during the Mexican Revolution was mobilized within a larger effort to eradicate a particular group and keep it from freely moving across the international boundary between the United States and Mexico. US officials saw air power as an instrument to protect the "lives and property of [US] citizens." To do so, they targeted populations that constituted some fabulous threat. In other words, by denying racialized Mexicans their means of subsistence, air power managed and controlled population interactions across vast expanses of terrain, surveyed land and people, and brought about an acquiescing border subject. Air power needs to be understood in relation to race; as a technology, it must also be understood for the ways it creates that which it polices. It is constitutive of a technopolitical regime that prioritizes the hierarchical relation between air and land to regulate space and people. Air power was not exclusively bound to the domain of "war." It was rather a crucial practice in the constitution of government power and the empire-nation's civilizing mission in "non-Western" spaces. In other words, air power is an articulation of a regime that operationalizes difference by governing the racial boundary between human and nonhuman, friend and enemy.

SAN DIEGO: AIR POWER AS BORDER TECHNOPOLITICAL REGIME

The city of San Diego holds a special place in the production of air power's imperial logics. From the "civilizing" endeavors of Spanish settlers to the "pacification" efforts of US settlers against Native Americans in the nineteenth century, imperial logics were continually rehearsed in San Diego through the displacement, dispossession, management, and eradication of peoples. These practices often materialized through an assortment of entities and discourses. Two are of note here. First was the conceptualization of San Diego as a testament to the success of the US frontier. In the early twentieth century, the California governor, James Gillett, and others argued that San Diego owed much of its growth to the pioneering duty of US citizens "to perform on the Pacific slope."[30] The western frontier, after all, opened the door to the Pacific frontier. The second assortment of entities and discourses through which imperial formations materialized was air power. From the early twentieth century, San Diego grew into the "Air Capital of the West" through the collaborations between the US Navy, the San Diego Chamber of Commerce, city hall, and a variety of manufacturers of aircraft parts.[31] Air power linked San Diego to the civilizing mission of "the West," which made the city into an experimental space testing the boundaries of technological and political imagination.

The civilizing mission of "the West," with its distinct racial hierarchies, was conveyed in what historian Genevieve Carpio calls the "Anglo Fantasy Past." This selective tradition is a discursive practice that emerged in the nineteenth century emphasizing certain elements, populations, and practices while negating others. White settlers occupy a strategic role as pioneers building the foundations for the empire-nation through Indigenous erasure and Mexican dispossession.[32] As a selective tradition, it legitimizes settler colonial logics and capitalist relations; it is the product and the producer of land enclosures, the whiteness of private property, and the exploitability and disposability of non-white populations.[33] Over time, individuals, organizations, and institutions made the Anglo Fantasy Past into an enduring structure of feeling of the settler colonial project on the US Southwest and a discourse shaping the technopolitical imagination of US empire.[34]

The Anglo Fantasy Past is informed by the settler colonial logics of elimination and exclusion. Anthropologist and ethnographer Patrick Wolfe argues that a central tenet of settler colonialism is land, "rather than [to] extract surplus value by mixing" the labor of natives "with a colony's natural resources."[35] Settler colonial formations emerge through the practices of colonizers who move into Indigenous territory with the goal of staying and dispossessing Indigenous peoples through their eradication—what Wolfe terms the logic of elimination. Yet, in the experience of Spanish settler colonialism, labor was never far removed from the occupation of land. Native laborers were integral to the establishment of settlements and the extraction of value from the "colony's natural resources." Spanish settler colonies developed elaborate and fluid systems of governance that regulated the participation of differently racialized populations.[36] These systems of governance operated through logics of exclusion. They produced barriers within the colonial and, eventually, the national cultures that protected and reinforced the social and political control of settlers.[37] Ethnic studies scholar Iyko Day argues that these two logics respond to the racializing assemblages at the heart of settler colonialism. The logic of exclusion, on the one hand, asserts and controls internalized alien populations such as enslaved Africans and Mexican laborers through practices of segregation, disenfranchisement, exploitation, police brutality, and detention.[38] On the other hand, settler colonialism's logic of elimination operates more forcefully through the extermination of Indigenous or native populations whose existence represents a threat to the land claims of settlers and their government apparatus. Extermination unfolds through physical violence just as much as it does through assimilation practices that eliminate Indigenous culture. The Anglo Fantasy Past represents the symbolic description of settler colonial logics that, since the turn of the twentieth century, elevated San Diego into a prominent space in the making of the infrastructural matter of the US empire-nation.

As the United States built the Panama Canal in 1911, people in Southern California argued that San Diego would "guard the gates of the first American port of call."[39] To protect San Diego was to "guard the gates" of the US empire-nation. The people and institutions that were a part of what Mike Davis calls San Diego's "private governments" gave the city a distinct flair among others in California.[40] Aviation entrepreneurs—often called pioneers, a term that beckons the frontier imaginary of old—did not merely perform aerial pirouettes. Aviators sought to make the city one of its chief experimental sites. Harry S. Harkness, a collaborator of aviation entrepreneur Glenn Curtiss, for example, flew in 1911 from Fort Rosecrans in San Diego to the Border Field near Tijuana to deliver orders from a commander to a subordinate officer stationed there. His flight proved the utility of air power to communicate with deployed troops—aviation was imagined already as an information technology linking multiple actors across space. In this sense, aviation helped produce a territory of remote control for the empire-nation with soldiers "on the line" connected to their command structure.[41] Aviators, boosters, political officials, and business folks built the foundations on which an incipient defense industry would rise. This defense industry was heavily invested—literally and metaphorically—in the articulation of the empire-nation (as the United States became involved in the world wars) and in imperial ventures in the Caribbean, Central America, and the Pacific.[42] The western frontier gave way to an imperial frontier to be exploited by aviation's pioneers.

North Island (see figure 1.2) is a paradigmatic manifestation of the materiality of San Diego's air power and border technopolitical regime and its spatial and social arrangements. At the beginning of the twentieth century, San Diego's military presence was dominated by defensive structures constructed during the settler colonial contest of the Spanish-American War. By 1906, the US Navy thought the city would be a good place to establish a naval training station.[43] Despite the help of the city council, the San Diego Chamber of Commerce, and the realty board, the Navy could not move forward with its plans. Among the main sites under consideration was North Island on the western edge of and entry point to San Diego Bay. Owned by John D. Spreckels, a real estate mogul and member of the city elite, North Island was thought to be too expensive. The organization of the Aero Club of San Diego in 1910, however, opened the door to the Navy. Colonel David Charles Collier, the club's president and staff member to California governor James Gillett, invited aviation entrepreneur Glenn Curtiss to hold an aerial exhibit—in part to drum up excitement for the Panama-California Exposition of 1915 and also to establish an aviation school on the island. Curtiss thought it was "the best location on the Pacific Coast for a permanent aviation school," and the Curtiss School of Aviation operated in North Island from 1911 to 1913.[44] Curtiss was invested in the notion that a "safe and sane method" of aviation training required "attention to mechanical or technical aerodynamics."[45] So he and other aviators taught members of the US Army and Navy how to take apart and reassemble a gas engine as well as instructed them on "the controls and art of balancing before attempting

FIGURE 1.2. North Island in the early 1910s with Coronado, Gaslamp Quarter, and Balboa Park in background. Source: San Diego Air and Space Museum.

actual flight."[46] By 1913, though, when the Curtiss School of Aviation closed, the Army and Navy were convinced that North Island was an excellent site for aviation training. After the beginning of hostilities in Europe in 1914, training resumed on the "island" under the Army's Air Service.

Through the work of Curtiss and other aviators, however, the island was transformed not only into a site for the proliferation of aviation knowledge but a space for experimenting with aeronautics. Harkness's flight to deliver communications to the Border Field close to Tijuana was merely one of many experiments. At the request of the Navy, Curtiss experimented in North Island with different aircraft configurations as aviators attempted to take off and land on water.[47] Hydroplanes emerged as a result of these efforts. In the 1920s, the Marine Base and Naval Training Center opened on land handed to the US government by the City of San Diego. The Marine Base expanded experimental work through its involvement in the research and development of cutting-edge technologies such as long-distance radio transmission, carrier aviation, and undersea and amphibious warfare.[48] Colonel Collier, the Aero Club, the Chamber of Commerce, Curtiss, Harkness, the US Army and the Navy, among others, sowed the seeds for the growth of a border technopolitical regime in San Diego.

Ryan Aeronautical, responsible for designing, developing, and fabricating the Firebee drone used in Operation Top Gun and Project William Tell, was one of the first companies to join San Diego's air power and border regime. Founded by ex-Army pilot T. Claude Ryan in 1922, the company entered the national and international spotlight when its plane, the Ryan NYP, also known as the *Spirit of St. Louis,* was flown by Charles Lindbergh in the world's first transatlantic flight. On May 10, 1927, Lindbergh initiated his odyssey to Paris from North Island, San Diego, with stops in St. Louis and New York before crossing the Atlantic.[49] His feat offered added currency to Ryan Aeronautical as an aircraft manufacturer, to San Diego as a hub for air power, and to the potential of civilian aviation. By the early 1930s, several aircraft manufacturers, including the General Aviation Corporation and Consolidated Aircraft, opened plants in Southern California.[50] A testament to the global and local reach of Ryan was its collaboration with the North Island Naval Air Station in San Diego, the first air station on the US Pacific Coast. The company constructed sport planes and trainers used to prepare World War II pilots during the 1930s. The Ryan School of Aeronautics was one of nine commercial schools chosen by the Air Corps in 1939 to conduct primary training of flying cadets.[51] In other words, Ryan Aeronautical contributed to the defense economy through the manufacture of aeronautical products (e.g., parts and planes) and the production of specialized knowledge. Toward the end of the 1930s, Ryan Aeronautical and San Diego became integral to the production of US air power and its strategic place within the border technopolitical regime.

Air power advocates fabricated a new domain, construed as independent from the ground or sea, from which to produce and order social space. The use of bomber aircraft to inaugurate atomic warfare in Hiroshima and Nagasaki at the end of World War II further entrenched air power's capacities to redefine legal and territorial boundaries. Military and government officials identified the persistent threats of nuclear annihilation and air power as justifications for an elaborate research agenda into remote control and push-button warfare.

"Cowboy in the Sky": The Firebee on the Settler Colonial Frontier

The specter of atomic destruction was simultaneously a source of fear and a boon. It was leveraged to justify the need for growing military research and funding, even as the prospect of nuclear holocaust haunted the US public.[52]

The same sites that were imagined as the "birthplace of the Atomic Age" back on July 16, 1945—Alamogordo and the White Sands Proving Ground in New Mexico—were soon after transformed into the testing stages for remote control and push-button warfare technologies. Guided missiles and other pilotless aircraft designed by various companies, among them Ryan Aeronautical, were tested there with the direct collaboration of the Air Force's Air Research and Development Command.[53] Military officials reasoned that remote control made unmanning possible and, thereby, removed humans from harm's way. These officials aimed to maintain safety for their soldiers even while bringing harm on others. To keep nuclear devastation far away from the citizens and soldiers of the US nation, the military and its industrial/corporate partners pursued push-button warfare, which more concretely relied on developments in electronics and computing. The unmanned technopolitics of push-button warfare promised two things: to provide the technical capacity of pinpoint accuracy that disavowed human effort and that stopped nuclear aerial attack, and to extend the reach of imperial and settler colonial entanglements. These entanglements came to the foreground through biopolitical scripts that inscribed unmanning within a racial order enrolling Indigenous and Mexican populations as unsettling threats. They were unsettling in a double sense of being anxiety-inducing and a disturbing source of the settler practices of US imperial formations.

THE MAKING OF THE FIREBEE: UNMANNED TECHNOPOLITICS

Remote control was associated with push-button warfare. Even the US Army in 1947 linked these two ideas when explaining that what made a weapon like the missile into a "push-button variety" were "the facilities" to control "its flight, after it is launched without the aid of a human pilot aboard."[54] Remote control, on the one hand, meant that a human agent could dictate the behaviors of a nonhuman entity over space and time. The "button," on the other hand, represented any kind of lethal force quickly unleashed with little human effort; it was catastrophic violence visited on humans by the offspring of modern science and technology: machines.[55] Push-button warfare endeavored to constitute a technopolitical arrangement that disavowed human labor and agency. In the wider public imaginary, it elicited the sense of automatic and precise deadly force that, once triggered, would be ungovernable.[56] Journalists imagined the "button," physically removed from the space of battle, as producing destruction elsewhere. Disenchantment and desperation were hegemonic affective dispositions toward push-button warfare.[57] But either as promise or far-flung fantasy, public discussion kept the idea of push-button warfare in wide circulation, which gave the US military ample justifications to fund its research and development. And this became a cornerstone of the Firebee and its unmanned technopolitics.

Policymakers, military officials, corporate actors, and members of the public sphere in the United States underscored the need for an aggressive military research agenda built around the notion of push-button warfare. With the Soviet Union becoming a nuclear power after detonating an atomic bomb in 1949, public pressure increased to ensure the United States would "remain militarily strong." This meant, a *New York Times* editorial argued, that the country would not have "to pay the inevitable penalty of weakness—submission to the will of others."[58] The editorial identified recruitment and training of soldiers as well as continued investments in air power as fundamental to "remain[ing] militarily strong." In a similar vein, a *Los Angeles Times* article said that "we must work very hard toward the push-button era, paradoxically, so that we may prevent, through our potential strength, just such a war."[59] Using the highly gendered dyads of strength and weakness, supporters of push-button warfare underscored their belief in a masculinist perspective of power. The US military needed to showcase its "muscle" and its brutal capacity to destroy the enemy.

Imperial violence was embedded, in this sense, in the instruments of push-button warfare. The public thought that *un*manning removed soldiers from danger and perpetuated their "strength"; their safety was premised on the exposure of the other to the machine's violence. Similarly, the dangers of nuclear destruction required, military officials and defense intellectuals argued, a more centralized yet dynamic military.[60] Unmanning unfolded through the automation of certain processes that, for example, allowed human labor to be redirected elsewhere while allowing for centralized and faster decision making. "Assist[ing] or replac[ing] human skill in aiming and operating advanced weapons," such as guided missiles, was one of the ways unmanning was integrated into military technology and practice.[61]

The drone program at Ryan Aeronautical grew out of its collaborations with the Air Material Command (AMC) Guided Missiles Section and the US military's pursuit of push-button warfare.[62] AMC initiated Project MX-873 in August 1946, a year after the United States launched two atomic bombs against Japan. Ryan won the contract on June 30, 1948, to initially develop and fabricate thirty-two experimental targets, though thirty more were requested a year later. With the lurking danger of enemy air power and nuclear devastation, the US Navy and Air Force sought to address the challenge of intercepting any prospective aerial attack. They supported the development of remotely controlled aerial targets "to simulate high-speed, high-altitude aircraft" and, in doing so, train ground-to-air gunners as well as pilots.[63] Ryan's prototype drone, the XQ-2, was the first jet-powered remote-controlled target in the US arsenal.[64] Its 1,800-pound airframe was made of aluminum, magnesium, and stainless steel. It had an overall height of 5 feet 4 inches, an overall length of 16 feet 8 inches, and a wingspan of 11 feet 2 inches.[65] Once its design was set, the subsequently known Firebee/Q-2 drone established the foundations for future drone development throughout the Cold War.

During and after World War II, drones generated little public interest, yet they had an important role to play in the development of warfare through their association with computing and push-button warfare.[66] Newspapers described them as "robot planes" or "robots in air" and, in doing so, signaled to readers that these remotely piloted aircraft were of a different kind.[67] They represented a new age of automation—a term that in the mid-twentieth century was often associated with cybernetics and computers. But what made the Q-2 a robot plane was the fact that it used an electronics package (see figures 1.3 and 1.4) designed to automatically execute some of its command-and-control functions as well as allow for a pilot on the ground to command the aircraft. Control was achieved through continuous wave radar techniques with equipment mounted on the Q-2 (AN/APW-11) and a ground tracking radar (MSQ-1 or SCR-584) plugged into a remote-control box.[68] Remote control was, as an article in *Ryan Reporter* stated, a literal "black box," the "push-button heart of the 'Firebee'" that allowed the aircraft to respond "ghost-like" to the commands of a human pilot.[69] The Firebee's on-board radar receiver processed informational inputs sent from the remote controller through a radar transmitter. A pilot on the ground monitored data captured by tracking equipment and displayed on a plotting board at the station. All these components created a closed cybernetic system of communication and control. Remote control made the robot plane an otherworldly entity, a spectral figure haunting the ground from the sky. The notion of a robot plane drew from the public mystique of new electronic digital computers and portrayed the US military as an advanced, modern enterprise. On the rise in the mid-twentieth century, computer technologies were imagined as harbingers of a different world, one enveloped by and understood through computational metaphors blurring the boundaries between human and machine.[70]

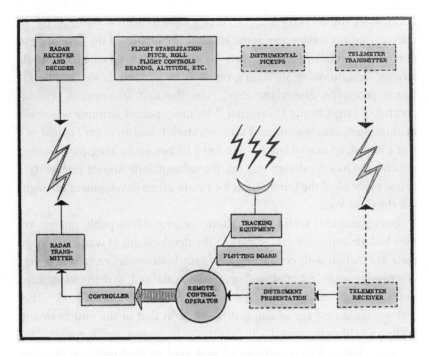

FIGURE 1.3. Firebee remote control. Source: "Mission 'Bullseye,'" *Ryan Reporter* 17, no. 5 (November 1956): 1.

In calling Q-2 Firebees robots in the air or "the bee with the electronic brain," Ryan Aeronautical described a sociotechnical arrangement that both disavowed human agency and the messiness of (imperial) politics.[71] Remote control and push-button technologies drew and articulated a desire for an automaticity that expedited action without having to deal with human volition—even while such mechanical action was imagined through the language of human bodies, push-button hearts, and electronic brains. This is what Chandler calls "unmanning": "a contingent set of situated practices imperfectly made by human, media, and machine." Unmanning makes human actions spectral by privileging the mechanical operations of the drone.[72] Writing about guided missile development for *Ryan Reporter* in 1950, Colonel Harry J. Sands Jr. expressed his skepticism with the ways that push-button technology was imagined. He insisted that for every push button there are "hundreds of thousands of manhours . . . invested in research, design, development, planning, tooling, fabricating, inspecting, and testing!"[73] But despite his attempts to remind the public of human action and control, these were obfuscated, embedded, and forgotten within the network of a drone's operations.

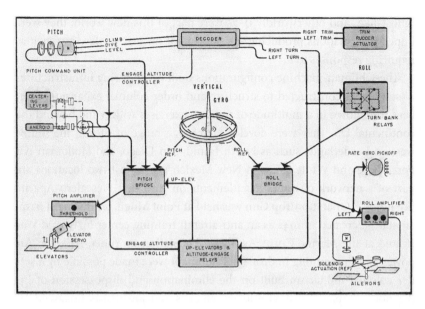

FIGURE 1.4. Firebee autopilot system. Source: "Mission 'Bullseye,'" *Ryan Reporter* 17, no. 5 (November 1956): 2.

This obfuscation produced a double disavowal of the human that, like a double negative, led to accumulation. In displacing the "hundreds of thousands of [citizen] manhours," the nonhuman drone machine represented an inhuman danger from which to ratify the liberty of the nation's citizens. Drones were surrogates for the capacity to be human. They were imagined replacing the human labor of actors in the border technopolitical regime just as they dispossessed, displaced, or eliminated the racialized surrogate labor of non-white populations in the frontier through the expansion of the network of US military settlements devoted to technological development. Surrogate labor, now embedded within drone operations, enabled the freedoms of US citizens.[74] Negating the drone's humanity was a translation of settler and imperial logics of differentiation and elimination. Flying robots in the air were the product of a vast border technopolitical regime working to govern the boundaries of inclusion and exclusion from the nation, which were the boundaries of the Other's humanity. In rejecting the drone/Other's humanity, citizens of the US nation accumulated rights. More importantly, their capacity to have rights was sustained. Human-machine configurations in the drone hid the human and built on existing anxieties of nuclear and frontier violence to conjure the deadly threat of an inhuman menace. The "ghost-like" and otherworldly Q-2s were part of this new world; they were imperial formations producing the dangers of nuclear warfare as much as requiring responses to it.

These human-machine configurations built on enduring infrastructures of settlement constructed to structure and order colonial expansion. Firebees were flown in a multitude of military exercises within and beyond the continental US. They were developed across a range of sites in the southwestern borderlands such as North Island, San Diego, and Holloman Air Force Base and White Sands in New Mexico—these last two locations are part of a network of military settlements on land that Mescalero Apache call home.[75] Operation Top Gun was held at Point Mugu, California, a naval air station created in 1942 as an anti-aircraft training center for World War II, and at the Marine Corps Auxiliary Air Station in Yuma, Arizona. Air power and unmanning in drone development were made possible by a settler colonial militarism built on the elimination and dispossession of Indigenous peoples.[76] Just as military officials and journalists imagined air power as subjecting the world to its violent view from above, remotely piloted vehicles were predicated on the paranoid fantasy that extending sovereign control over the Other and their space both imperiled and promised the protection of the nation. In Alamogordo, New Mexico, the Chamber of Commerce felt so proud of its city's role in the development of the Firebee that it installed a decommissioned drone on top of its downtown building in 1959. "The citizens of Alamogordo have," an article in *Ryan Reporter* told its readers, "placed these test vehicles on display as symbols of the vital link between the community and the missile, aircraft and space research conducted at nearby Holloman."[77] The drone atop of the Chamber of Commerce was a reminder and remnant of the entanglements between industry and the military in sustaining the community. More importantly, it suggested that the configuration of human-machine relations by the border technopolitical regime was also a spatial operation enrolling actors differently reifying imperial formations.

FRONTIER BIOPOLITICAL SCRIPTS

As an assemblage of human and nonhuman entities, drones were designed by Ryan Aeronautical and the US military to play unique roles in situations that called on the wider border technopolitical regime to put their plans into action. That is, the border crossing maneuvers of drones into US territory triggered the activations of a predetermined sequence of actions designed to defend the nation.[78] These plans and situations built on frontier biopolitical scripts as to what kinds of bodies were to be included and excluded from the nation.

Weapons meets during the Cold War often conjured doomsday scenarios for which US soldiers and their weapons systems must be ready. Among these scenarios was the possibility that the Soviet Union would unleash an all-out nuclear aerial attack. Writing for *The Aircraft Flash*, the editor of the Air Force periodical Jeff Wilson explained to his readers, mainly the civilian volunteer members of the Ground Observer Corps, what "the basic concept of air defense" was all about. The Corps was tasked with supporting air defense by spotting and plotting the movements of (possible) hostile aircraft.[79] That meant that Cold War "[air defense] is designed to keep an atomic war out from over our heads."[80] Operation Top Gun and Project William Tell were military exercises that trained US pilots in the Navy and the Air Force, respectively, in the basics of air defense: early identification of enemy presence close to US territory, attack of intruder forces, and maneuvers to deny them access to their targets. Military officials like General Curtis E. LeMay thought US national survival relied on the preparation of soldiers to fend off any aerial attacks.[81] Ryan Aeronautical's Firebee drone was mobilized to protect the nation by tackling what was called the "interception problem"; the drone "simulated," the *Los Angeles Times* said, "almost exactly all piloted jet plane maneuvers."[82] Q-2 drones offered a way to mimic high-speed jet aircraft and, in so doing, gave fighter plane pilots a "realistic target." Military officials arranged the interception of intruder aircraft into a cornerstone of national defense and, concomitantly, national survival. These exercises were plans on how to avoid the conjoining of air power and "an atomic war" from raining death and destruction "from over our heads." Positing intruders as central targets for the defense of the nation, however, was not merely a technical matter of concern for the border technopolitical regime.

Military exercises with drones like Operation Top Gun and Project William Tell prescribed frontier relations through the execution of biopolitical scripts. As military and government officials negotiated public anxieties around nuclear devastation and the status of US imperial power, they set out a series of plans to manage intruders and enforce US sovereignty. These plans enmeshed concerns over enemy air power with visions for settler colonial control in the southern borderlands. Experiments with air power came to embody pursuits of an authentic national self. Military exercises drew from a robust structure of feeling that elicited stories of frontier pioneers that did not merely eliminate Indigenous peoples but represented "a heuristic encounter with the primitive" to integrate their authenticity and ruggedness to the nation.[83] Air power's material investments in settler log-ics took center stage during the performance of military plans designed to respond to situations of danger. Drones embodied the role of the racialized Other. As an intruder, they were considered unauthorized and extraneous actors threatening to destroy (the defensive forces of) the nation.[84]

Plans against future Soviet intruder operations were paramount for the US military. The US Navy organized Operation Top Gun in 1959 to prepare naval and aerial defense operations on the "gates of the first American port of call" to the Pacific. The weapons meet, held over five days simultaneously at Point Mugu near Los Angeles and the Marine Corps Auxiliary Air Station in Yuma, Arizona, included the participation of Navy and Marine teams from Atlantic and Pacific fleet squadrons. Project William Tell, on the other hand, was a weapons meet organized in 1958 (though held well into the 1960s) by the US Air Force's Air Defense Command. Held at Tyndall Air Force Base in Florida and over the Gulf of Mexico, Project William Tell initially consisted of a ten-day war game exercise in which targets, weapons, and carriers (interceptor aircraft and pilots) were deployed to test the na-tional defense system.[85] Air Defense Command was armed with "modern" intercepting jet-powered aircraft, guided missiles, and rockets to tackle the threat of intruder operations. "Our [US] survival," *Ryan Reporter* argued in 1959, "still depends on whether the enemy gets through our air defense system to dump his lethal charge."[86] And to make sure the enemy did not penetrate US aerial defenses, Air Defense Command and the Atlantic and Pacific fleets rehearsed plans to protect the nation. Like aerial cowboys in the US Southwest, pilots were out to institute order in the lawless frontier.

And the "push-button target" in this frontier play was Ryan Aeronau-tical's Firebee Q-2. In an ad appearing in *Ryan Reporter*, the company described the Q-2 as an "'enemy' jet over America."[87] The Firebee was an enemy intruder in both Operation Top Gun and Project William Tell, simulating high-speed jet aircraft and bomber planes threatening to unleash nuclear terror on US cities. Across both weapons meets, drones flew in pre-planned circuits within firing ranges between 50 and 170 nautical miles.[88] For Project William Tell, for example, Firebees flew in high (above 30,000 feet) and low (5,000 to 15,000 feet) missions over the Gulf of Mexico with-out warning.[89] They allowed military officials to assess the proficiency of their pilots by testing their skills against a high-flying, quick-evasion target that replicated real combat conditions and, thanks to the absence of an on-board pilot, allowed the use of live ammunition. Throughout both weapons meets, electronics scoring systems were used to record performance data on military technologies, such as weapons and aircrafts, and pilot actions.[90] As a result, the use of Firebees in military exercises gave officials an opportunity to evaluate the overall performance of air defense.

Q-2s played two other important roles in the maintenance of air power and the border technopolitical regime: the coordination of entities in national defense as an informational problem and the prescription of enmity through racial imaginaries. According to the 4756th Drone Squadron stationed at Tyndall Air Force Base, this "weapons system had three prime factors: the pilot, his aircraft, and the ground controller who directed him to the 'intruder.' The [Firebee] drone assumed the role of the 'intruder' and acted the part well."[91] Air defense was the integration of a detection and monitoring system that alerted armed forces personnel of the prospective intrusion of national territory and a communications network that would coordinate intruder interceptions. As part of Project William Tell in 1961 and again in 1963, the Air Force employed the still experimental Semi-Automatic Ground Environment (SAGE) system. SAGE was part of a Cold War drive to produce a "closed world" governed through computerized command, control, and communications systems.[92] SAGE's functions during the weapons meet were to detect and identify enemy aircraft and to direct interceptors toward the enemy.[93] The Navy described its air defense system through the coordination of interceptors in the air and a ground control interceptor (GCI). GCI monitored radar systems in case of an intrusion that, once detected, would lead them to "vector the aircraft to its target." In other words, GCI was a "vital link" because it directed pilots, as part of the human and nonhuman "airborne weapons system," toward their targets to stop the attack.[94] Descriptions put forth in military publications and in Ryan Aeronautical's promotional materials show that Firebee drones were part of the closed world that imagined warfare through the frameworks of cybernetics. The sociotechnical arrangement put together by the Air Force and Navy treated intrusion as an informational problem. The US armed forces abstracted intruder operations into data to sense, communicate, and control. Defense of the nation was made computable, and the plans put forth by military exercises sought to make responses to imminent danger automatic, habitually incorporated into system operations.

In the images of the Firebee used by Ryan Aeronautical, we find some of the imperial and settler logics of the border technopolitical regime. In figure 1.5, the Firebee hovers over a vast rugged, mountainous range. This kind of perspectival approach to the Firebee was often used in Ryan Aeronautical's magazine ads and promotional pamphlets.[95] It sought to convey

FIGURE 1.5. Q-2 Firebee. Source: San Diego Air and Space Museum.

to viewers how the technopolitical regime built by Ryan Aeronautical, the Navy, the Air Force, and the Army articulated command of the air. A seemingly desolate and boundless landscape occupies the secondary plane of the image. Drawing from historical depictions of the US Southwest as a void space, no human trace can be found within the frame of the shot. This is a practice that feminist STS scholar Felicity Amaya Schaeffer contends "erases longer histories of settler theft of land considered wild and empty, or void of inhabitants."[96] In this image, technical descriptions are left behind as the

Firebee is attributed agency over this supposedly void space where Indigenous communities have lived for centuries. STS scholar John Law calls this the distribution of active and passive agency, which is also the distribution of vulnerability and invulnerability.[97] The photograph drew a boundary of contrasts through physical proximity and viewpoint. The unmanned drone flies as if by its own will—though it is actually piloted from a ground control station. Inverting the romantic conceptualization of the sublime, the perspective articulated in the image inscribes the Firebee as an imposing figure, an entity that dominates the landscape down below. The image diminishes the enormous mountains in the background. Technology acts over the natural world, making the latter vulnerable to the former's supposed invulnerability. The imagined (drone) automaton, a symbol of Western (imperial) science, triumphs over the frontier and its unruly people. They are all reduced by the sharp contrast and the larger volume of the flying machine of war. The flight of this Firebee is most likely taking place in one of the many Air Force bases constructed on Indigenous lands, like the Holloman Air Development Center in New Mexico.[98] The disappearance of humans from the frame, in the air and on the ground, is emblematic of the "vanishing logic" of settler colonialism. This is a logic that dispossesses and displaces Indigenous peoples to evade the question of ongoing settler colonialism.[99] The dominating presence of the robot plane operationalized the US empire-nation's racializing claims over land and people, while the image worked to document the creation of its territory.

Operation Top Gun was pre-inscribed through the tropes of and practices in a wild west story, part of the grand "American" epic. Pilots, aeronautical engineers, aircraft manufacturers, the US military, and their aircrafts were "pioneers" settling new territory for the US empire-nation.[100] During the opening scene of Ryan's informational film about Top Gun, the morning sun creeps over a shadowy mountain ridge, a kind of generic image of the borderlands. The film's narrator frames the event: "As the vast western frontier open[ed] to settlement," these lands require "forces of law and order" vested "with the belief in the ideals of liberty with justice for all, [and] a willingness to fight for those ideals with deadly accuracy." The men of law and order were the "top guns of the west," an allusion to the geographical area to be made into US territory and to the racial project of Western civilization. Indigenous communities were but unspeakable subjects in this film, the unmentioned targets of the top guns. The "western frontier" was, after all, "open to settlement," imagined as devoid of its Indigenous inhabitants. Settler practices in the "western frontier" are partially alluded to yet not elaborated.

These are what Latina/o studies scholar Nicole Guidotti-Hernández calls "unspeakable violence."[101] Settler violence is not some foregone conclusion, left in the dustbins of history. Instead, it is constantly rehearsed and reproduced, a concomitant practice of the US empire-nation. Operation Top Gun was one of many contemporary reenactments of settler violence. Sailors and pilots of the US Navy were, the narrator promptly concludes, "the top guns of the space age," and on their shoulders and aircraft rested "the survival of our nation and the free world."[102] Many of the images and symbols used by Ryan Aeronautical and the Navy to promote Operation Top Gun—pistols, saloon fonts, cowboys, and horses—linked the exercise to the wild west.[103] With air power construed as an "infinite frontier," military aircraft were envisioned as flying mechanical horses while Navy pilots took on the role of "hard-riding keepers of the peace."[104] But if they were the heroes, then Firebees were villains and intruders. They were the nonhuman embodiment of unspeakable Indigenous subjects whose mere presence challenged sovereign claims over the western frontier.

The high-flying pirouettes of Firebees coproduced settler colonial practices in time and space through a theater of war prescribing relations of enmity. In his work on control systems before cybernetics, historian of science David Mindell argues that all control systems worked with three core elements: perception, integration, and articulation.[105] The border technopolitical regime of US air power constituted such a control system. In Operation Top Gun and Project William Tell, drones enabled relations of enmity by embodying the role of an intruder. Drones oriented the human-machine configuration of pilots and aircraft by shaping their attention and behavior. This perception of a threatening enemy intruder was integrated into the conception of the borderlands of the nation. The presence of seemingly extraneous entities in this area habituated the human-machine assemblage into a distinct response—the articulation of a violent posture to repel it. The outcome of this iteration of the border technopolitical regime was the lethal exclusion of bodies construed as foreign to the nation.

Frontier biopolitical scripts can also be found in the name of Project William Tell, which reproduced a structure of feeling whereby foreign subjects were imagined and felt as inherently suspect and, at worst, enemies of the nation. In their film about the military exercise, the Air Force argued that "yesterday and today, a nation's defense forces must keep alert, ready to counter an invader's approach. That is what military training is all about: setting up and maintaining defense capable of repelling enemy attack. Principal enemy during William Tell meets is the Ryan Firebee."[106] Calling attention to those "invaders" that threatened the nation "yesterday and today"—a shape-shifting abstract reference that can be read as an allusion to British imperialism, Mexican forces at the Alamo, Native Americans undoing US sovereignty in the western states, or Villa's border crossing attacks in New Mexico—the Air Force naturalized its animosity toward intruders. This imagined persistent threat resonates with what historians Pekka Hämäläinen and Samuel Truett argue about borderlands stories as romances. They "were tales of movement and adventure with indefinite end points." Borderland tales were told "as prologues to frontier tales in which the United States completed the unfinished work of conquest."[107] Yet, paradoxically, borderlands romances challenge such closure by underscoring the persistent need of settlers to reenact—that is, to reaffirm their purported victory. Frontier biopolitical scripts were fundamental in how military and corporate officials sought to make sense of drones. These scripts not only made sense of new technologies, they also worked to structure sociotechnical relations and operations.

The name of the military exercise entangled two stories about masculine violence in the making of "the West." First is the story of William Tell, a Swiss folk hero whose story functions as a foundational myth for the Swiss confederacy since at least the sixteenth century.[108] The second is the story of the Lone Ranger. William Tell was known for his expert marksmanship, having shot an apple off his son's head. Framed within the context of an ideological and geopolitical struggle with the Soviet Union, the US Air Force came to imagine William Tell as a "symbol of man's freedom, of man's resistance to a tyrant oppression."[109] Practicing their marksmanship during the Cold War, US pilots were thought of as modern William Tells striving to protect the nation. Since the inception of aviation, pilots were also depicted as contemporary reiterations of the self-contained, self-reliant, and courageous pioneers of yore. They were linked with the rugged individualism that people had come to associate with the frontier in US history.[110] William Tell's legend made its way to the opera stage when Gioachino Rossini adapted it in 1829. The opera's overture finale became, more than a century later, the theme song for *The Lone Ranger* in radio, television, and film.

Another fighting spirit, the Lone Ranger translated William Tell into the context of the US Southwest borderlands. He was a former Texas Ranger—a paramilitary, settler colonial organization created in the nineteenth century for the "pacification" of Mexican and Native American communities.[111] Together, the Lone Ranger and his Native American partner, Tonto, protected vulnerable individuals or groups by fighting powerful adversaries in the "southwest territory of the US." Clearly operating within a revisionist framework, the Lone Ranger took on (white) villains to bring forth what Michael Ray Fitzgerald calls a "benevolent white supremacy."[112] As the narrative voiceover in the 1949 pilot episode states, the Lone Ranger "was a fabulous individual, a man whose presence brought fear to the lawless and hope to those who wanted to make this frontier-land their home."[113] Following a frontier mentality, only the development and modernization of western territories could, in the end, protect inhabitants from the evil forces of noncivilized life. The story of the Lone Ranger dramatized the making of US settler colonialism's surveillant infrastructure through the enrollment of the Native scout. Tonto's worldmaking practices and his engagements in the Southwest represented the historical integration of Indigenous techniques in the late nineteenth century into, as Schaeffer convincingly shows, the repertoires of US imperial formations. The instrumentalization of Indigenous knowledge for border making articulated the perspective of the state and, in doing so, erased Native peoples and their worldviews.[114] *The Lone Ranger* television series ran from 1949 to 1957—the dawn of the Cold War—and reimagined the past to think the present. The male bravado exuded by the Lone Ranger was crucial in deterring all menaces. Like William Tell before him, he resisted a somewhat tyrannical force—lawlessness—and championed the cause of liberty. The television series portrayed the expansion and territorial consolidation of the US nation in conjunction with the reproduction of US government power, both private and public. Together, these functioned as protective factors in the face of a different kind of "lawless" threat.

By the time jet-propelled drones were integrated into US military weapons meets in the 1940s, another kind of intruder was already the focus of government officials and the wider US public. The largely "Mexican migratory agricultural proletariat," Mae Ngai suggests, came to the fore through government projects such as the Bracero Program (1942–1964) and the efforts of agribusiness.[115] Comprising Mexican Americans, legal and unauthorized Mexican immigrants, and imported contract workers, this Mexican transnational labor force was the target of concerted attempts to monitor, contain, and manage it. An integral part of the Bracero Program, for example, was the careful and systematic control of migrant populations. The US Border Patrol, Kelly Lytle Hernández shows, was ordered to "prevent Mexican laborers from surreptitiously crossing into the United States and to aggressively detect and deport those who had successfully affected illegal entry." Among its strategies, which were generally coordinated with Mexican government officials, was the use of airplanes to airlift deportees from Holtville, California, and Brownsville, Texas, into central Mexican states like Guanajuato, Jalisco, and San Luis Potosí. These airlifts were used in 1951 and 1952 in the deportation of 85,561 Mexicans.[116] Just as it was experimentally employed in managing Villa's border crossing exploits during the Mexican Revolution, air power continued to be integral to the border technopolitical regime in the management of Mexican populations in the borderlands and in border making itself.

Within and beyond the US Southwest, this migrant population came to embody the intractability of the border—their presence signaled a sense of bounded "foreignness." The legal concept of "alien" placed some bodies within and beyond the bounds of the US body politic. US law's definition of an alien was "any person not a citizen or national of the United States."[117] Immigrant aliens were those who had been formally admitted for residency in the United States while nonimmigrant aliens were those given temporary admission into the country under one of the more than twenty-five visa categories. The category of alien signaled both an intent to administer how certain bodies participated within and how they could be excluded from social space.[118] In their sociolegal inquiries into the US production of Mexican-migrant "illegality," Ngai and Nicholas De Genova show how the systematic targeting of Mexicans shaped and was shaped by a specifically spatialized sociopolitical imagination. The US southern border and Mexican bodies occupied privileged positions in the collective construction of foreignness. These supposed migrants were racialized through the legal category of "illegal alien," which, in the US public imaginary, further entrenched their place as "invasive violators of the law, incorrigible 'foreigners,' subverting the integrity of 'the nation' and its sovereignty from within the space of the US nation-state."[119] The making of a sovereign nation was thought to be dependent on the constitution of a legal territory, and illegal aliens challenged such attempts. They represented the transgression of said territory while also inhabiting it. As subversive subjects of US sovereignty, illegal aliens constituted a permanent and enduring foreign threat. In their foreignness, they resonated heavily in the US imaginary with the condition of intruder.

The US Air Force, Navy, and Ryan Aeronautical imagined themselves as pioneers in the unsettled lands of the frontier. The technopolitics of aviation, read through the popular tropes embodied by William Tell and the Lone Ranger, were redrawing the boundaries of belonging on the land and in the air—and on people. The Swiss legend afforded visions of an ideological and geopolitical struggle between liberal capitalism (freedom) and communism (tyranny). Pilots were trained in emulating William Tell's targeting precision and proficiency while defense systems were tested in "realistic" simulations. Dressed and often imagined as cowboys in the sky (see figure 1.6), perhaps flying to the tune of *The Lone Ranger*, US pilots helped retrace the frontier imaginary, informing and materially shaping US air power. In assuming a role like the Lone Ranger, as cowboys instituting law and order over the skies on the western frontier, folks in the US military and at Ryan Aeronautical renewed their commitments to settler colonialism.

"Indian play" was enmeshed with unmanning when the military conscripted US pilots to perform frontier practices of border control. Their humanity and the inhumanity of their targets was actualized through unmanning. Push-button warfare and remote control of drones were reflexively constitutive of a distinctly situated human-machine configuration.[120] These techniques and artifacts were shaped by the material practices of settler colonialism in the frontier as much as they constituted contemporary settler colonial practices themselves. In targeting the nonhuman and semiautonomous Firebee, pilots sought to defend the nation and its people. Their humanity—that is, their capacity to live "in freedom and liberty"—was protected. Yet such discourses

FIGURE 1.6. Champion Team during tactical fighter weapons meet in 1958. Source: Dave Karten, "Weapons Meet," *The Airman* 2, no. 5 (December 1958): 43.

reveal how border technopolitical regimes rely on what Neda Atanasoski and Kalindi Vora call the surrogate effect of technology—sociotechnical arrangements that, like unmanning, asserted the position of "human" to a limited range of actors.[121] The non/inhuman threat of the robot plane played with frontier biopolitical scripts prescribing the violent submission of racialized populations in the borderlands. Contrary to excited, even if conflicted, universalist proclamations of the posthuman cyborg, the cowboy human-machine configuration of the border technopolitical regime in the mid-twentieth century was designed to evacuate Indigenous and Mexican folks from the "human."[122] Their destabilizing and threatening qualities were embedded in the flight maneuvers of the unmanned Q-2. These drones obfuscated the racialized and gendered surrogates that historically enabled the freedom of the top guns of the West.

As the United States entered a new age of military engagements against the Soviet Union and negotiated the seeming threat of nuclear devastation, actors in the military, government, and industry worked to develop systems to defend the nation. Computers, guided missiles, and jet airplanes entered the elaborate arsenal of the United States in the mid-twentieth century. And while geopolitical considerations were present in their development, other political objectives and imaginaries shaped and were shaped by Cold War technoscience.[123] In the production and control of an intruder to the empire-nation, US government officials along with the military and industry worked to develop a border technopolitical regime through the racial politics of unmanning.

Drone operations were incorporated into military weapons meets as theaters of war, where human-machine configurations enacted frontier biopolitical scripts. Operation Top Gun and Project William Tell were part of the border technopolitical regime's efforts to arrange plans against the imagined threat of nuclear and aerial destruction. These plans conceived a series of situations for which US military forces ought to be prepared, such as the aerial intruder operations of an enemy power. Firebee drones were enrolled as intruders of the nation; they were imagined as enemy targets threatening lethal force on the United States. But just as much as drones were scripted to play the role of intruder, US weapons systems—an assemblage of human pilot, aircraft, and armaments—were construed as heroes of the modern frontier. Narratives of intrusion built on an enduring settler colonial structure of feeling that posited racialized populations in the southern borderlands as dangerous threats to the survival of the nation. Indigenous and Mexican populations had historically been targeted for their purported menace to

US sovereignty. When it came time to design the themes for weapons meets, aircraft manufacturers and the US military drew on frontier tropes to interpret their technological systems in relation to the kinds of values they envisioned these systems to embody.

This chapter shows that to speak of drone operations is to grapple with the racial politics of unmanning. Drones were surrogates of the human. Their automated and unmanned flight maneuvers were premised on the survival of the subjects of the nation at the expense of the lives of others. Unmanning translated settler colonial and imperial logics of differentiation that organized whose lives were protected and whose ought to be eliminated. The technoscientific scenes in Operation Top Gun and Project William Tell underscored the commitments to treat racialized others as expendable subjects of the nation. Consequently, these technoscientific scenes reveal the cultural power of drone operations; they shape how people think about the boundaries of inclusion and exclusion of the nation.

More than five decades before a Predator B unmanned aerial system flew surveillance operations in border enforcement, there was the Firebee, which was developed as the target of an emerging technopolitical regime anchored in air power and remote control. The "origin" story for the drone as a technique for border making and border control is found in Operation Top Gun and Project William Tell. The story reveals an expansive series of associations—of institutional, technological, and discursive relations linked to governing the racial and territorial boundaries of the empire-nation.

2. AUTOMATING BOUNDARIES

Information as a Regime of Border Control

For two straight days, sensor No. 139 sent radio signals to the US Border Patrol's station in San Ysidro, California. A light flashed intermittently, as if someone or something activated it. To Border Patrol agents, the sensor's uninterrupted activation was a clear sign that it was malfunctioning. The light for sensor No. 103, by contrast, was off when it suddenly turned on. The activation data were automatically recorded on magnetic tape back at sector headquarters, where a desk officer radioed the nearest patrol car. "Minutes later," James P. Sterba wrote in the *New York Times* in 1973, "three Mexicans, attempting to sneak into the United States, were tracked down and caught as a result of the electronic detection system" installed "along the Mexican border."[1] The system described by Sterba was commonly known as the "electronic fence." It relied on the operation of different components: ground sensors, radio waves and transmitters, signal processors, computers, magnetic tapes, and Border Patrol agents, among others. "It [was] a far cry from the Patrol Inspector of fifty years ago," agents reflected, "who rode miles of desert on horseback or who walked miles of tote roads or border slash on snowshoes in search of foot prints to track down illegal aliens."[2] Sensors were programmed to detect different kinds of phenomena, from seismic sensors measuring the applied stress of footsteps to infrared sensors that measured body heat. Components of the electronic fence were meant to work in concert to monitor, record, and circulate information about those the *INS Reporter* called "intruders" (see figure 2.1).

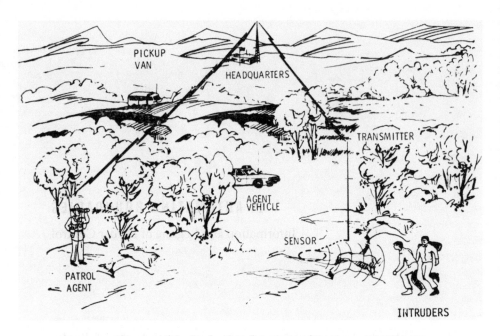

PICKUP VAN

HEADQUARTERS

TRANSMITTER

AGENT VEHICLE

SENSOR

PATROL AGENT

INTRUDERS

FIGURE 2.1. Diagram of the Border Patrol's intrusion detection system. Source: Harry D. Frankel, "INS Research and Development Programs," *INS Reporter* 26, no. 3 (Winter 1977–1978): 35.

This chapter examines who these intruders were that, like the Firebee in chapter 1, surreptitiously crossed the borders of the nation. But unlike the Firebee, these intruders shifted government efforts in border making from a nonhuman target into a human one. The chapter also explores how the electronic fence and its routines became the sociotechnical arrangement of choice for the Border Patrol in the management of such targets. What did it mean for border crossers to be treated as sensory data to capture? And what were the emerging data technopolitics of the electronic fence?

In the US public debate of the 1970s, the southern border was imagined as out of control because of the "thousands" of migrants that crossed it, overwhelming an understaffed Border Patrol.[3] In 1963, the Border Patrol, the enforcement arm of the Immigration and Naturalization Service (INS), located around twenty-one thousand migrants who attempted entry without inspection across the border.[4] For these apprehended migrants, INS used the category of "deportable alien," which included migrants who entered without inspection or violated their conditions for admission. Ten years later, in 1973, that number rose to more than half a million deportable aliens for an average increase of 41 percent per year. After the end of the Bracero Program in 1964 and passage of the Immigration and Nationality Act of 1965, anxious federal officials and engineers struggled to control the border and those they named as intruders. In the span of a decade, the total number of apprehended deportable aliens on the US-Mexico border was almost two million.[5] INS officials and the public at large associated deportable aliens with the southern border and, more specifically, with Mexicans. They were the intruders drawn in the INS *Reporter*'s diagram (figure 2.1); they were the targets of intrusion detection systems.

Officials at INS answered this logistical challenge by mobilizing cybernetic ideas around communication and control to make sense of the border and address the imagined failures of the immigration system. Cybernetics emphasized that systems depended on information to execute their control mechanisms. Intrusion detection systems, like the one mapped by the INS *Reporter*, were designed to expand the reach of the Border Patrol by automatically monitoring and recording accurate information from phenomena. "These supersensitive devices," INS Officer Robert J. Seitz held, "allow one officer monitoring the 'control box' to cover a far wider territory than could be observed on ordinary 'still watch.' Through use of the device he can call in patrol units to areas where the instrument indicates movement."[6] Ground sensors placed on different border locations operated as what media theorist Marshall McLuhan called "extensions of man."[7] They translated border crossing phenomena into sensory data, multiplying the capacity of agents who monitored activations on a "control box." Detecting the presence of those the system classified as intruders, agents would now coordinate and support enforcement actions in a specific border sector. Intruders, in turn, were shaped by the technology into data-producing subjects—data inputs of an ongoing border technopolitical regime that I call the cybernetic border.

To study the cybernetic border is to grasp the intersections between nation making, automation, and racial sorting logics. This chapter explores these intersections by discussing how populations classified as "illegal aliens" and "deportable aliens" were perceived as racial problems threatening the nation in the twentieth century and how INS responded to them. Officials thought border enforcement efforts had to be revamped through the power of numbers and "making up people" through their classification.[8] Cybernetics' emphasis on information, communication, and control offered INS officials the conceptual apparatus through which to build on enumerative power and render border enforcement, and the border itself, as an information regime. The Department of Defense (DOD) and the Border Patrol drew material support and inspiration from military operations in Southeast Asia, where an intrusion detection system known as the "McNamara Line" was used to automate security operations along South Vietnam's borders. The McNamara Line and the electronic fence exposed, more importantly, how the US empire-nation sought to police and undo its own boundaries through information, or what media studies scholar Jonathan Beller, through cybernetician Gregory Bateson, calls the "difference that makes a *social* difference."[9] The intrusion detection system that came out of this conjuncture is predicated on the material entanglements between electronic technology, race, and conceptions of the frontier.

The electronic fence is part of the racial politics of unmanning—that is, disavowing human agency and the political in the pursuit of enacting remote control. But as we saw in chapter 1, military exercises like Operation Top Gun and Project William Tell inscribed unmanning with "Indian play," a settler and imperial racial script where non-white populations embody the roles of enemy intruders. Government and military officials and technicians designed a distinct regime in the 1970s that folded unmanning within the abstract imaginary of cybernetics to make sense of the world and all its entities through information. Automatic, remote control in border enforcement means that the problem of unauthorized border crossing is thought to be legible—that is, knowable and manageable—through data. In this sense, the electronic fence was among the first systems to abstract all entities in the operations of border enforcement, from Border Patrol agents and their surveillance techniques to intruders; it reconfigured them into seemingly nonpolitical data subjects and objects even while operationalizing the borderlands through settler and racial scripts with enemies to eliminate.

Cost-saving rationales in the 1970s were not uncommon for advocates of automation and new electronic technologies. A *Washington Post* reporter commented that government actors found in technology a way to "save many precious man hours" and maximize the work executed by Border Patrol agents.[10] But, as the same reporter argued, sensors along the Mexican border were not just a cost-saving solution to a staffing problem. They were designed to help Border Patrol agents control "wetbacks and narcotic smugglers." In depicting Mexicans through racist epithets that marked them as unauthorized border crossers, cheap labor, and criminals, the electronic fence was encoded to reify the racial order of the US empire-nation.

Despite its repeated failures to command territory and people, the electronic fence is part of an imperial control fantasy that spans the globe—from the jungles of Southeast Asia to the southwestern borderlands. Technical breakdowns, such as the case of sensor No. 139, are endemic to the system, but they do not keep actors from trusting it to deliver on its promise of mastery. The design and use of the electronic fence responds more to a paradoxical desire for a clearly bounded national space, with neatly defined borders and racial categories, all the while undoing and redrawing such boundaries through the exercise of US military and political force worldwide. Decades before the post-9/11 increase in cybersecurity measures (discussed in chapter 3) the US-Mexico border of the 1970s was one of the critical spaces where (non)government actors reconfigured the foreign and the domestic through experiments in automation—experiments in the production of territory and the control of racialized populations.

To examine the technopolitical regime of the electronic fence, I trace associations or relations between ideas, institutional arrangements, and technical operations. Such tracing makes possible an analysis of the data technopolitics of INS. Intrusion detection systems were products of a classification regime committed to producing gaps and omissions in the public record about technological and military research.[11] Classification regimes, as the introduction to the book argues, multiply domains of knowledge to be removed from wide debate, and this chapter works to connect the ever-expanding material networks of secrecy around border enforcement. New ideas about the border circulated through short articles written by INS officials in the *I and N Reporter* (later renamed *INS Reporter*) and through their statements in the press. I analyze how journalists described the "illegal alien" problem and the electronic fence to show how they were entangled. In addition, technical reports, congressional hearings, annual reports, authorization and budget requests, and press coverage reveal the institutional rearrangements of the agencies responsible for managing the border. One such rearrangement was the focus on apprehension measures and their relationship to the electronic fence. The system was meant to improve not just the capture of unauthorized border crossers but also the operational data generated because of their incursions within US territory. The electronic fence intensified the process whereby border metrics became critical artifacts in the practices of the border technopolitical regime. And such practices called on more information technologies, regardless of their unproven efficiencies.

Boundary Configurations: The "Illegal Alien" Problem and "Deportable Aliens"

To understand the automation of the border requires an examination of who the state and the wider public named as its targets. Who were made into illegal and deportable aliens? The construction of categories and classifications through which to name, define, and manage populations offers insights into the boundary politics they enact and the kinds of technologies deemed appropriate to leverage against these populations. The construction of "illegal" and "deportable aliens" in the mid-twentieth century worked through processes of racialization that positioned attributes of criminality as bound to the bodies of ethnic Mexicans. While Mexicans initially troubled the Black and white racial line, criminalization discourses helped produce them as enemies of the nation. They were a problem object against which to leverage government power.

The restrictive immigration policy of the US empire-nation was pivotal to the construction of the illegal alien problem. In the twentieth century, the National Origins Act of 1924 instituted a quota system that limited the number of entrants to the United States from outside the Western Hemisphere and differentiated those entrants according to their national origin. The National Origins Act, immigration historian Mae Ngai argues, "defined the world formally in terms of country and nationality but also in terms of race. The quota system distinguished persons of the 'colored races' from 'white' persons from 'white' countries."[12] Some people deemed to be part of the "colored races" were granted entry into the United States, except for those identified as excludable people ineligible for citizenship (e.g., Chinese and Japanese). These populations embodied a sense of foreignness that placed them outside the bounds of the US nation. Inside its territory, Ngai concludes, illegal aliens had "no right to be present"—they were "at another juridical boundary."[13] Numerical restriction contributed to the construction of a subject whose existence was an expression of the limit of the law. While numerical restriction became a distinct biopolitical practice after 1924, one that relied on specific knowledges—from eugenics to statistical analyses—the practice was at its core a method through which the US empire-nation, with its peoples and territory, was made.

As part of the Western Hemisphere, Latin American countries were not constrained by the quota system, although this did not mean migrants from these countries were free from government and corporate attempts to monitor, restrain, and deport them. Mexican migrant workers in the Imperial Valley during the 1930s and 1940s, for example, were the targets of a concerted effort to make them into what US historian Natalia Molina calls "deportable immigrants."[14] Targeted for their participation in organized labor activities and their border crossing practices, Mexican workers were construed by government officials at INS and the Border Patrol as potential carriers of disease. US officials relied on the language of disease written into law since the Immigration Act of 1882, which prohibited the entry of any "convict, lunatic, idiot, or any person unable to take care of himself or herself without becoming a public charge."[15] Carriers of disease could, officials believed, become public charges or trigger others to become public charges. This imagined potential for disease opened the door for Mexican migrants to become deportable. The category of "deportable alien" was an accounting category used by INS officials to track, measure, and sort the interactions between Border Patrol and targeted populations. Deportable aliens were identified for transgressing the conditions of their admission or crossing the border without authorization.[16] The category helped differentiate bodies, between those that deserved to remain within and those that ought to be removed from the nation. Molina argues that "racializing Mexicans and Mexican Americans alike as dependent disease carriers helped to mark both populations as deviant, dangerous, and outside the bounds of social membership within the United States."[17] The category of deportable alien, combined with the spatial focus on the southern border, signaled that officials at INS made it a priority to target Mexicans who were imagined as intractably foreign. Even when these populations were outside the 1924 quota system, public and private actors developed different mechanisms through which their inclusion in and exclusion from the US nation was managed— preserving the existing white racial order.[18]

The category of deportable alien forms part of the INS participation in the long history of the avalanche of printed numbers. Philosopher of science Ian Hacking's work offers insight into the foundations of enumeration as a biopolitical technology since the mid-eighteenth century. Biopolitics is concerned with administering and managing populations—at the levels of both the group and the individual—which meant it relied on the production of data about its object. Even when the common refrain in critical commentary is that statistical data on populations are designed to inform and control, Hacking counters instead that such data often result in disinformation and mismanagement. Statistical data struggle to capture what is counted and classified. "Counting," he tells us, "is hungry for categories."[19] And categories, like geopolitical borders themselves, cannot but have their boundaries overflown by the phenomena they aim to contain. Categories and systems of classifications are necessarily contingent spatiotemporal cuts of the world.[20] They are context specific or situated in the process of segmenting aspects of the world through distinction and comparison. The contingency of categories, however, should not discount them as epistemological instruments. Rather, we should carefully understand categories and classification systems according to the work they do and the networks within which they are embedded.[21] Categories and classifications, like the biopolitical projects out of which they spring, are productive.

And deportable aliens, as a category and the groups of people associated with it, were at the core of the border technopolitical regime. INS operations since at least 1933, when INS started publication of its annual statistical reports, were built on the power of enumeration. Enumerative power or numerical technologies, as Latina/o studies scholar Jonathan Xavier Inda calls them, are strategically situated as authoritative practices "of knowing and producing truths about the social body"; they sort and divide people.[22] INS annual reports dealt with myriad immigration issues like naturalizations, asylum requests, temporary admissions, and apprehensions. "Once particular categories [were] operationalized in government data, they enter[ed] not only the language of administration but also generally that of society at large (i.e., the mass media, academia, the public, and so forth)."[23] Deportable aliens and the proximate category of illegal aliens entered the official language of government and public discourse about migrants, with a distinct emphasis placed on Mexicans during the mid-twentieth century.

Vigilance of deportable aliens was among the key functions of the Border Patrol. Hired as temporary agricultural workers through the Bracero Program (1942–1964), Mexicans were made primary targets. Brought to the country as braceros through bilateral agreements between the United States and Mexico, they were to be made modern by learning new farming techniques and adopting a new work ethic that, on their return to Mexico, would help the Mexican nation also become modern.[24] And to guarantee their presence was not permanent, historian Kelly Lytle Hernández argues, the Border Patrol was directed to police unsanctioned Mexican migration. Such a narrow focus "drew a very particular color line around the political condition of illegality. Border Patrol practice, in other words, imported the borderlands' deeply rooted racial divides arising from conquest and capitalist economic development into the making of US immigration law enforcement and, in turn, transformed the legal/illegal divide into a problem of race."[25] Prioritizing the policing of Mexican laborers betrayed a racial capitalist dynamic through which agents contributed to the differential management of a transnational labor force. The Border Patrol, however, constantly struggled to achieve full control of border crossing, both authorized and unauthorized, given the significant direct and indirect incentives generated by the Bracero Program for migrants and agricultural capital. INS officials imagined effective control would mean reducing unauthorized border crossings down to a "negligible" (unnumbered) level and instilling in guest workers the sense that overstaying their visas would inevitably lead to capture.[26] US historians have argued that the consistent increase in apprehensions of deportable aliens is evidence of "the unprecedented nature of undocumented migration during the bracero era."[27] In its 1947 *Annual Report*, INS held that "during the year the force became more concentrated along the Mexican border because of the unprecedented number of aliens entering illegally there." That year, the Border Patrol had 734 officers, or about 60 percent of its total force, authorized on the southern border, while 117 officers were on the Gulf Coast and Florida. By contrast, 378 officers patrolled the entire Canadian border.[28] The higher presence of agents on the southern border demonstrates that, on the one hand, as INS annual reports stated, the problem of deportable aliens and surreptitious entries was racially construed as a Mexican one, since "most of the immigration violations were created by an influx of Mexican aliens across the land border of the Southwest Region."[29] On the other hand, the Border Patrol was a police force meant to discipline and punish Mexicans as migrant labor and a racially othered population.[30] Governmental surveillance of Mexicans responded to an understanding that the US nation could not include them; a Mexican presence in the United States represented the failure of controlling the US-Mexico border.

Anxieties about rising illegal migration in the 1950s and early 1960s converged with panics around drug smuggling and consumption. In California, moral crusades held "dope peddlers" and "narcotics pushers" responsible for the distribution and consumption of narcotics in white suburban spaces. The flow of narcotics was often associated with ethnic Mexicans, which infused a racial imaginary into urban crime control efforts.[31] In the Texas borderlands, meanwhile, these panics had repercussions on Mexican families targeted by local and federal actors. Government officials mobilized images of Mexican domestic spaces as harbingers of disease and illegal narcotics throughout the 1950s, with the aim of construing them as criminal. Mexican families were rounded up, arrested, and photographed in attempts to document and make evident their supposedly deviant proclivities.[32] Moral panics around drug smuggling and consumption intensified the criminalization of Mexicans who, as potential deportable and illegal aliens, continued to be, as Inda argues, problem objects of a growing regime of truth that targeted them.[33]

Imagined as criminal, Mexicans and Mexican Americans were treated as threats to the stability of the US nation, and so actors pushed for the development and deployment of practices and technologies to control them.[34]

By the time President Richard Nixon embarked on his war on drugs in 1971, associations between ethnic Mexicans as criminal and the southern border as a nefarious zone were ingrained in the US public imagination.[35] A double process of criminalization and racialization of drug trafficking had marked Mexican and Black communities as targets of a bipartisan effort to protect the middle-class suburbs and its imagined whiteness.[36] Newspapers constrained the ongoing pursuit to solve "the problem of illegal aliens" and the "drug-smuggling war" to the southern borderlands.[37] Federal government efforts like Operation Intercept in 1969, which instituted harsher inspection procedures on border crossing from Mexico through land ports of entry, perpetuated the sense of the border and of its foreign subjects as lawless. The steady, circulating mobility of Mexican migration to the US Southwest that characterized the period before the Immigration and Naturalization Act of 1965 ended and a new phase began whereby temporary migrants were increasingly sorted as criminalized deportable aliens.[38]

By the 1970s, the sense of foreignness with which immigrants were entangled, through categories like intruder and deportable alien, also invoked the idea of "the enemy" to a larger US public. In an article for the *Los Angeles Times*, Bob Williams told readers that US authorities had failed to prevent "illegal aliens" from establishing "a beachhead for the Third World" in the United States.[39] Williams adopted the language of war to identify Southern California as a beachhead, a defensive position where landing forces could launch attacks. Illegal aliens, linked to the Third World but thought of as mostly Mexican, represented the landing enemy force. Williams concluded that Mexicans were responsible for carrying out a "silent and sometimes invisible invasion." In a similar vein, INS Commissioner Leonard F. Chapman Jr. described "illegal immigrants" as constituting a "vast and silent invasion . . . fast reaching the proportions of a national disaster."[40] Referring to their entry in these terms positioned illegal aliens as untrustworthy, threatening, and unknowable subjects. They acted covertly whenever and wherever no one could perceive their presence. Illegal aliens, such discourse posited, were not migrating to contribute to US society; they hid their true intentions. They were a surreptitious, silent invasion.

The propensity to use the language of war to talk about immigration and border enforcement colored these efforts with an existential hue. The "Latino threat narrative," as anthropologist Leo R. Chavez has called it, identified Mexicans as people who could not become part of the United States because they represented a danger to the continuity of the United States as an imagined community.[41] Their linguistic, kinship, religious, and other cultural practices marked them as inexorably separate from dominant conceptions of "America." Mexicans, euphemistically named through border and immigration enforcement categories, were the targets of a war about who could belong to the nation and who could not. Heightened anxieties over the safety of a national body supposedly overwhelmed by illegal migration and drug smuggling characterized the situation where cybernetic ideas left their mark at INS—with the result that a new information regime took shape.

Cybernetics and the INS

A new technopolitical regime meant to manage illegal and deportable aliens emerged from the entrails of what scholars have come to call the military-industrial complex. This regime understood the physical world through abstract processes of information, communication, and control. Known as cybernetics, this epistemological reordering of the world blurred the boundaries of the human and nonhuman. And such reordering opened new pathways for computational logics meant to model and govern all kinds of systems, from the microscopic at the biological or the individual level to more macroscopic levels, like that of the population or the organization. Information was the key. While the airplane, radio, and sign cutting operations were already in use since at least the 1930s, the confirmation of Chapman as commissioner in 1972 gave the INS a significant impetus toward configuring the border as an information regime.[42] Nixon named Chapman, a former Marine Corps general and chief of staff, to reinvigorate the INS.[43] Prior to his confirmation, Chapman was a decorated administrator for his work promoting new management techniques and integrating computers and other information processing machines into the Marine Corps in the 1960s.[44] With him at the helm, government officials finally came to view INS through the language and logic of cybernetics. Actors understood and reorganized US immigration and border enforcement as a shifting network of entities bound together through information and communication. How did cybernetics figure into the technopolitical regime of the INS?

CONTROL THROUGH THE "DIFFERENCE THAT MAKES A DIFFERENCE"

At the Massachusetts Institute of Technology (MIT) radiation laboratory, cybernetics helped researchers work out solutions to military problems during World War II, such as how to shoot an airplane from the sky. Academic and military researchers worked on how to track the course of the plane, measure its movements, and predict its future position. Anti-aircraft guns, gunners, airplanes, pilots, projectiles, and aerodynamics were imagined as an interlocking system that could be statistically defined in the pursuit of a goal—shooting down the plane. At the center of it all were messages that allowed for these different entities to be intelligible to each other. Cyberneticians like Norbert Wiener, one of the field's foundational figures and a mathematician at MIT who drew from the neurophysiological work of Arturo Rosenblueth, thought that the production and circulation of messages and information explained how an entity sustained itself. Informational processes helped show how it related to, cohered, or clashed with other entities.[45]

By centering information, cyberneticians understood human and nonhuman entities in analogous terms. Blurring the boundary between one and the other allowed them to abstract and articulate a universal language that would effectively name processes in both flesh and metal. In other words, "Wiener believed," as historian of media technologies Fred Turner contends, "that biological, mechanical, and information systems, including then-emerging digital computers, could be seen as analogues of one another. All controlled themselves by sending and receiving messages, and, metaphorically at least, all were simply patterns of ordered information in a world otherwise tending to entropy and noise."[46] Latching on to the production, circulation, reception, and processing of messages allowed cyberneticians to propose an abstract language attendant to behavior, purpose, and feedback, a language that cut across human and nonhuman entities. *Behavior* constituted "any change of an entity with respect to its surroundings"; the concept described the relations between an entity and its surrounding environment.[47] These relations were interpreted through an assessment of the behavior's *purpose*. Most entities behave following a given objective: a pencil "seeks" to leave a carbon trace on a porous surface, and an electronic ground sensor aims to be triggered by distinct phenomena such as terrestrial vibrations. For this behavior to be purposeful, which is an aspect of complex systems, it must integrate *feedback* mechanisms. Feedback is the process through which an entity's output energy returned to it as an input, governing or modifying and guiding its behavior. The engineering concept of feedback helped cyberneticians to frame the circulation and processing of information.[48] This meant that a complex entity or system required the existence of some mechanism by which the inputs, transmissions, and outputs of information were monitored, ordered, and regulated. Wiener, relying on his collaborations with Rosenblueth and Julian Bigelow, argued that feedback was about the *control* of a machine or organism based on its *actual* performance rather than its *expected* performance.[49] Feedback, in other words, concerned a circular causality, or the ordering of an entity's purposeful behavior and its subsequent responses relative to its given goal.

A set of conferences organized by the Josiah Macy Jr. Foundation from 1946 to 1953 helped cybernetics reach beyond the confines of the military and gain a strong footing across a range of academic fields in the natural and social sciences.[50] These conferences brought together social scientists like Gregory Bateson, Warren McCulloch, Margaret Mead, and Oskar Morgenstern with an assortment of mathematicians, logicians, electrical engineers, physiologists, and neurophysiologists like Wiener, John von Neumann, Walter Pitts, Bigelow, and Rosenblueth. Talking about the first of the Macy conferences, Wiener thought scholars from the social sciences convened with other scientists in part because they all agreed that "the importance of information and communication as mechanisms of organization proceeds beyond the individual into the community."[51] Wiener held that what unified the different disciplines at the conference was concern over *the message* and its role in shaping relations.[52] A focus on the message created a pathway for cybernetics to move past military applications.

The social sciences, art, design, and the burgeoning closed world of computing all quickly made use of the abstract language of information.[53] Conceptions of the human and other appropriately complex ensembles of entities (e.g., brain, nervous system, communities, organizations, cities) were soon construed as self-corrective systems. In the words of Bateson, the behavior of such systems was the result of "a difference that makes a difference."[54] That is, bits of information were apprehended by a sensor in a system that must emit a message noting this difference so that the whole system effectively responded to it. In other words, attention to the "difference that makes a difference" led cyberneticians and the cybernetic-inclined to be attuned to perception or the ability of a system or one of its integral components to respond.[55] Information, following Bateson's ecology of mind, was not some event or thing but an "abstract matter" that produced effects. In the case of the system, information processed by a sensor triggered other sensors, which in turn modulated the behavior of the system.

Emblematic of the influence of cybernetic principles at INS is the way Chapman made the Office of Planning and Evaluation (P&E) a central node in the assessment of immigration and border enforcement. When P&E was created in 1974, Chapman told officials "to look at INS operations" and "come up with innovative ways" for the service to execute its work.[56] One of these innovations was implementing a management-by-objectives (MBO) regime that relied on a systems understanding of INS. The service was imagined as an interlocking hierarchy of offices and branches or "subsystems," each with individual tasks and objectives to be achieved but that still had to work in concert for the success of the overall system.[57] Chapman's MBO regime, which became known as the Commissioner's Planning System (COMPS), mobilized cybernetic principles like *purpose* by linking all INS resource requests with objectives. In other words, this management approach was designed "to identify and budget critical Service needs and to channel I&NS efforts in new, directed, and purposeful ways through the development of long range forecasts and short term impact plans."[58] Of note here is the emphasis on purposefulness to *steer* INS plans and efforts. P&E, even if it was often seen by other INS officials as nothing more than a performance management office, was meant to operate as a governor—a term found in the Greek root of the word "cybernetics" (κυβερνάω or kubernáo), meaning "to steer, navigate, or govern." P&E guided the system and its chief officer by processing informational inputs and outputs; operations of the system and its interlocking subsystems were to be shaped through an attentive assessment of goals achieved and missed.

In its diagrammatic description of border enforcement and the Border Patrol (see figure 2.2), P&E was keen to stress the importance of objective-oriented operations. The office embodied the beliefs and aims of a mid-century designer steeped in cybernetics. The role of the designer, according to artists Ray and Charles Eames, was "to design a particular flow of information."[59] As designers of what P&E called the Border Patrol subsystem, officials produced a clear and accessible model of how information entered the agency's "prevention system." They abstracted the different components and operations of the system and found that the practices of prevention comprised three key facets: an input, a processor, and an output. All activity began when the system was triggered by the input, which was "aliens contemplating illegal entry and those who have entered illegally and have not yet been employed." Prevention, in other words, revolved around the actions of aliens entering the country without authorization. Engaging these subjects required that Border Patrol agents employ a variety of processor practices like "line watch," "sign cutting," and "air patrol." By reframing these techniques and technologies as processors, INS officials construed them as clearly identifiable and standardized methods of action designed to generate a legible goal or output. Among the outputs of processors were the apprehension of aliens or their avoidance of Border Patrol prevention

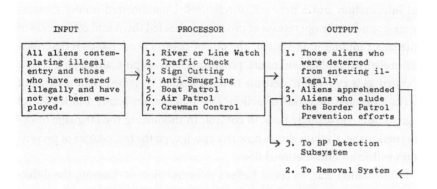

FIGURE 2.2. Diagram of the Prevention System: Border Patrol Subsystem. Source: INS, Office of Planning and Evaluation, "Section II. Detection System Part II. Border Patrol Subsystem (1974)," Folder 2, Vertical File, "United States, Immigration and Naturalization Service, Office of Planning and Evaluation," USCIS.

operations. Each output prompted the activation of different systems ("removal" or "detection").

What the diagram highlights is the fact that well after INS installed the electronic fence and made use of a range of electronic technology in 1970, officials sought to manufacture the field of the borderlands as a coherent and structured space of information. Diagrams like the Border Patrol subsystem draw relations. They visually describe how entities relate, and they might even reveal under what conditions and to what ends. Diagrams are configurations. Like the plans rehearsed during the war games discussed in chapter 1, they are structured and structuring artifacts that guide how actors comport themselves and how situations are interpreted. The prevention diagram enacted a visibility that was historically situated within a Western tradition of knowledge making, a vast infrastructure designed to know—that is, to produce and control subjects. It produced each entity involved in prevention as discrete and manageable. In this sense, the diagram participated in the development of what science studies scholar Donna Haraway argues is the history of science's entanglements with militarism, capitalism, patriarchy, and empire. "The eyes have been used to signify a perverse capacity"; technological vision is the "unregulated gluttony" of a knowing subject distanced "from everybody and everything in the interests of unfettered power."[60] From a distance, P&E's diagram configured the operations of prevention as a carefully built loop of circular causation with distinct entities inhabiting the once incontrollable zone. Prevention became a specific and ordered flow of information and a network of relations. Unauthorized border crossers were bound to the operations of processors that fed them into other areas of the larger immigration system. The out-of-control borderlands is described as an abstract problem of inputs, processors, and outputs, although it is now posited as a cybernetic, self-maintained system.[61] Armed with a range of techniques and methods of action, INS officials, especially Border Patrol agents, are reassuringly back in control. In mobilizing the language of cybernetics, the diagram shows how INS configured the boundaries of prevention within an informational flow.

Information was, to recall Beller's reformulation of Bateson, the difference that made a social difference when integrated into the Border Patrol subsystem. Some might interpret processor practices included in the diagram as an evident sign that enforcement followed a visual control. However, as the book's introduction argues, I caution against such formulations. Enforcement practices like "river or line watch," "air patrol," and "traffic check" clearly involved ocular inspection. They engaged the borderlands environment through the materiality of vision and the logics of visibility—of producing, as science and technology studies (STS) scholar Orit Halpern contends, evidence about bodies, subjects, and populations.[62] Yet the prevention diagram demonstrates that P&E treated these technologies of vision as processor practices. In doing so, they were incorporated within a larger and more abstract technopolitical regime that, as the electronic fence discussed later makes plain, relied on a broader perceptual field and prioritized information as both an object and a biopolitical vector.

The abstraction or abstracting capacity of cybernetic language constituted them all as governable, following an imperial logic. Cybernetics was a spatializing governmentality, ever expanding its field of operations by bringing a wider range of phenomena under its purview. There was nothing that the abstract language of cybernetics could not incorporate within its framework. This has led critical information studies scholar Syed Mustafa Ali to posit that cybernetics and informatics need to be understood in relation to racial formations. Building on Bateson's understanding of information, Ali argues that information involves a process of "implanting form or, alternatively, allowing form to become sedimented"—that is, coterminous to processes of racialization.[63] Race, as both a system and a process, names dynamics of differentiation that are embodied or that position specific practices of knowing and meaning making within a taxonomic and hierarchical structure of relations.[64] Ali cleverly makes the connection between cybernetic conceptions of information and Stuart Hall's argument that "race is a shape-shifting signifier" to stress the extent to which the two realms are tightly entangled.[65] The imperial logic of cybernetics to subsume whatever exceeds it is further complicated by its permanent engagement with information as "a difference that makes a difference." This logic—or, perhaps more accurately, this imperial control fantasy—becomes sharper when we consider, as Ali concludes and the previous section on boundary configurations shows, that race is perhaps "*the* difference."[66] It was information that the INS P&E identified as a key actant in the Border Patrol subsystem. Information was central to enforcing the border in order to implant its form and make a difference in the control of populations.

INFORMATION AS ENFORCEMENT

Facilitating the integration of cybernetics into the everyday operations of the Border Patrol was the fact that, to some extent, the border was already treated as an information environment. Evidence of this was the processor practice of sign cutting. Formally taught at the Border Patrol Academy, sign cutting was defined by one INS official as "recognizing and interpreting physical signs of the movement and activities of persons who have crossed the border without inspection."[67] Changes imprinted on the natural landscape, such as footprints and vehicle tracks, were a priori understood as suspect. They were "signs" or evidence of the presence of someone or something that should not have been there. Traces left behind were data that Border Patrol agents could use not only to identify the presence of an intruder but also to figure out their direction. To cut meant two things. First, agents broke the large border terrain into discrete or manageable segments to scrutinize. And second, agents severed the path of those attempting entry without inspection; track-producing subjects would be removed from the border, and their tracks would reach a dead end. Sign cutting strove to transform unauthorized border crossers from unknowable entities into knowable, excludable intruder subjects.

As a central enforcement practice, sign cutting is also how the Border Patrol recreates its exclusionary desire and its role in frontier making.[68] In an article celebrating the fifty years of the Border Patrol, the *I and N Reporter* described sign cutting as "a skill practiced by the American Indian, long before the arrival of Columbus. Later, it was practiced by hunters, frontiersmen, and trappers who left the beaten trail to locate game or to detect an enemy in the area. Also, during the settlement of the West, sign cutting was used successfully to track down cattle rustlers and other outlaws."[69] Like the Navy and Air Force during Operation Top Gun and Project William Tell, INS imagined Border Patrol agents as "playing Indian" when sign cutting.[70] They were in fact, as Xicana and feminist STS scholar Felicity Amaya Schaeffer demonstrates in her work on unsettled borders, repurposing a Native American cosmological practice, whereby "the study of material and ephemeral ancestral imprints left on the land" and in "storied relations" helped guide collective worldings in time and space.[71] The relational orientation of Indigenous tracking of traces on the land embodies an entanglement of one's position with the land and its beings. "Frontiersmen," an expression of a masculine and imperial desire, transformed the tracking of footprints into a technology for settling "the West," a method whereby land was made into resources and territory to control. Folding Indigenous knowledge within Western technologies and their associated political objectives, Schaeffer concludes, preserved and vanished Indigeneity.

Border Patrol agents imagine sign cutting as an ancestral practice drawn from an Indigenous past to make possible a settler (and thereby non-Native) present. Participating in the long history of integrating Indigeneity (Native scouts and their practices) for settlement, the Border Patrol's sign cutting is an everyday practice through which settler sovereignties are enacted.[72] Border Patrol use of sign cutting articulates what Stefan Aune calls "Indian/fighting," or the competing discourses positing "US military violence as both 'fighting against Indians' and 'fighting *like* Indians.'"[73] The targets of the practice shifted depending on context—at times they were game, at others they were enemies or even law transgressors ("cattle rustlers and other outlaws"). In the end, they were subjects that sustained or disturbed the tenuous balance of the settler project. Practiced in the modern borderlands, though especially the Southwest, sign cutting rearticulates the frontier politics of managing and containing the Other. All the while displacing and dispossessing Indigenous communities, Border Patrol agents act "*like* Indians" as they track and apprehend unauthorized border crossers in the making of US sovereignty. Sign cutting perpetuates the settler project by enforcing immigration law and severing undesirable "deportable" subjects from the national body.

During the 1960s and 1970s, INS officials continued treating the border as a rich communication and information landscape with its set of practices and sign-producing subjects and objects. What shifted slowly was treating the border as an information *system*. Officials were insistent that they lacked the adequate tools to manage both immigration requests and the growing influx of unauthorized entries.[74] One constant in their articles for the *I and N Reporter* was the centrality given to communication. George F. Klemcke, deputy assistant commissioner for enforcement at INS, even argued that "effective law enforcement requires a rapid, accurate, and smooth-flowing communications system for transmitting information and messages to the office responsible for taking action."[75] Though the term "cybernetics" was not used, the usage of some of its key concepts (e.g., communication, information, messages) makes evident the influence the interdisciplinary science had at INS. "Modern" and "efficient" law enforcement was imagined to depend on neatly circulating data flows that would direct INS personnel and resources wherever they were needed. This was, after all, as science studies scholar Paul N. Edwards shows, a period marked by business schools "theorizing management as a problem of information processing" and Rand Corporation strategists "increasingly formulat[ing] command as information processing and war itself as a problem of communication."[76] Officials at INS were immersed in a discursive milieu marked by the language of cybernetics and systems thinking that permeated business, policy, and military circles.

The border was an information system where control depended, among other things, on what Klemcke stressed ought to be "rapid, accurate, and smooth-flowing communications." Actors believed the effective circulation of information would give Border Patrol and investigative agents the most accurate data whenever they engaged unauthorized border crossers in the field. Communications operators, for example, were tasked with aiding officials by providing data from the INS Main Index. This contained different data from forms like the G-361 (used for "alien files" and visa petition files) and the I-94 (used for stowaways, excludable aliens, and "unable to locate persons").[77] The role of communications operators within the immigration system was, as Klemcke suggested, to facilitate all necessary information to agents in the field so that they could act. Using radio systems, they linked different border sectors and their actors to INS offices. By managing the flow and processing of information, communications operators and other INS agents controlled the border. Control of the border, like shooting down an airplane, meant agents had to make sure the "right" people were identified before they were removed from US territory or new information was incorporated into the system's database. Through technology such as radio communications, the chaotic flows of immigration and border enforcement were rendered manageable.

Government officials and the public insisted the country was under threat of a racialized "silent" and "invisible invasion."[78] These two recurring tropes reinforce treatment of the border as an information system and showcase the strategic value given to techniques of sound and vision. Actors believed that to reveal surreptitious entries, they had to intervene in the field of the perceptible. Only then could they make the unknown knowable. The desire to "instrumentalize" the aural and visual fields built, as Haraway has argued, on the "unregulated gluttony" of imperial science. This desire conveyed an interest in building specific modes of perception and gathering information. To look at and hear something meant that its existence was objectified. This existence was made into extractable matter. Techniques of sound and vision on the US-Mexico border governed populations by extracting information: Was there an intruding presence (i.e., human body or vehicle)? When and where did they intrude, and where were they headed? Such data, as the ensuing discussion of the McNamara Line and the electronic fence shows, were necessary for the capture of subjects and their subsequent removal. Without these, unauthorized border crossers would continue resisting the security infrastructure of the US empire-nation.

Actors thought that the structured and ordered logics of computers, built on what *Time* magazine called "reliable and cool" components, would produce a return of order to the border and immigration enforcement.[79] The cybernetic border is this epistemological order of things and beings at the border that is simultaneously technical and discursive. Returning to the diagram from INS *Reporter* (see figure 2.1), the cybernetic border was made up initially of ground sensors, transmitters, radio links, computers, Border Patrol agents, vehicles, and intruders, among others. More importantly, the cybernetic border was a southern borderlands formation of what Edwards calls "the closed world." It was the kind of "chaotic and dangerous space rendered orderly and controllable by the powers of rationality and technology."[80] The cybernetic border automated techniques of sound and vision in its attempts to territorialize the borderlands. It was made up of tropes, practices, techniques, and artifacts that were embedded in the matter and investments of administering and managing racialized populations.[81] Prior to the techno-solutionism of drones and smart walls at the turn of the twenty-first century (discussed in chapter 3), the Border Patrol's intrusion detection system sought to govern the border as an empire of patterns of order.

The automation of US border enforcement through cybernetic logics and information technology follows unexpected circuits of development that link Vietnam and the (settler colonial) southern borderlands. Intrusion detection systems, developed for use by a regime comprising the US military, industry, and universities during the Vietnam War, contributed to the creation of the cybernetic border. Examining the operations of the McNamara Line and, subsequently, the electronic fence reveals that the circuitry of modern border enforcement relies on an enduring settler colonial structure of feeling that positions the intruder as an unruly, racial Other to subject to order.

VIETNAM AND THE McNAMARA LINE

The development of intrusion detection systems was one way that the boundaries of US empire were redrawn during the Cold War. During this period, the US government and its military sought to reinforce as well as expand the boundaries of their domains of influence. The Vietnam War (1955–1975) marked a critical moment when the United States aimed to contain the spread of communism by intervening in the region through the deployment of financial and military resources, including personnel, weaponry, training, and soldiers. This interventionist approach meant actors imagined US territorial boundaries were negotiable whenever their interests were thought to be affected.[82] Like the case of drones developed in the US Southwest during the Cold War to make and police the border, intrusion detection systems were also developed in the US Southwest for use elsewhere. But they never quite left the US-Mexican borderlands and its racial order. They were imperial remainders, enduring away and at home in their aims to produce boundaries of distinction.

One critical problem the US military confronted during the Vietnam War was the surreptitious movement of Vietcong fighters within South Vietnam and the North Vietnamese forces across the country's borders.[83] As the war grew in intensity during the mid-1960s, Secretary of Defense Robert McNamara tasked a group of academic scientists, known as the JASON Committee, to propose a solution to the military's Southeast Asia problem. They recommended the creation of an information system that the Defense Communications Planning Group (DCPG) was tasked with implementing. At its most basic, the system consisted of electronic sensors, signal processors, and electronic transmitters placed along the demilitarized zone "to prevent infiltration and supply from North Vietnam across South Vietnam's 43-mile frontier."[84] The McNamara Line or "McNamara Wall," as it was known by the public, would "detect enemy personnel and vehicles" attempting to infiltrate South Vietnam. Future iterations of the system integrated computers to accelerate the analysis and circulation of intruder data such as site of intrusion, rate of movement, and direction while weapons were used "to counter the enemy incursions thus detected."[85] This system worked (see figure 2.3) through a variety of sensors (e.g., seismic, magnetic, acoustic) dropped by parachute into or installed by soldiers in a zone with enemy troop movements. Sensors were triggered by phenomena that a signal processor later interpreted as human- or machine-generated. A radio signal was then sent to a display terminal or "readout equipment," where ground movement was mapped for a "readout operator" to observe. Depending on the probable location of intruders, attack coordinates were radioed by a "unit commander" to fortified troop positions, artillery, or fighter jets to intercept the enemy force.

The McNamara Line was among the first attempts to bring forth the technological dream of an "electronic battlefield" and its distinct regime. Sensors, sensor signals, readout equipment, unit commander, fire support base, and the delivery of lethal force operated through and as information. Together, they produced a new territory, a rational perceptual field wired through data flows to monitor and control. Surreptitious enemy entries that relied on "cloaks of bad weather, jungle, and darkness" were made knowable by the system.[86] Military officials hoped electronic and computer technologies like "sound and seismic devices" would substitute "visible and endangered human patrols that [led] to casualty lists."[87] The large numbers of dead US soldiers had been a decisive factor in growing antiwar sentiment throughout the 1960s. Automation, officials thought, would save the life of soldiers because "[a sensor] doesn't bleed, and if it dies out there in the jungle, you don't have to write a letter home to the wife or parents."[88] Military outposts near the demilitarized zone no longer relied on soldiers patrolling nearby areas to prevent intrusions. Their patrolling labor would be embedded in multiple, unmanned sensor devices that operated ceaselessly. Those watching and hearing were far removed from the sites and objects under scrutiny. Their remote location was part of a technopolitical drive to extend the reach of government and military actors by mastering distance and living beings. Automation of the battlefield offered military officials a scenario in which the risk of death was minimized for their troops yet maximized for their enemy. The McNamara Line also reconfigured

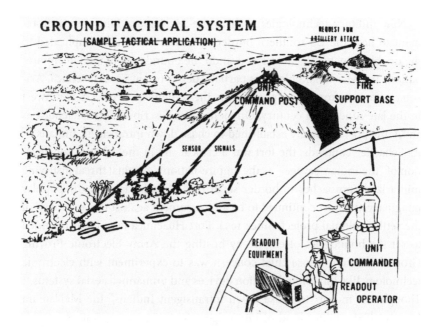

FIGURE 2.3. Diagram of the McNamara Line as a "ground tactical system." Source: *Investigation into Electronic Battlefield Program: Hearings before the Electronic Battlefield Subcommittee of the Committee on Armed Services*, 91st Cong. (1971), 12.

the geopolitical border between South and North Vietnam from one visibly devised on the landscape into an informational one. Like many other Vietnam-era projects coming out of the US military-industrial complex, the system "sought to extend computerized control to the battlefield, in a kind of information panopticon where nothing and no one could move unobserved."[89] These projects, however, were not only about controlling battlefields; they also enacted imperial sovereignties through a layered regime of perception. Disturbances or activations of the McNamara Line's perceptual field were immediately made suspect as covert behavior was interpreted as a transgression to the system's order. Humans imagined as enemies were now construed as mere technical matter—data-producing entities across a plotting device to be eliminated. Geopolitical boundaries were recoded through informational feedback loops: annihilation of the disturbance meant the restoration of order; repeated activations of sensors required continued military response until elimination was achieved. The border, as a result, was the product of the McNamara Line, and it existed within the closed world propped up by a technopolitical regime.

New military technologies such as the McNamara Line were a testament to how the US southern borderlands continued to be implicated in the double impetus to enforce and undo the boundaries of the US empire-nation. The McNamara Line was partially developed at Fort Huachuca, Arizona, a former frontier outpost during the settlement of the US Southwest in the late nineteenth century. One journalist described Fort Huachuca as an "Army post originally established to chase down intransigent Indians."[90] As Schaeffer contends, the fort was a critical site in the colonial construction of "the Indian 'savage'" as the empire-nation's "original threat justifying militarized approaches to border security."[91] Decades later in the popular imaginary, the post continued to be an instrument against the "enemies" of the settler colonial project. Since 1954, Fort Huachuca tested and intended to set the boundaries of empire by hosting the Army Electronic Proving Ground (AEPG), whose chief concern was to experiment with electronic technology like intrusion detection devices and unmanned aerial systems.[92] Though not meant "to chase down intransigent Indians," the McNamara Line tracked another kind of intransigent force. Sensor operators for this system were trained by the AEPG's Combat Surveillance School to provide "security through vigilance."[93] Security from an "intransigent" Other was again, as the term "vigilance" betrays, intertwined with techniques of sound and vision. Sensor operators had to be in a state of alert and watchful while they closely monitored the McNamara Line. Trained in a settler outpost for operations in a foreign territory, US soldiers in the Vietnamese borderlands embodied the role of a frontiersman enforcing, undoing, and expanding the boundaries of the US empire-nation.

The relations of enmity embodied in the racial settler violence that Fort Huachuca produced against Native Americans during the nineteenth century were reconfigured through the McNamara Line. In this instance, military actors targeted intransigent Vietnamese bodies during the Cold War. As figure 2.3 shows, Vietcong and North Vietnamese were imagined as an infiltration force that had to be monitored. The force's movements, represented in the diagram by dark, shadowy armed figures wearing *nón lá* (conical leaf hats often made from palm leaves and bamboo), constituted a threat to South Vietnam (land) and US soldiers (life). Because of their efforts to produce a unified nation and communist society, Vietcong and North Vietnamese forces were commonly referred to in public debate as enemies. To soldiers, however, they were "gooks."[94] This racial epithet was previously used during the Haitian Revolution and Indian Wars of the nineteenth century as well as during the Philippine-US War. American studies scholar Sylvia Chong argues, by way of David Roediger, that naming enemy fighters using a pan-racist term like "gooks" linked US empire to racial oppression and war in Vietnam.[95] In the specific case of the McNamara Line and its development in Fort Huachuca, the system's targeting of an Other "intransigent" force entangled the historical yet ongoing frontier violence of colonial settlement to the present racial violence of US imperial ventures in Southeast Asia.

THE SOUTHERN US BORDER AND THE ELECTRONIC FENCE

The McNamara Line was endemic of how the porous borders of the empire-nation allowed for the foreign and domestic to converge. What McNamara proposed, an anonymous Pentagon official told the *New York Times*, furnished the military with the "ability to monitor even the most rugged border anywhere in the world."[96] Remote control unfolded through automated techniques of sound and vision. The McNamara Line offered a way to automate some of the Border Patrol's gatekeeping function at the "rugged border" with Mexico. In spring 1970, an engineer of the DCPG, the group responsible for the development of the McNamara Line, made an on-site survey of the Chula Vista, El Centro, and Yuma sectors. Though sensors had already been in use in some areas like Nogales, Arizona, it was not until the visit of the DCPG engineer that a concerted and systematic approach was pursued by INS. The Chula Vista sector in California, which consisted of sixty miles of international land border, was chosen as the experimental site for the Border Patrol's new intrusion detection system because it was the busiest crossing point for entries without inspection. Soon after DCPG's visit to the border, the Sandia Corporation, an Albuquerque company operated by Western Electric, assisted in the installation of 177 sensors. An agreement was reached for experimental data to be collected from Border Patrol operations so that DCPG could improve sensors and operational techniques.[97]

The early seeds for a new border technopolitical regime were sown when INS was associated with the Department of Defense. Research and development of the McNamara Line recruited a network of academic partners, including researchers at the MITRE Corporation and the Syracuse Research Corporation.[98] MITRE was founded in 1958 as a federally funded research center, and initially, most of its workers were transferred from MIT's Lincoln Laboratory—the same laboratory that pursued foundational cybernetic and systems research under the leadership of Jay W. Forrester.[99] The Syracuse Research Corporation, on the other hand, was a nonprofit research and development company founded in 1957 by Syracuse University. Sources examined show that while INS did not directly fund the development of the electronic fence, it did offer the military and its partners an experimental space so that they could test and improve the system. In addition to having access to detection techniques developed by the Pentagon's academic partners, INS was also involved with electronics manufacturers. From 1970 to 1976, Sandia Corporation, Magnavox, Teledyne Geotech, and AEC were four of the electronics manufacturers that supplied expert knowledge and ground sensors for the electronic fence. INS spent $8,742,457 from fiscal years 1971 to 1976.[100] Though the amount spent in intrusion detection systems accounted for a minute fraction of the INS budget, it set the conditions of possibility for, on the one hand, future collaborations between the Pentagon and INS, and on the other, continued reliance on electronic technology for border control. INS and its military, academic, and industrial partners constituted a new regime. With information as the difference that makes a social difference and information technologies as structuring and coordinating entities, the cybernetic border became a racial technopolitical regime for making and governing the boundaries of the nation.

Defense and INS collaborations were also the result of the intersection between military engagements and law enforcement. This is what the book's introduction highlights as an entanglement of military and police power in the making of the empire-nation—that is, integral to US state formation. When government officials announced that INS would test intrusion detection systems on the southern border, Attorney General John N. Mitchell was quoted as saying, "We are piggybacking [the DOD's] R&D to a greater and greater degree" particularly for "military gadgetry . . . to detect narcotics of all kinds."[101] Nixon's declaration of drug abuse as "public enemy number one" in 1971 coincided with growing public opposition to the Vietnam War. The program for de-escalation in Southeast Asia seemed to have made the war against narcotics on US soil an attractive proposition for electronics manufacturers already invested heavily in defense.[102] To manage the integration of INS as a node in the defense technopolitical regime, Chapman pushed for better defined collaborations between the INS and the Pentagon. A new research and development (R&D) branch within P&E was created to that end.

R&D funded work on devices, techniques, and systems for border enforcement meant to improve control between ports of entry by detecting and apprehending subjects.[103] In his reflection of paradigmatic INS R&D programs, Harry D. Frankel commented how, before the creation of this branch in 1974–1975, the INS had made minimal use of modern technology.

Among the technologies previously used by the Border Patrol were airplanes, autogiros, cars, and radio communications.[104] The installation and use of the electronic fence since 1970 laid some of the institutional groundwork for relying on electronic and digital technologies. But what changed with the R&D branch was that the INS could now play a role in the development of technology used "to cop[e] with such problems as illegal entries, apprehension of illegal entrants, case backlogs, and access to central files."[105] Frankel, who was the programs manager at R&D, documented the array of projects pursued at INS, such as the use of intrusion sensor systems, radars, and night vision devices. These projects were pursued in cooperation with various institutional partners, among them the Customs Service, the Drug Enforcement Administration, the Army, Navy, Marine Corps, and the National Aeronautics and Space Administration. For example, "test and evaluation of long-range, infrared imaging devices," Frankel argued, were thought to possibly "extend the Border Patrol Agent's capability to detect and apprehend undocumented aliens at or near the borders under virtually any weather or terrain conditions."[106] Technically speaking, the use of infrared imaging devices meant that migrants were handled as heat-generating entities to be measured and statistically differentiated from the surrounding environment. Projects were, in other words, framed by a cybernetic vision that imagined the border environment as a system of interconnected entities, all producing data that could be tracked, circulated, and registered. Electronic technologies like infrared imaging devices and intrusion detection systems were used to reveal the intruding body. Doing so would lead, Frankel and other INS officials thought, to more effectively controlling the flows of drug smuggling and unauthorized immigration.

In revealing the intruding body, the electronic fence was also linked to the prevailing operational statistic for the Border Patrol since its inception in 1924: apprehensions. The statistic of apprehensions was maintained by the INS, and subsequently the Department of Homeland Security (DHS), the next chapter shows, as a measure that records the number of "inadmissible aliens" arrested by the Border Patrol after violating US immigration law.[107] Apprehension statistics turn unauthorized border crossings into an issue of magnitude both as a quantifiable entity and as something of significance. INS officials name the total number of apprehensions as evidence of the Border Patrol achieving its stated mission to detect and prevent unlawful entries.[108] While the measure of apprehensions can be interpreted as the product of successful Border Patrol operations, shadow data related to this statistic are the total number of attempted entries without inspection, and this number has been a permanent item of controversy among government officials and think tanks.[109] Apprehensions were haunted by its excess and by those the statistic could not capture—fugitive border crossers. They were data haunts, something I elaborate on further in chapter 4, in the sense of a sociotechnical figuration resisting the reduction of individuals and populations to statistical control. How many border crossers avoided apprehension? What is the statistical difference between those captured and those who escaped? Sensors in the electronic fence were meant to help augment Border Patrol capacities to apprehend more people and shine a light on those escaping capture, the haunting surplus of apprehensions. The relation between the electronic fence and measures for apprehensions and missed apprehensions are further evidence that the 1970s constituted an important reorganization in the history of the INS. The historical forces deploying informatics and biopolitics were now structured through the recursive logics of cybernetics and information technology.

Public debate, government policy, and Border Patrol practices shaped which populations were identified as intruders to be detected. According to the INS, Mexican nationals constituted 88 percent of all located "deportable aliens" by 1973. Officials believed that the problem of intrusions beyond ports of entry, especially post-1965, was predominantly a Mexican one.[110] A similar sentiment was expressed by Border Patrol officers who explained the growth of the policing force after 1970 because of "the resurgence of the illegal Mexican alien problem."[111] This rationale justified the installation of intrusion detection systems on the southern border and, as a result, tracking Mexicans as intruders. Expenditures for the electronic fence from 1970 to 1972 show that it was first budgeted for the Border Patrol sectors of Chula Vista, Del Río, El Paso, and Swanton.[112] But the fact that three of the four sectors were along the US-Mexico border signaled an investment in the management of Mexicans. Installation of intrusion detection systems on the southern border reproduced the logic that, as Hernández argues, "the legal/illegal divide" was "a problem of race."[113]

The Electronic Fence and the Technopolitics of Data

The electronic fence was a racial technology that centered information in making a social difference. It targeted Mexicans through its higher use on the southern US border, yet officials and engineers attempted to dissociate it from such murky politics by stressing its purportedly technical means. Though it preceded the nomination of former Marine Corps general Chapman as INS commissioner, as well as P&E's efforts to implement cybernetic principles to restructure the service, the electronic fence was in part the product of the same technopolitics. The closed world of computing, Edwards shows us, prioritized information and communication as the means through which to structure, enact, and sustain US global military power.[114] The intrusion detection system used on the southern US border was part of this imperial control fantasy that positioned data as decisive for biopower. The technopolitics of data at the heart of the electronic fence were like those of unmanning and automation during drone operations in the 1940s and 1950s. The electronic fence sought to disavow the human and make the political process of intrusion into a technical one. But the perceptual field produced through the electronic fence was pre-inscribed to target some populations instead of others—Mexicans categorized as intruders. Sensor triggers called their humanity into question. Their personal stories were displaced as the border technopolitical regime emphasized the enumerative power to count sensor activations (alien intrusions) and apprehended deportable aliens/intruders. And despite myriad failings and limitations in the 1970s, the allure of mastery and control embedded in the cybernetic border endured still.

Intrusion detection systems, like other electronic technology later developed or funded by INS R&D, aimed to break down the circulation of things and beings along the border by automating perception. Sensors in the system were programmed to cut for sign. Just like Border Patrol agents interpreted data on a discrete segment of the border, ground sensors recorded data from the border environment. These sensors registered different kinds of signals, and the signal processor they were wired to deciphered whether the signal was produced by a human being or not.[115] In the case of seismic sensors, signal processors known as variance frequency discriminators (VFD) were programmed using "pattern recognition techniques" to discriminate between signals. This allowed "separating valid targets from false alarm sources with least errors."[116] VFD were meant to discriminate between the seismic data generated by different phenomena like vehicles, people, rain, and helicopters. In the context of the southern border, breaking the movements of a border crosser into electrical outputs transformed a human body into an abstract data-producing entity. The behaviors and movements of intruders were at the center of the cybernetic border. These were broken into discrete bits of data for careful study. Patterns of information were traced by a computer as it assessed the "nature" of the triggered sensor. Determining the presence of a person was key, officials and journalists held, to prevent "both illegal aliens and drug smugglers [from] moving across the border."[117] Preventing intrusions was among the chief objectives of INS. Officials and journalists mobilized a Mexican threat narrative that stressed how the nation's survival was dependent on such an endeavor. As urban unrest rattled the country throughout the 1960s, newspapers like the *Los Angeles Times* argued that the way forward was for "America [to] bring its hard-core unemployed into the economic mainstream."[118] The presence of Mexicans in the labor market, however, was imagined as undermining this political objective. And the *Los Angeles Times* insisted that "it is wasteful and short-sighted to permit a system that virtually encourages employment of illegal aliens in jobs that should be filled by needy Americans." Targeting Mexicans as intruders was the political objective assigned to the cybernetic border.

The technopolitics of data multiplied the labor of border enforcement rather than minimized or simplified it. Ground sensors were used to make surreptitious bodies into knowable quantities and categories (e.g., "alien intrusions," "apprehended aliens")—that is, into problems to be resolved through "manpower." The interest of the INS in sensor activations, the nature of their trigger, and the precise measuring of these in statistical assessments was grounded in the power of enumeration as a policy and operational instrument. Sensor activations were not attached to an individual but, instead, were an event. Triggers by a single person could multiply across the system's readout equipment. Every moment these sensors were triggered by human movement, data were collected pertaining to the time of activation, date, sensor location, sector area, and probable direction. Once agents were dispatched, their name and the status of their actions were entered into the system's memory.[119] Collected data were used in reports, INS electronics engineer Thomas C. Henneberger Jr. explained, "as sources of intelligence on border crossing activities, or as analytical tools for evaluating the effectiveness of [the system's] sensors." Sensor data were analyzed to determine potential shifts in border crossings such as an increase or decrease in activations in an area of a border sector. Statistical analyses and models made individuals into populations. By analyzing these data and identifying "alien intrusion patterns," sensors were relocated to higher transit zones or around them to broaden the system's monitoring capacity.[120] Agents were equally reallocated and distributed because of data analysis. Agent positions grew by only 349 positions between the years of 1960 and 1974, while Border Patrol apprehensions increased over 2,000 percent in the same period (from 29,881 to 640,848).[121] Because INS constantly failed to obtain increases in funding and staffing, officials argued that automating detection through sensors helped maximize their limited resources. Sensors allowed agents to identify high-volume crossing areas, which, in turn, let the INS make the most of the time and efforts of its Border Patrol force.

To highlight the purported successes of the electronic fence, INS stated that the system permitted "better control of operational activities." This meant that agent deployment and resource allocation along the border was informed by an analysis of sensor data. And, as a result, improvements to sensor technologies "increased the effectiveness of the overall system both as an aid in apprehension and as an intelligence gathering tool."[122] Almost half a decade after the use of the electronic fence along the southern border, P&E justified the INS R&D plan by implicitly foregrounding what they imagined the electronic fence resolved. The R&D plan was invested in a range of surveillance information technologies because P&E claimed that "illegal aliens are difficult to find, apprehend, and physically deport, especially those suspected of residing in urban areas."[123] Enacting the border depended on a human-machine assemblage supposedly automating data detection and apprehension about "difficult to find" intruders. Information was the key to shape the purposeful operation of this new cybernetic border. Intrusion data, like intruding bodies, awaited capture.

Yet no data on what amount of intrusion detection system activations led to alien apprehensions were included in any of the INS annual reports of the 1970s. Only anecdotal evidence was presented to the public about the effectiveness of the system. Examples included the *New York Times* article that opened this chapter or the story in the 1975 INS report about how, only hours after installation in the El Paso Border Patrol sector, the electronic sensors had led to "the largest known marijuana seizure made by officers of the Border Patrol"—two 2.5-ton grain trucks carrying a combined weight of 16,130 pounds of marijuana.[124] Both of these stories frame the relation between the electronic fence and unauthorized border crossers through the racial politics of illegal aliens and drug smuggling. By 1982, however, the General Accounting Office (GAO) concluded that efforts to estimate the total number of the illegal alien population had been fraught with inaccuracies and errors. The same could be said of the number of "entries without inspection," a significant category for assessing the efficiency of the electronic fence, which had relied on specious ratios between detected and undetected illegal entries. No constant ratio existed, nor could it be empirically demonstrated.[125] And though the electronic fence was meant to ameliorate the effects of the avalanche of printed numbers, success in this regard was limited.

The electronic fence enacted an imperial control fantasy by attempting to actualize an imagined capacity to master the messiness of the borderlands. Returning to the chapter's opening story in the *New York Times*, it is evident that the system was not without its failures and limitations. Sterba's story began by mentioning that the readout equipment or alarm display map (see figure 2.4) showed a sensor was steadily activated for two days. This was not supposed to happen. Lights on the display map should have only flashed whenever a sensor was activated and, in so doing, let operators know the specific sensor triggered and its location. But its constant activation was indicative, as Sterba stated, of "an obvious malfunction." Starting his story with the failing sensor No. 139, Sterba conveyed to readers that failure was integral to the electronic fence. Sometimes, "the electronic readout console becomes a Christmas tree, and stopping the swarm of illegal aliens crossing the border is an exercise in futility."[126] Not only could sensors fail, but the Border Patrol was also restrained in its capacity to respond to accurate activations. It was hampered by not having enough agents who could react to every triggered sensor. Dependent on the kinds of resources the Border Patrol had available to respond to sensor alerts, automatic detection did not translate to automatic apprehension and removal.

Since the installation of the experimental electronic fence on the southern US border, failure and error have been and (as chapter 3 shows) remain integral to the cybernetic border. Stories abound in INS publications and official materials of other kinds of failures interfering with effective Border Patrol operations. Initially, sensors in the system were developed to operate for brief periods of time and, consequently, could not endure long-term, wide-area operations.[127] This led to sensors losing power or failing to keep up with the harsh southern desert environment. Meanwhile, cattle and helicopters triggered sensors, sometimes leading to signals being erroneously processed by the system as human-generated.[128] Personnel were then dispatched to corroborate the source of such signals only to find no one there. This was indicative, Henneberger concluded, of how "technological improvements [invariably] introduce new and often unanticipated problems."[129] False positives, like cattle sensor activations processed as human ones, became a new problem for the immigration system at a moment when budgeting and personnel resources were hard to come by. Not only did the Border Patrol fail to achieve an operational goal of 90 percent response rate to sensor-detected intrusions, it also had to contend with the movements of nonhuman actors "confusing" ground sensors.[130] But just as unauthorized border crossers develop methods to avoid apprehension and their

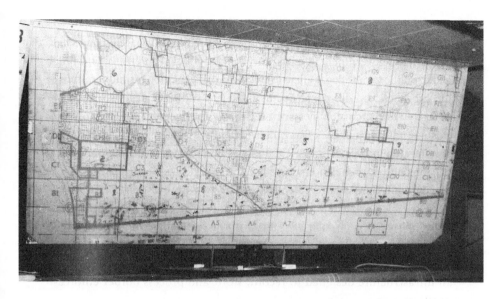

FIGURE 2.4. Alarm display map. Source: Thomas C. Henneberger Jr., "The Electronics Support Program of INS," *INS Reporter* 26, no. 4 (Spring 1978): 59.

sheer exercise of mobility constitutes a challenge and resistance to US border enforcement, the border technopolitical regime reinserts these issues as justifications for system improvements. Errors call attention to embedded structures of collaboration between DOD, INS/DHS, industry, and the academy responsible for correcting them. Error, as information studies scholars Cindy Lin and Steve Jackson argue, is not an edge case or an anomaly but a structuring site that works to redeploy existing structures of collaboration, call into being new forms of collaboration, or redeploy old sites and actors in new ways.[131] In this regard, emphasis on data and information technologies must be understood not as the simplification or elimination of the labor of border enforcement but as its multiplication. Error, failure, and border crossers' avoidance have renewed the commitment of actors to test, improve, and deploy more information technology to govern the southern border.[132]

The technical operation of the electronic fence could not stand separate from the political objectives it was meant to fulfill—racialization, criminalization, and datafication. The system was programmed to produce a perceptual and informational territory that only some people could enter while others classified as intruders could not. The electronic fence installed mostly along the southern US border in the 1970s guarded against the purported threat of Mexicans who, throughout the twentieth century, were conceived by many US government officials, government policies, and members of the wider public as an illegal alien problem to solve. No longer hidden, those the cybernetic border construed as intruders and their actions were now perceived and recorded by a sociotechnical arrangement attuned to their existence. Their presence was quantified, processed, and subjected to the enumerative power of statistical analysis by INS officials. Data about intrusions and apprehensions were used to reorganize Border Patrol agent deployments across border sectors. A one-way flow of practices was superseded by a cybernetic reconfiguration. Border enforcement since the 1970s operates via circular causality with discrete objectives—a feedback loop that guided operations. The electronic fence was integral to the expansion of numerical technologies through its capacity to contribute to an infrastructure designed to record, store, and process border enforcement data.

This chapter moves historical studies of science and technology beyond export and import models. Where historians have sought to show how ideas or technologies move in one direction, from an empire's center to its peripheries, I drew imperial practices and technologies together across space and time. Frontier making shaped the material infrastructure on which the US military could rely in developing intrusion detection systems. Fort Huachuca, once a frontier outpost created to manage "intransigent Indians," provided soldiers with the technical know-how to be vigilant against another kind of intransigent subject in the Vietnamese borderlands. There, infiltration forces were racially marked through the epithet of "gooks." In this sense, the McNamara Line represented an articulation of frontier politics, racial oppression, and war. When it was transformed into the electronic fence, the system became an instrument of a technopolitical regime designed to target Mexicans in the management of the boundaries of exclusion from the US empire-nation. "Imperial encounters," anthropologist Fernando Coronil writes, "entail the transcultural interaction of the domestic and the foreign under changing historical conditions. This process does not involve the movement of discrete entities from one bounded body into another across fixed borders, but rather their reciprocal transformation."[133] What both export and import models miss is that technologies such as the Firebee (discussed in chapter 1) and the electronic fence (in this one) were co-shaped locally and internationally through the articulations of border technopolitical regimes.

The cybernetic border that emerged during the mid-twentieth century through the electronic fence set the conditions of possibility for future entanglements between border enforcement and automation. Chapter 3 discusses new articulations in the US government's pursuit of a "system of systems." Such a technopolitical arrangement—built on the convergence of drones, CCTV systems, ground sensors, computers, and databases—continued to treat the borderlands as a data-filled environment to be sensed, managed, and ordered. In short, to make the border and the nation is to draw a racial line through investments in informational platforms of enmity.

3. PLATFORMS OF ENMITY AND
THE CONSOLIDATION OF THE NETWORKED
INFORMATION REGIME

The border has never been a mere line in the sand. It is not an undeniable entity or a legal construct that stands ahistorical and unmediated over time. The operations designed to enact the border merit critical attention for they allow deeper understanding of their political objectives as much as of the practices and arrangements that materialize sovereignty. In the previous chapters, I showed how drones flown during military exercises in the 1940s to the 1960s helped articulate the racialized figure of the intruder as a menace to the nation in the borderlands. US military and government officials and aeronautical companies inscribed the intruder's settler colonial temporalities and racial imaginaries into the making of Cold War US imperial formations. The ambivalent acceptance of the predominantly Mexican migratory agricultural proletariat in this period was superseded by a border technopolitical regime designed to discriminate between the movements of those meant for inclusion and those meant for exclusion from the nation. Drones, the electronic fence, and intruders produced the border as much as they were embodiments themselves of the border, which is to say that they were part of the political project of territorialized sovereignties.

Since 2002, the Department of Homeland Security (DHS) has sought to create "smart borders" in its efforts to police intruders and enact spatial control. Perhaps there is no better-known effort to create a smart border than the "system of systems," which integrates multiple platforms under a networked architecture. In the system of systems, US government officials and the defense industry brought together the technopolitics of air power and unmanning (chapter 1) with those of data (chapter 2). While the electronic fence collected intrusion data and, in some instances, automatically processed it to determine the nature of the intrusion, data were isolated from other enforcement systems. The system of systems has, in contrast, sought to deliver the unfulfilled dreams of an integrated electronic battlefield. One DHS official described it during a congressional hearing in 2005 as "an architecture" combining a range of platforms to "gather, process and distribute real-time knowledge of the border and transportation situation."[1] The US Border Patrol's diagram of "elements of change detection capability" (figure 3.1) translates this networked arrangement into a plan. Shadowy figures kick up dirt as they approach the imagined southern boundary of the United States, while others succeeded in crossing it. According to the 2012–2016 Border Patrol Strategic Plan, these figures constitute threats and risks for agents to guard against.[2] Along the southern line and well beyond it, a range of systems work in concert to produce the Border Patrol's "change detection capability": unmanned aerial systems (UASs), agents performing sign cutting, relay towers, remote video surveillance systems, imaging sensors, and unattended ground sensors, among many others. These systems and practices are drawn together under the construct of change detection by their collection of diverse information and intelligence. The system of systems gathers, processes, and integrates platform data to shape the operations of agents in each sector of the border.

I argue this arrangement *prototyped* the border as a networked platform. To say the border is prototyped as a networked platform means that actors approach it as a complex, interlocking system of information. It performs a tangible even if provisional arrangement. As a prototype, it "reconfigure[s] material and discursive practice[s]" already present in border enforcement efforts.[3] The border as a networked platform is a distinct materialization of the more general understanding that borders are infrastructural. It is a platform in the sense suggested by Peter Andreas: the stage upon which policing, generally understood as the coercive hand of the state, is also a performative practice that communicates the commitment to mark and maintain the boundaries of territorialized sovereignty.[4] This reasoning leads one to think of the border as the figurative elevated stand from which actors announce a political vision for the nation. In this sense, the border-as-platform is architectural, figurative, and political, three of the four semantic territories of platforms identified by information studies scholar Tarleton Gillespie. This means that the border is the physical infrastructure dedicated to the production of

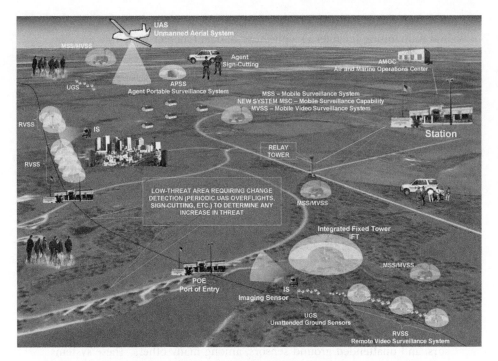

FIGURE 3.1. Elements of change detection capability. Source: DHS, CBP, Office of the Border Patrol, *2012–2016 Border Patrol Strategic Plan* (Washington, DC: Customs and Border Protection, 2012), HSDL, 14.

territorial demarcations as much as one of the symbolic foundations of the nation as an imagined community and a material reality. But the border as networked platform brings into purview the fourth dimension proposed by Gillespie: the computational. The border is "an infrastructure that supports the design and use of particular applications," either computer hardware, operating systems, or fixed and mobile information devices.[5] In figure 3.1, we see DHS's change detection capability and its interconnection of practices, ideas, human actors, computer hardware, devices, and buildings. The type of border such an arrangement produces is networked and datafied; this platform orientation, in turn, supports further research and development into other sociotechnical arrangements meant to produce the border. As the chapter demonstrates, this approach has been ever-changing due to ongoing events in and beyond the borderlands as well as the inconsistent efficiencies delivered by specific versions of it. Therefore, the border as a networked platform is not a finished product but a perennial prototype.

This chapter approaches the border as networked platform through a fractal structure whereby the parts are reduced-size copies of the whole. Surveillance studies scholars Tamara Vukov and Mimi Sheller describe borders in the twenty-first century as fractalized because they are dispersed, ubiquitous, and multi-scalar, produced through ever-more datafied processes and techniques.[6] Each section of the chapter delves deeper into this fractal structure by digging into the networked platform's technopolitical arrangements. The fractal structure of the chapter should not be read as following a hierarchical or causal order but a rhizomatic one. Each element is simultaneously shaped and shaping the other. The first fractal is devoted to the political shifts informing how the United States imagined itself just before and in the aftermath of the attacks of September 11, 2001. The paranoid politics of the War on Terror built on "settler native" discourses that multiplied the racialized bodies imagined as existential threats to the nation; those threats were no longer limited to Mexicans and Latina/o/es more broadly but now included Arabs and Muslims. Efforts to produce security simultaneously expanded and closed the boundaries of the empire-nation so that, as the 9/11 Commission concluded, "the American homeland [was] the planet."[7] The age of anxiety is how commentators described the world made by 9/11.[8] And it was to be managed through information. When it came to the southern border, discussed on the second fractal, US government officials, technicians, and the broader public identified information technologies (e.g., drones and so-called smart walls) as integral to their strategic approach to execute operational control. These were platforms for revealing and governing the hidden enemies of the empire-nation; these machines and the interlocking institutional, social, and technical arrangements that brought them forth are at their core platforms of enmity. Since the 1970s, the pursuit of these platforms consolidated the organization of the borderlands as a data-filled environment to be governed and controlled by the electronic fence and other efforts led by the Immigration and Naturalization Service (INS). The third fractal is devoted to the prototyping boundaries of these platforms of enmity: the system of systems, Predator B UASS, and BigPipe. Together, this networked platform worked to produce a common operating picture through which to control the risks and threats of the nation.

Border enforcement operations are the materialization of sociotechnical relations and knowledge practices in the management of populations. These relations and knowledge practices are the products of historical processes that draw boundaries on objects and subjects. And while these processes are not neat but unfold in shifting and uneven ways, it is important to approach them as situated becomings—that is, to describe and analyze the ideas that value specific methods and means of knowing at a particular conjuncture. Who becomes a target of the border technopolitical regime, and how are they known? To what ends are they known? Answers to these questions do not follow tidy causal chains but co-shape one another. The logics of war and security after the attacks of 9/11 led to the enjoining of Latina/o/es, Arabs, and Muslims as enemy threats of the nation. Their purported dangers were governed through an approach that understood the border as a networked platform. When it comes to the networked platform of the system of systems (and drones within it), I rely mostly on materials produced during the period from 2004 to 2012 because it was a period of relative stabilization. The prototyping of the data networked platform, however, continued long after this period, and I engage materials produced during the presidencies of Barack Obama, Donald Trump, and Joe Biden to show the insistent entanglements between such a platform and operational control.[9]

Logics of War and Security: Retracing the Boundaries of Enmity

Border enforcement has undergone two fundamental transformations in the last three decades. The first was the North American Free Trade Agreement (NAFTA), which liberalized the cross-border mobility of goods, services, and capital through the integration of Canada, Mexico, and the United States as trade partners, all the while opening security challenges.[10] These challenges resulted from the paradox of decreasing restrictions on capital and trade flows just as governments worked to tighten the mobility of labor and clamped down on the flow of illegal goods such as drugs.[11] Nativist and conservative activists like Pat Buchanan and Samuel P. Huntington succeeded in pushing the US government to continue approaching Latina/o/es as targets of migration and drugs enforcement. While Latina/o/e migrants were imagined throughout the second half of the twentieth century through tropes of intrusion and invasion, US nativist populism, as a settler colonial and imperial project, rewrote these biopolitical scripts as wide civilizational ones whereby Latina/o/es were distinct, inferior, and a menace to (white) Western civilization. "Upon being equated with a specific national-origin migrant group," Nicholas De Genova succinctly notes, "the sociopolitical category 'illegal alien'—inseparable from a distinct 'problem' or 'crisis' of governance and national sovereignty—has consistently come to be saturated with racialized difference." This differentiation of Mexicans as impossible subjects constitutes part of a hegemonic project that, as De Genova argues and this book shows, promoted the priority of settler "natives" since the mid-twentieth century as the incommensurable "we" pressed against external threats and risks.[12] The "settler native" is a variation of Genevieve Carpio's "Anglo Fantasy Past" discussed in chapter 1, which only validated the internal mobility of white settlers as means of erasing colonial narratives and practices.[13] Within this enduring structure of feeling, debates about the border are practices that draw out the racial boundaries of the nation.

The second transformation occurred after the attacks of September 11, 2001, which led government officials and the public at large to imagine border security in the United States as inextricably linked to the exploits of terrorists.[14] The Latina/o/e threats of migration and drugs were enjoined to the terrorist threat scripted for Arabs and Muslims. What were often separate realms of policy, national security and border security were now entangled through a new framework of homeland security. The paranoid politics of the War on Terror multiplied enmity by putting pressure on the boundaries of the nation as theaters for security operations. Those imagined to be enemies and the border (as a spatialized articulation of sovereignty) were redrawn through the logics of war and the logics of security—a dimension that in the aftermath of 9/11 brought together government officials and conservatives with the populist right. Both logics come sharply into relief through the classification system developed for "apprehended" subjects during border enforcement operations by the DHS. Attention to the collection of data about these subjects (i.e., "Mexican," "Other than Mexican," "person from special interest country") highlights the paranoid narratives of border control. As digital studies scholar Wendy Chun contends, "Paranoia stems from the reduction of political problems into technological ones—a reduction that blinds us to the ways in which those very technologies operate and fail to operate."[15] Enmity was no longer reserved for the Mexican "silent invasion" but for other Latina/o/es, Arabs, and Muslims. Enmity was to be interpreted through a civilizational framework invested in the supremacy of whiteness and embedded in bureaucratic classificatory schema.

In producing homeland security—the entanglement of border and national securities—US government officials, defense manufacturers, and members of the public brought the local and the global ever more into contact with one another. And when the United States was imagined as territorially extended throughout the whole world, foreign threats were never far removed or external to the empire-nation. They were internal to it, and territorial boundaries were imagined equally, as far away as Afghanistan or Iraq or as close as the southern border with Mexico. To secure the borders of the United States meant that leading figures in government and in the public at large raised something to a new status on the political agenda and, in doing so, justified extraordinary policy efforts and responses.[16] Efforts in security were meant to reassure the secured that they were protected and kept safe from harm. More fundamentally, securitization here was the valorization of one kind of life and one kind of territorial sovereignty over another.

MEXICAN ENMITY AFTER NAFTA

The early 1990s continued to be marked by long-lasting anxieties about the southern border and ongoing Latin American migrations to the United States. The paranoid narratives about the "invisible" and "silent invasion" that former INS Commissioner Leonard Chapman decried in the popular press materialized now in debates about the establishment of multilateral trade treaties like NAFTA in 1994 and about the integrity of the nation because of demographic changes. This period was marked by the efficacy of the settler nativist (populist) right in leveraging the logics of war by making Mexico and Mexicans into enemy threats against whom to prioritize efforts in border security.[17]

Samuel P. Huntington's "clash of civilizations" thesis was a paradigmatic framing device through which responses to NAFTA and immigration were described. Reflecting on the meaning of the end of the Cold War, the Harvard political scientist suggested a new era awaited where "conflict between civilizations will supplant ideological and other forms of conflict as the dominant global form of conflict."[18] He argued that the main challenge to Western hegemony was Islam, a source of conflict that was historically linked to its rivalry against a Judeo-Christian heritage.[19] From Huntington's vantage point, the main conflict with Islam would finally reach a new phase of clear and present danger after 9/11 (discussed later in the chapter.) Within this clash of civilizations, regional economic blocs would help enforce an ethnic, racial, and cultural commons that he called a "civilization-consciousness." Yet NAFTA unsettled this formation because it brought together what Huntington identified as clashing civilizations: "Western" (United States and Canada) and "Latin American" (Mexico). Critics of NAFTA were found across the political spectrum as they levied arguments considering the treaty's negative effects on labor rights, the environment, and the undoing of national sovereignty.[20] Among the treaty's forceful opponents were political conservatives and self-proclaimed members of the "populist right" like Pat

Buchanan. They saw in their opposition to NAFTA a civilizational defense—it was the articulation of "a new patriotism" that fought for "our way of life."[21] "Contemptuous of states' rights, regional differences and national distinctions," Buchanan argued, "NAFTA would supersede state laws and diminish US sovereignty."[22] The multilateral trade treaty was seen by the populist right as an affront to the nation. In political terms, NAFTA was thought to undo the state's right to govern by, among other things, transferring some of its responsibilities to newly created multilateral institutions.

The US nation, as a settler colonial project, was felt to be under threat in cultural terms as well because Buchanan and like-minded folks imagined that closer collaboration and interaction with Mexicans would eviscerate what he called "national distinctions." Buchanan made this point forcefully when he stated that "no matter the cash benefits, we don't want to merge our economy with Mexico, and we don't want to merge our country with Mexico." The nativist opposition to NAFTA was a prescient articulation of Huntington's clash of civilizations thesis, whereby economic rivalries supposedly did not materialize along "ideological" lines—as was the case during the Cold War—but between the "fault lines" of civilizations. US nativist discourse simultaneously displaced Indigenous peoples and appropriated for themselves the position of "native" by imagining white (Anglo) folks as the original inhabitants of the land. Settlers positioned themselves as natives while holding nativist attitudes against those they imagined as foreign to the nation; their discursive maneuver was an expression of settler nativism.[23] The illegal alien within this discourse represented a menace to the settler project for it threatened the apparent homogeneity of the nation. It was no surprise, then, that the civilizational fault line was made manifest, to quote Gloria Anzaldúa, "where the Third World grates against the first and bleeds," on the border between the United States and Mexico.[24] There, it was already reimagined as a "front line."

Nativist and populist right gained ground in the Republican Party by identifying illegal immigration and border enforcement as key areas of intervention. Left in the past was the 1980 Republican platform championed by then presidential candidate Ronald Reagan, a platform that claimed party supporters "have opened our arms and hearts to strangers from abroad" and that "we favor an immigration and refugee policy which is consistent with this tradition."[25] By the early 1990s, some Republicans in California blamed "unchecked immigration" for the state's economic and budget crisis.[26] In 1994, as California governor Pete Wilson stood for reelection, he became the champion of a draconian ballot initiative (Proposition 187) meant to establish a citizenship-based screening system that would prevent unauthorized immigrants ("illegal aliens") from accessing basic public services such as health and education. As he stated in an op-ed published in the *Wall Street Journal*, "the fundamental and very serious flaw of current federal immigration policy is that the US, a nation built on the rule of law, now rewards people who have broken the law by illegally crossing our borders."[27] Governor Wilson's criticism was, in part, an allusion to Reagan's signature project—the Immigration Reform and Control Act of 1986—which provided amnesty to large numbers of unauthorized immigrants and seasonal agricultural laborers. Underscoring "the rule of law," Wilson made use of the long-standing US tradition of criminalizing non-white migrants by portraying them as disorderly "lawbreakers." The California governor, through his public interventions and policy measures, legitimized the xenophobic and racist sentiments that nurtured the anti-immigrant movement not just in California but across the United States.[28] The paranoid defense of the empire-nation continued to approach the border and criminalized migrants as threats.

The settler nativist politics espoused by Buchanan and Wilson became a fundamental new force in the Republican Party, all the while putting pressure on moderates in the party and on Democrats to respond to popular reactions against immigration. The Illegal Immigration Reform and Immigrant Responsibility Act (IIRIRA) of 1996, approved by the Republican-led Congress and signed into law by President Bill Clinton, targeted illegal aliens and the border. Clinton and the Democratic Party embraced calls to be tough on illegal immigration and to make the border a lawful place. The legislation expanded the ground for removal under criminal law.[29] It also made support of security technologies, fortifications, and the expansion of Border Patrol personnel key budget priorities. More fundamentally, approval of IIRIRA reified and legitimized the anti-immigrant fervor espoused by US settler nativism and the populist right, which depicted the border as a space of threats to the nation.[30] The racialized criminalization of unauthorized border crossers and drug smuggling turned the southern borderlands into spaces for military and security logics. As a sign of the heightened focus that NAFTA placed on managing and discriminating between mobilities across the border, operational budgets at INS grew significantly between 1993 and 2000, from $1.5 billion to $5 billion, and the number of Border Patrol agents increased from 4,000 to 9,000.[31]

IIRIRA's funding for border enforcement expanded the sociotechnical arrangements put in place through a strategy known as "prevention through deterrence." Throughout the 1990s, the Border Patrol implemented a series of operations to exert control over unauthorized border crossings. Among them were Operations Hold the Line and Gatekeeper. The immigration and border enforcement agency combined fence structures, high-intensity lighting, large amounts of mobilized agents near the international US-Mexico boundary line, and different sensing technologies (e.g., ground sensors, cameras) in its efforts to prevent and deter unauthorized migrants and smugglers. Operations Hold the Line and Gatekeeper were re-instantiations of the intrusion detection systems of the 1970s, sociotechnical arrangements designed to exclude, remove, and endanger intruder threats. These operations were soon reframed through the strategic concept of prevention through deterrence, which meant that a "proper balance" of personnel, equipment, technology, and border infrastructure was needed to dissuade people from attempting to cross the border without authorization.[32] The Border Patrol described the strategy in 1996 by stressing that its objective was "to close off the routes most frequently used by smugglers and illegal aliens and to shift traffic to areas that are more remote and difficult to cross illegally, where INS has the tactical advantage." This "proper balance" of humans, technology, and infrastructure would "deter, detect, and apprehend illegal aliens."[33] Funding from IIRIRA further entrenched the belief that border enforcement equated sociotechnical arrangements that, in this strategy, prevented unauthorized border crossings through sheer intimidation of force and an increase in danger.

Furthermore, the strategy of pushing unauthorized border crossings through remote areas subsequently led to construing these zones as "gaps" and "voids" to be remediated. Felicity Amaya Schaeffer's work shows that these constructions occur in relation to settler surveillance and Indigeneity. After all, prevention through deterrence shifted crossings from California into Tohono O'odham land, which straddles across the US-Mexico border in the Sonoran Desert. The incursion of new information infrastructures and their technopolitics of enmity "into the O'odham reservation rehashes the making of this land as a wild and sparsely populated frontier in need of conversion into a securitized border."[34] Even when the federal government did this, it could not avoid demonstrating the fact that the southern borderlands are "unsettled borders." Understanding US borders as unsettled, as Schaeffer proposes, foregrounds their instability in the face of historical and ongoing unauthorized crossings as much as the contestations of Indigenous peoples. Prevention through deterrence is part of the historical and current settler struggles of the US empire-nation.

The effects of the strategy on human life, however, were quite ominous. Border anthropologist Jason De León has shown that the strategy "made migration less visible and created a scenario in which the policing of undocumented people occurred in areas with few witnesses"; worse yet, it conscripted the desert environment "to act as an enforcer while simultaneously providing [the Border Patrol] with plausible deniability regarding blame for any victims the desert may claim."[35] In mid-2001, the Government Accountability Office (GAO) noted that before the implementation of the strategy, unauthorized border crossers had faced danger and even died crossing between ports of entry; however, prevention through deterrence was thought to have caused "an increase in deaths from exposure to either heat or cold."[36] Prevention through deterrence disregarded the lives of unauthorized border crossers by placing them into more vulnerable, life-threatening positions. Working to secure the border, the US government makes the lives of migrants more insecure. Its operations articulated a form of "social death." According to American studies scholar Lisa Marie Cacho, social death is a condition of ineligible personhood that defines who does not matter—people such as "undocumented immigrants, the racialized poor of the global South, and criminalized US residents of color in both inner cities and rural areas." The corollary of such a condition is that mattering is made meaningful—as meaningful as having one's right to live recognized.[37] But I would argue, drawing on Black studies scholar Fred Moten's reading of Frantz Fanon, that this maneuver to produce the social death of the Other is incomplete.[38] What folks have theorized as the condition of social death is the product of a political practice without closure: the attempt to draw boundaries of inside/outside, inclusion/exclusion, integration/expulsion. In the context of the border enforcement strategy perpetuated by IIRIRA, future sociotechnical assemblages were meant to "deter" unauthorized border crossers and, as a result, to leave them exposed to the ravages of the desert environment.[39] Technologies were sold, jobs were paid for, and profits were made in determining who mattered and who did not. Settler nativist discourse refashioned the technopolitics of intrusion by naming Mexicans as threats and risks. In other words, this discourse and its eventual legitimation in government policy has worked to eviscerate their legibility to human and constitutional rights by endangering their lives. These populations are forced to navigate the violence of the empire-nation.[40]

And yet, the migrant Other, especially the unauthorized border crosser, set to live a life of social death challenges this totalizing orientation by moving toward and against death. Unauthorized border crossers recognize the dangers that lurk in the weaponized desert landscape of the US southwestern borderlands. In traversing such landscape, their sovereign practices transgress the bounds of the possible set up by imperial formations. Their actions create another sociopolitical world—a world within the sovereign machines of empire where there is a gap, an absence.[41] Such absence reveals the limitations of imperial formations. Their transgressions make evident the imperial disorder of things and the immanent constraints to the project of producing social death.

ARAB AND MUSLIM ENMITY AFTER THE WAR ON TERROR

Settler nativism and the populist right laid the groundwork for the Islamophobic orientations of the emerging security regime after 9/11. These political movements built on the historical legacies of US settler colonialism and racial formations positing the supremacy of white communities. While Mexicans and Latina/o/es were treated as risky intruders and dangers to the imagined purity of the nation, Arabs and Muslims were treated by a range of government organizations and members of the public as architects of terror. The ensuing "War on Terror" was, as ethnic studies scholar Junaid Rana holds, a project in the management of fear. The rhetoric of terror enabled the fiction of racialized Arabs and Muslims as enemies of the nation. This security fiction went beyond any specific, individual actions; it was, instead, projected onto this racialized community.[42] A generalized sense of anxiety and panic overwhelmed a variety of actors because of the surreptitious movements of the attackers and the failures of the US national security apparatus.[43] In the face of fear, pessimism, and loss of control, the War on Terror became the clearest expression of a need and a desire for security.[44]

A hegemonic field of meaning was constituted through government and media discourses targeting Arabs and Muslims for their identities, not their purported criminality.[45] Passage of the PATRIOT Act in 2001 (and its subsequent renewals in 2005, 2006, 2010, and 2011) legalized previously illegal acts that, in turn, enabled anti-Arab and anti-Muslim racism, such as "monitoring Arab and Muslim groups; granting the US Attorney General the right to indefinitely detain noncitizens whom he suspects might have ties to terrorism; searching and wiretapping secretly, without probable cause; arresting and holding a person as a 'material witness' whose testimony might assist in a case; using secret evidence, without granting the accused access to that evidence; trying those designated as 'enemy combatants' in military tribunals (as opposed to civilian courts); and deportation based on guilt by association (not on what someone has done)."[46] A legal framework to manage and administer the lives of Arabs and Muslims legitimized and generalized a sense of suspicion toward these populations. These communities were envisioned as terrorist or potentially terrorist. The "terrorist," in this instance, was a "composite figure, and like previous menaces, this figure drew upon and 're-assembled' the body of existing dangers to bring into being a 'new enemy.'"[47] Arabs and Muslims, entangled with the figure of the "terrorist," were now critically marked for monitoring as enemy Others of the US empire-nation.

The legal framework was part and parcel of the global political and military strategy demanded by *The 9/11 Commission Report*—that its target be "the Arab and Muslim world, in all its variety."[48] A global threat demanded a global response. In the announcement of his administration's *National Strategy for Homeland Security* (summer 2002), President George W. Bush stated, "We are today *a nation at risk* to a new and changing threat. The terrorist threat to America *takes many forms, has many places to hide*, and *is often invisible*."[49] Even though the new threat was not a particular nation, it was thought to target specific collective imaginaries: the US nation and Western civilization. Because terrorism did not distinguish between US targets abroad ("over there") or at home ("over here"), the 9/11 Commission concluded that "the American homeland [was] the planet."[50] The commission proposed through this formulation a security framework that redrew the boundaries of the empire-nation as it imagined the foreign in the domestic and the domestic in the foreign. Talk of national security—defense from foreign adversaries—would not unfold at the expense of homeland security. In effect, to prevent, monitor, and curtail the spread of risks—in many instances thought to be specific populations—became a global strategic objective of the US empire-nation and its political rationale. The War on Terror, then, as Rana forcefully argues, was a global project, not unlike the settler colonial one, meant to destroy an enemy Other deemed less than human.[51]

If the US homeland was the planet, then why did government officials insist on policing the physical borderline between the United States and Mexico? Empire scholars have shown that imperial formations permanently do and undo boundaries; they expand territorially while integrating and displacing populations. Through boundary making, imperial sovereignty attempts to regulate the flows of goods and people and their presence.[52] In the United States, imperial sovereignty did not shed its entanglements with nation making and its heightened proclivity to bind citizenship through sorting practices and constructs like race, gender, and sexuality, among others.[53] It is through citizenship that belonging to and participation in an imagined community is granted, recognized, and legitimated. Citizenship is a boundary technology that regulates the terms of inclusion or exclusion of individuals and of communities in the nation. Consequently, the multiplication of the border post-9/11 meant that the borderlands, like settler nativism did in the 1990s, were treated as a "front line" in the defense of citizenship from ever-shifting threats and risks.

One such way that otherness in the borderlands was managed was in field processing by the Border Patrol, one of the law enforcement arms of Customs and Border Protection (CBP).[54] The classificatory schema used by the Border Patrol and other officials at DHS give insight into how the sensory regime of the system of systems and its associated operative image were prescripted to police the presence of racialized populations. Whenever "an alien attempting to enter the country illegally" was apprehended by agents of the Border Patrol, a file (Form I-826) was created where information such as name, date and place of birth, and country of citizenship was recorded.[55] An integral part of processing was identifying the apprehended border crossers within the Border Patrol's classificatory schema: Mexican, OTM (Other than Mexican), and person from special interest country. Because the vast majority of people apprehended by the Border Patrol were Mexican nationals, a Congressional Research Service report stated that "the agency categorizes the aliens it apprehends as Mexican or 'Other Than Mexican.'"[56] The expansive OTM designation identified "people who come up through the Southern border of Mexico from Central America, maybe South America," but it could also be used for people from countries elsewhere in the world.[57] "Person from special interest country" was used for people from countries designated by the US intelligence community as places "that could export individuals that could bring harm to our country in the way of terrorism."[58] This last subject type, a legacy of post-9/11 security efforts, was for the most part a euphemism for Arabs or Muslims. Field processing, in the end, was designed to be hyper-focused on subject types meant for removal.

The conceptual focus on these field processing subject types and these populations reveals a racializing logic operating at the center of the border technopolitical regime. They are categories that, as the work of Geoffrey Bowker and Susan Leigh Star shows, segment the world into contingently defined spatial, temporal, or spatiotemporal unities.[59] Subject types redeploy a political imaginary built through scripts of enmity; populations identified by these categories were marked as exogenous enemies by nationalist and settler nativist discourses. "Mexican," "Other than Mexican," and "person from special interest country" helped narrow the field of operations for Border Patrol agents. These subject types sorted who were expected to be the target of oversight (a direct translation of the French *surveillance*) and who, by omission, would not. They executed what digital studies scholar Simone Browne calls "racializing surveillance"—a technology of social control that reifies "boundaries, borders, and bodies along racial lines" and whose outcome is the discriminatory treatment of racialized subjects and populations.[60] When an apprehended subject was placed within the bounds of any of these categories, their citizenship status and their possibility of belonging was irremediably questioned.

The racializing logic of subject types produces a border understood through control of territorial and citizenship boundaries. Failure to execute control over land and its inhabitants does not lead to a reformulation of border enforcement itself. On the contrary, commitments are renewed because much is imagined to be on the line. "Calls for more border enforcement continue," Douglas S. Massey, Jorge Durand, and Karen A. Pren contend, "because the Mexico-US border has become the preeminent symbolic line separating Americans from any and all external threats."[61] Illegal alien and terrorist are both tightly associated with the border zone as a liminal space of insecurity. The production of US citizenship relies on the enactment of logics of security against those populations identified by subject types. Their existence is, as field processing subject types demonstrate, pre-inscripted as a transgression of the law because they undo the boundaries of what is codified as lawful.[62] In a controversial statement before Congress in early 2005, then DHS deputy secretary James Loy said that "information from ongoing investigations, detentions, and emerging-threat streams strongly suggest that Al Qaeda has considered using the southwest border to infiltrate the United States."[63] This kind of unsubstantiated formulation came to view the border as a site of terrorist futurity, a space through which terrorists might materialize. Because of the invisible threats of terrorists and illegal aliens, the border continues to be imagined as a site of national vulnerability. Remediating such vulnerability is, as CBP commissioner Robert C. Bonner held in 2004, "an existential objective."[64]

Human-Machine Configurations of Operational Control

The strategies pursued by INS/DHS to secure the existential objective cohered around understanding the border as a networked platform. The War on Terror articulated a grammar of global empire in need of an infrastructural apparatus to operationalize it. The multiplication of threats across the imagined territory of the "American homeland" led US officials and engineers to propose a sociotechnical arrangement that would produce security through enclosure. The US military's human-machine configurations of control drew from the world built by the Cold War—a world "of automatic, rationalized systems" that would turn the chaos of modern warfare into neat order.[65] It was a world interconnected through techniques of unmanning and automation, supplanting and supplementing human labor through self-regulating systems. The cybernetic border produced through variable enactments of operational control draws self-reflexive routines of enforcement that make the border a permanent prototype.

Some of the rationales for a networked border were based on the notion that illegal aliens and terrorists were surreptitious and deceitful figures who hid from the reach of the government. Unauthorized border crossers were described as a silent invasion while those who led the attack of 9/11 did so through asymmetry, a dominant concern in US military circles a decade prior.[66] They exploited US weaknesses in border security to attain greater freedom of action and maximized those conditions favorable to their operations. Among the security vulnerabilities found by the 9/11 Commission was the lack of information collaboration across the various US military and civilian intelligence agencies. Intelligence, security, and travel officials missed relevant and precise data at various moments before and on September 11; they operated in an environment of heightened uncertainty.[67] In an op-ed published a few days after the September 11 attacks, historian David M. Kennedy argued that "whoever our adversaries are, their objectives are not measured in terms of geography, trade, or any of the usual markers of political rivalry . . . [they are] an elusive foe impervious to the military might we have spent decades building."[68] The seeming elusiveness of the enemy made it harder for US actors to know who, how, and when to engage them. Paranoia, a familiar disposition throughout the Cold War, gripped the public. As New York Times columnist Maureen Dowd asserted, the "faceless enemy . . . could live among us as a fifth column."[69] Data precision and, whenever possible, interagency data integration were identified as antidotes to a "faceless enemy" and the uncertainty of "an elusive foe."[70]

The emphasis on control, as a structuring component in design as well as a political objective, brought "operational control" into being. Before its subsumption into the newly formed super-department of homeland security, INS devoted itself to establishing control on travel and the domestic sphere through a regime of inspection on all entries to US territory or through practices of border and immigration enforcement—preventing illegal entry, locating aliens that violated immigration law, and initiating deportation proceedings on apprehended subjects. INS defined effective border enforcement through its capacity to quickly locate and remove deportable aliens. Control of the border meant removing "surreptitious entries," 99 percent of which occurred "over the Mexican border."[71] Once DHS was founded, pursuit of control morphed through one of its major initiatives: the creation of smart borders as measures for securing the homeland. The *National Strategy for Homeland Security* stated such borders would "be a continuum framed by land, sea, and air dimensions, where a layered management system enables greater visibility of vehicles, people, and goods coming to and departing from our country."[72] Integration of territorialized sovereignties—land, sea, and air—unfolded through the creation of an integrated ("layered") sensory regime for recording data flows about the movement of people, goods, and services across borders and then leveraging such data to differentiate between reliable and legitimate entities and those ("illegal contraband and people") requiring exclusion from the nation.[73] Operational control grew out of historic efforts in racialized control, enrollment of electronic and information technology, and efforts rebranded through the concept of smart borders. It is within this conjuncture that the border technopolitical regime approached the border as a networked platform.

The meaning of the actions performed by sociotechnical arrangements like smart borders "is found in and through the very same methods" employed "to enact them intelligibly in the first place."[74] The technopolitics of smart borders as human-machine configurations are observed in the strategic plans for border enforcement and the evaluative assessments made of these border enforcement efforts by various government organizations. Plans often identify purposes, practices, and relations according to distinct circumstances. Science studies scholar and anthropologist Lucy Suchman argues that plans are about structuring behavior "in reflexive relation to circumstances that are themselves in the process of being generated, through the same actions that they in turn work to make comprehensible."[75] The goal for DHS's smart borders at first was to have a range of interconnected systems create an informational net that captured the data signatures of "intruders" crossing into US territory without authorization. And smart borders were to a great extent the responsibility of the CBP. Triggered unattended ground sensors alerted agents at a "command center" within a Border Patrol sector that a potential intrusion was underway. Agents used radar and camera towers to examine phenomena activating the sensors. Information was relayed and displayed to agents in the field through a "mobile data

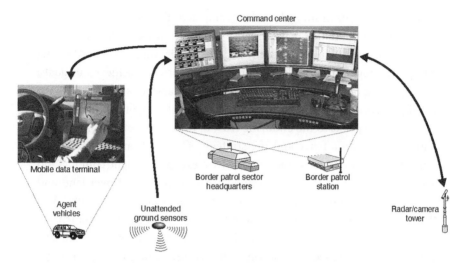

Command center

Mobile data terminal

Agent
vehicles

Unattended
ground sensors

Border patrol sector
headquarters

Border patrol
station

Radar/camera
tower

FIGURE 3.2. Diagram of DHS plans for a Common Operating Picture. Source: Government Accountability Office, "Secure Border Initiative: DHS Needs to Address Significant Risks in Delivering Key Technology Investment," GAO-08-1086 (Washington, DC: Government Accountability Office, 2008), 9.

terminal" that allowed them to search the area of activity more precisely. Figure 3.2 visualizes the plan to treat the border as a networked platform, where combined elements execute distinct responsibilities in the making of operational control and, more broadly, the establishment of sovereign territory. These plans, as the following pages demonstrate, were not immutable or inflexible—failures, inaccuracies, the avalanche of printed numbers, and electoral shifts often led to reformulations of strategy. Across DHS documents, actors envision a smart border embedded with self-reflexivity, the kind that was a cornerstone of cybernetic systems. Government plans and assessment imagined a smart border that responded to the behaviors of intruders and Border Patrol agents by shaping their future behaviors. And this is what operational control is all about.

CBP and Border Patrol proposed operational control as a strategic goal in 2004, as part of DHS's efforts to reorganize homeland security post-9/11. The goal described by CBP commissioner Bonner initially had six core elements, though these were described differently in documents, and some of these changed slightly over the years. Among the core elements were "(1) securing the right combination of personnel, technology and infrastructure; (2) improving mobility and rapid deployment to quickly counter and interdict based on shifts in smuggling routes and tactical intelligence; (3) deploying defense-in-depth that makes full use of interior checkpoints and enforcement operations calculated to deny successful migration; (4) coordinating and partnering with other law enforcement agencies to achieve our goals; (5) improving border awareness and intelligence; and (6) strengthening the Headquarters command structure."[76] The notion of a "right combination" of components speaks to the enduring trust in the arrangements once tested with the electronic fence and the strategy of prevention through deterrence in Operations Hold the Line and Gatekeeper. A right combination acknowledges that border enforcement enacted command over land and people through human-machine and infrastructural arrangements. And that belief in the existence of some fitting interconnection of elements— that is, a mix of entities that are suitable and capable—must follow an empirical approach based on knowing what correct and incorrect arrangements were. "Border awareness and intelligence," meanwhile, conveys the sense that a networked platform was a kind of self-conscious entity that blurs the boundary between human and machine actants within it. Establishing and maintaining operational control was to "leverage 'smart border' technology to multiply the effect of enforcement personnel."[77] Actionable data produced by ground sensors and other surveillance equipment used to monitor remote areas along the extensive US-Mexico geopolitical boundary, as figure 3.2 shows, were meant to affect the behaviors of Border Patrol agents.

By associating smart border technology with notions of awareness, DHS drew on the work of military strategists and technicians from the 1990s. What they called "situational awareness" became a central concern when the Cold War enemy of communism gave way to a new age of uncertainty, risks, and threats. The term is connected to network-centric warfare, a US military concept of operations centering data as vectors in the management of the contemporary battlespace. Network-centric warfare (NCW) aimed to rearrange human and organizational behavior in the military and increase "combat power by networking sensors, decision makers, and shooters to achieve shared awareness, increased speed of command, higher tempo of operations, greater lethality, increased survivability, and a degree of self-synchronization."[78] Data flowing from linked sensors were integrated to create a common operating picture or situational awareness across the military hierarchy, from deployed soldiers all the way to the branch's chief. Battlespace awareness emerged from sharing the same information with all or with a subset of actors.[79] Increase in speed became a factor as information was shared more quickly, in "near real time," through the chain of command. More importantly, well-informed actors on the front lines and in lower levels of command were afforded the ability "to organize and synchronize complex warfare activities from the bottom up."[80] NCW, through its relation to computing systems, was defined in terms of efficiencies and optimizations because nodes were integrated into a network with data stored, processed, and held in common.[81] Networked human actors and programmable sensors were articulated by data flows.

Situational awareness works to rearrange and standardize the labor of border enforcement and the borderlands themselves as a varied assortment of informational nodes and links—hence its reliance on metaphors of networks and intelligence. The smart border was said to create common awareness by "having and disseminating information and tactical intelligence, while also responding to that intelligence quickly and nimbly."[82] Speed ("quickly") and flexibility ("nimbly") in situational awareness speak to the rationales embedded in the institution of protocols of enforcement. The protocols of situational awareness allude to an acceleration of perception beyond what might be possible by a sole agent. New prospects grow in the constitution of a networked, intersubjective perspective. Border Patrol agents are abstracted to become nodes that access, process, circulate, and respond to information. The relations of border enforcement drawn out in CBP plans are datafied and executed by a human-machine assemblage already standardized by uses of the electronic fence. When confronted with triggered unattended ground sensors, this reconfiguration expects agents to observe and note the activated sensor's location within the border sector and to identify, if possible, the nature of the data signature (i.e., who or what caused it). Once this is done, the agent must inform agents in the field where to intervene. If more information is needed, other DHS platforms (e.g., drones, helicopters) are called in to provide further awareness. Situational awareness in border enforcement is about working to organize and order heterogeneous flows of informationalized entities into coherent and actionable data.

With information a strategic vector in the management of the borderlands, CBP construed operational control as a standardized technical matter to be managed through circular causality. It also depended on the logics of war and security to produce and target stable and clearly bounded risk objects. The strategy pursued both agent capacities to influence and engage those deemed threats to the nation as well as the use of data to guide current and future CBP operations. In other words, operational control required a human-machine configuration that could inform the behaviors of actors on the ground by defining their relations through the difference that made a social difference. This objective followed and executed racial scripts whereby some populations played the roles of targets tracked, captured, and excluded from US territory.

Risk objects were emplaced in operational control, and their ongoing presence in apprehension statistical data between 2004 and 2010 generated the sense at the GAO of an unfulfilled strategic objective. At its simplest, DHS defined operational control as the Border Patrol's "ability to detect, respond, and interdict cross-border illegal activity."[83] But analysis of border security operations by the GAO in 2010 found that most of the areas of the Southwest border (about 1,120 miles) were only monitored, not controlled. The agency said CBP only had "substantial detection resources in place, but accessibility and resources continue to affect ability to respond." Furthermore, studies commissioned by CBP showed that apprehension statistics bore "little relationship to effectiveness because agency officials do not compare these numbers to the amount of illegal activity that crosses the border undetected."[84] This is what the measure of apprehension rate was meant to solve. Operational control was briefly abandoned during President Barack Obama's second term as a strategic goal because of the absence of measures that could confirm DHS successes. Risk objects, however, lingered as threats to resolve, even if the purported danger of terrorism decreased.

The temporary demotion of operational control from border enforcement strategy did not lead away from DHS's initial goal of creating a smart border to institute control and security. President Obama's administration favored an approach in 2012 based on three pillars: "information, integration, and rapid response." Gathering and analyzing data would inform and ensure operational planning and execution across spaces and organizations. The integration of operational partners and integration would then instruct what actors deemed as an appropriate response to existing or probable risks and threats.[85] In contrast, Donald Trump's racist project was made plain when he announced his presidential candidacy on June 16, 2015, and explicitly called out non-white populations as national menaces.[86] Among the first acts of his presidency days after taking office in 2017 was signing Executive Order 13767, which charged DHS with achieving operational control of the nation's borders. This meant "the prevention of all unlawful entries into the United States, including entries by terrorists, other unlawful aliens, instruments of terrorism, narcotics, and other contraband."[87] The Border Patrol's return to operational control during the Trump administration consisted of situational awareness, impedance and denial, and response and resolution. Officials stressed enforcement operations should either stop illegal crossings or slow them down and thereby improve the response time of agents to apprehend subjects. But this approach to operational control mostly reified the concept of operations from the Obama administration by emphasizing the role of information to guide and improve operations.[88] DHS officials argued smart border technology had furnished Border Patrol agents with the situational awareness necessary "to understand how much illegal activity agents are encountering" and how they should respond.[89] In this sense, operational control was tied to the deployment and enactments of smart borders that would inform agent decisions on how to intervene against the imagined threats to the nation.

While operational control was superseded by "operational advantage," an approach proposed by President Joe Biden's administration, it is still tethered to informational processes that allow agents "to detect, identify, classify, prioritize, and mitigate threats . . . through innovation and data analytics."[90] Accentuating *advantage*, the CBP aims "to match or exceed the capability of the threats we face, as well as to improve our ability to anticipate and predict emerging threats." CBP moves away from the abstraction of control to identify practices that are binary, either successful or unsuccessful, by matching or exceeding the efforts of targets. Technology is described through "innovative" platforms, a sign that the organization finds purchase in the symbolic capital assigned to it by the public. Innovation is represented by "autonomous capabilities like machine learning and artificial intelligence," techniques that CBP says will improve its capabilities to detect and identify threats—in short, to intervene in and influence the operating environment. The "Digital Border Patrol" planned by DHS today is a rearticulation of the promises of unmanning and automation found in the human-machine configurations of operational control.[91]

Measures of control remain elusive. DHS was ordered by the Consolidated Appropriations Act of 2017 to publish "metrics developed to measure the effectiveness of security between ports of entry, including the methodology and data supporting the resulting measures."[92] Border security measures or metrics speak to a cybernetic technoaesthetic already found in the reorganization of INS by Commissioner Chapman and the efforts of the Office of Planning and Evaluation—a recursive loop of evaluation that carefully examines inputs, processors, and outputs to control the border through logics of efficiency. This is border enforcement not as a finished set of arrangements but an ongoing set of practices and routines that structure the sensible and the knowledge cultures of the border technopolitical regime.[93] It is a technoaesthetic arrangement to be permanently tested and submitted to statistical measure. As a prototype, arrangements in border enforcement are tested against their contributions to identifying unauthorized border incursions and apprehensions. Since 1997, INS/DHS has attempted to implement a range of statistical measures to demonstrate the effectiveness of its enforcement practices.[94] The measure of "apprehension rate," used consistently since 2011, helps convey the sense that control is built on an empirical approach that is recorded, verified, and tested. DHS defines apprehension rate "as the proportion of attempted border crossers that is apprehended" by the Border Patrol. Methods for determining the total number of attempted unauthorized entries without inspection include statistical modeling and direct and indirect observations by agents.[95] While the measure has suffered extensive critique, least of which because there is no way to identify all attempted entries without authorization between ports of entry, it continues to be used and be the subject of numerous studies.[96] It is used because DHS understands the apprehension rate as an output measure that identifies actions taken by the Border Patrol that help produce risk objects—Jonathan Xavier Inda calls them "problem objects"—not just as thinkable but as calculable and manageable entities.[97] These are the targets of government.

Security in the twenty-first century is made through the Border Patrol's project to govern racialized threats through information supremacy. Information is the difference that makes a social difference. In the book's opening pages, I showed how tech startup Anduril Industries installed and tested its Lattice system to support border enforcement operations in 2018. The latest iteration of the pursuit of smart borders, Lattice is not dissimilar to the one conjured by CBP's system of systems. The following fractal shows that the supposed innovations of Anduril are but the reification of older platforms and their technopolitics. They are all part of the cybernetic border regime's plans to prototype the border as a networked platform.

Prototyping Boundaries

Border Patrol enforcement operations conceptualized as prevention through deterrence were celebrated at the organization itself as well as among some government circles throughout the 1990s and the early 2000s.[98] California governor Pete Wilson, part of the nativist and populist right wing of the Republican Party, said in 1994 that the approach "produced a new tranquility on both sides of the international boundary."[99] A year later, Texas governor

George W. Bush penned an op-ed calling for amity with Mexico but sub-scribing to the "highly successful program" and calling for its expansion.[100] A Department of Justice (DOJ) report in 1996 was said to proclaim that "progress is clear and successes are many" in the Clinton administration's efforts against "illegal immigration," which included prevention through deterrence.[101] An integral part of the strategy was the notion that a right mixture or a "proper balance" of elements existed in effective border en-forcement. Even when studies by CBP and GAO showed the strategy led to an increase in migrant deaths and that its impact preventing migration was inconclusive, Border Patrol continues to pursue a proper balance.

This proper balance existed as a perpetual prototype. It has changed slightly over time with specific devices adopted and later discarded, and others linked together under one name only to be called something else later. And yet a constant over the past twenty years of border enforcement arrangements is what in 2005 was called the system of systems, part of the Secure Border Initiative network (SBInet) program that underwent difficult and uneven development until its cancellation in 2011.[102] The architecture of the system of systems, as described by Kirk Evans, director of the Mission Support Office at DHS Advanced Research Projects Agency, was like NCW in that it connected distributed platforms collecting border information into a single system designed to "provide decision support tools and labor saving devices for our [homeland] security forces."[103] The system of systems prototyped the integration and use of a range of existing systems such as the network of electronic ground sensors and the incorporation of a new border enforcement platform: UAS. It prototyped how operational control would be produced and maintained through a "common operating picture," which is DHS's version of situational awareness. This human-machine configura-tion, government officials argued, assisted law enforcement activities in tar-geting risk objects and thereby producing secured national boundaries.

SYSTEM OF SYSTEMS

With SBInet, DHS sought to reconfigure past surveillance systems under a new arrangement. This included the electronic fence, which by 1988 was turned into the Integrated Computer-Aided Detection (ICAD) system and later renamed ICAD II from 1994 to 1998. ICAD used low-level television cameras to monitor high-traffic locations beyond ports of entry and system-recorded sensor activity; it tracked agent response and recorded results. ICAD II was then redesigned and renamed again in 1998 as the Integrated Surveillance Intelligence System (ISIS). It placed weight on creating a layered system of data flows to orient Border Patrol labor in space by maximizing available resources. Integration was predicated on logics of optimization that, despite purported promises, did not materialize because, in the words of a GAO report, the system "provided limited command, control, and situational awareness capability."[104] ISIS was subsequently folded into America's Shield Initiative, which was quickly redesigned as the Secure Border Initiative in 2006.[105] And it was then that DHS proposed SBInet as a systematic approach to border enforcement and border security.

The SBInet program had two main goals. The first was continuing efforts to produce some "proper balance" of operational technologies, infrastructure, rapid response capabilities, and personnel to "enable CBP agents and officers to gain effective control of US borders." Control, we have seen, has been a permanent, even if differently understood, goal for DHS. With SBInet, control was a relation agents enacted through detection, identification, classification, and response to "illegal entries into the United States" which ended their threat to the nation.[106] DHS was convinced that this could only happen through sociotechnical arrangements, especially those associated with Command, Control, Communications, and Information (C3I). The second goal was to employ C3I technology such as unattended ground sensors and drones in use since experiments were conducted in Arizona from 2004 to 2007.[107] These technologies would create a common operating picture—"a uniform presentation of activities within specific areas along the border."[108] C3I technology would gather information on these activities and circulate it to data terminals in the field and at command centers and to other necessary law enforcement partners. In sharing information streams across time and space, DHS constructed a "uniform" territory for border enforcement, a singular data space populated with data bodies.

The common operating picture was DHS's and CBP's implementation of situational awareness. The objective was to allow CBP agents to quickly learn about "intrusions" on the border and to disseminate this information expediently to those in a better position to intervene. BigPipe (see figure 3.3), created in 2005 and described by a DHS official as "a robust information sharing environment," was one way to construct a common operating picture. The platform linked CBP aviation assets with "federal, state, local, and tribal law enforcement and public safety agencies to provide near-real time and sensor data—enhancing situational awareness for officers and rescue personnel across the public safety community."[109] Data fed into BigPipe included a spectrum of media and software applications such as video, audio,

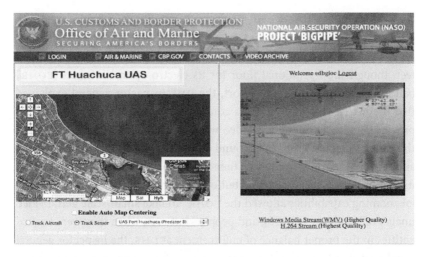

FIGURE 3.3. Interface of DHS's BigPipe platform. Source: DHS, CBP, Office of Public Affairs, Visual Communications Division, "CBP UAS B-Roll," *Defense Visual Information Distribution Service*, 2012.

geospatial information, and chat. The data technopolitics of BigPipe were informed by the logics of war and security that were said to provide "situational awareness and fidelity in combating threats." Such capabilities, DHS believed, were unparalleled in command and control operations.[110] The drone in use here was the Predator B UAS from General Atomics, and the actual operator/sensor screen can be seen on the right side of figure 3.3 (and in figures 3.5 and 3.6). In this sense, BigPipe users were allowed to participate in what the UAS sensors picked up from high above. The Predator B used during this specific operation took off from Fort Huachuca, yet its reach went well beyond Arizona. It flew over the coast of Corpus Christi, Texas, as its geolocation was mapped on the left of the image by a Google Maps interface. Sensors mounted on the Predator B interpreted a variety of signals (e.g., infrared, electromagnetic) while offering near-real-time video feeds. Data flows from these various sensors were aggregated into "an operational picture" that alerted CBP agents and sent them toward "areas of likely activity and interest."[111] Tracts of land, objects, and people were imagined to be enclosed by and within the sensory regime's common operating picture. Data generated within these enclosures were interpreted by human-machine configurations that determined the nature of a target (who or what they were) and its placement in the border zone.

A few facts might prove useful for understanding the Predator B as an object and system. It weighs 10,500 pounds, measures 36 feet in length, and has a wingspan of 66 feet. It operates at an altitude between 19,000 to 28,000 feet, though the operational floor for its electro-optical/infrared (EO/IR) ball is 19,000 feet. In a 2013 report, the DHS inspector general explained that the EO/IR ball was a camera containing a fixed-focus lens capable of providing video to operators. Video was sent by an encrypted feed relayed through a satellite to the UAS ground control station. Data were decrypted and sent behind the DHS firewall, then the video would be streamed through its BigPipe image and video distribution network to relevant parties.[112] Digital zooming capabilities allowed the EO/IR "to take small-scale aerial video images of buildings, vehicles, and people." But even when they were trusted entities in the proper balance of enforcement at DHS, the inspector general concluded that "video, still images, signals information, and/or radar images [from Predator Bs] do not clearly identify individuals. The only information about individuals that is collected and/or retained is the indication of a human form."[113] This human form, the report contended, supposedly lacked an identity. But, as I have shown throughout this book and in this chapter, it is the silhouette of a body pre-inscripted for exclusion along racial lines by public discussions and government policies.

The Predator B is a product of the United States's technopolitical frontier and its capacities to redraw the territorialized boundaries of sovereignty. Though it was originally envisioned by Abraham Karem, the Predator was finalized and manufactured in the 1990s by San Diego–based General Atomics. The first version of the Predator, known as the GNAT750, flew intelligence, reconnaissance, and surveillance operations from 1993 to 1994 for the Central Intelligence Agency over Bosnia.[114] One Department of Defense (DOD) official saw it as an "eye in the sky," a platform that could deliver near-real-time information of battlespaces to US forces.[115] In a 2002 informational packet (see figure 3.4), General Atomics described the Predator UAS as an aircraft for "Anywhere, Anyplace, Anytime." The packet contains a map of the globe showing only the continents of Europe, Africa, and some parts of Asia, and hovering over the globe is a Predator B, marking "a new dimension in worldwide awareness." This UAS is imagined for launch, recovery, and control from anywhere across the globe. Its sensing systems expand the reach and influence of US actors as they collect data from foreign territories now transformed into battlespaces and integrated into the sovereign space of the US empire-nation. Just as the 9/11 Commission had envisioned, Predator Bs underscored "the American homeland [was] the planet."

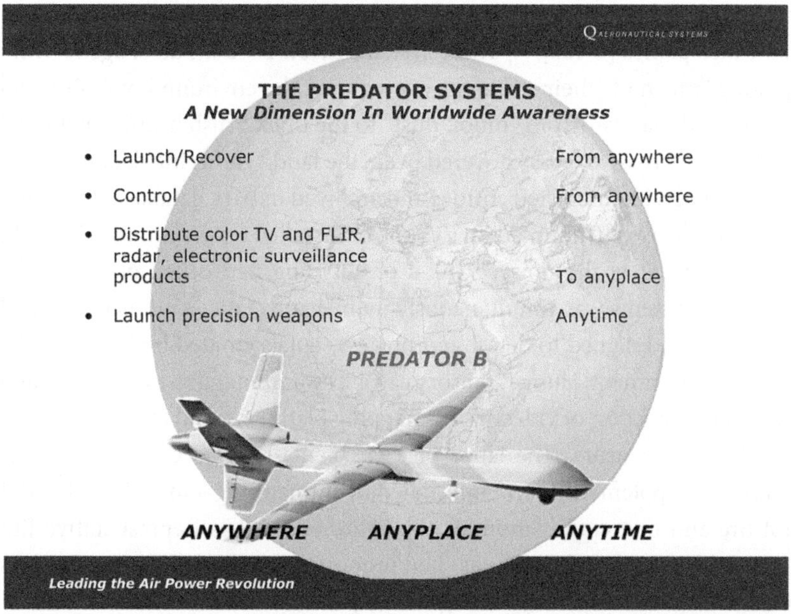

FIGURE 3.4. "The Predator Systems: A New Dimension in Worldwide Awareness." Source: General Atomics Aeronautical Systems, "Predator B: The Multi-Role UAV," June 2002, https://apps.dtic.mil/sti/pdfs/ADA427459.pdf.

Like the frontiersmen in US popular imaginary, Predators sought out "empty" lands for future settlement. Data collected by Predator B UASs circulated across the US global network of bases and sites of operations; they revealed how the borders of the empire-nation operated through networked (data)bases. The omniscient imaginaries of UASs helped blur the boundaries of the domestic and the foreign as well as of those classified as risk objects to target.

Drones and their sensors were positioned as strategic C3I technologies of the system of systems. They offered what Evans called "the advantage of height of eye," an advantage *over* an imagined enemy Other that hinged on the hovering capacity of unmanned aircraft equipped with sensors to "look out over a long range." For example, in a 21-mile stretch of the border in Papago Farms, Arizona, two Border Patrol agents were tasked with covering the large and complicated terrain at night: "They were often forced to drive slowly to avoid 'moon dust,' a thick substance covering back roads. His vision obscured by tall shrubs, [Border Patrol agent Nicholas] Greenig had to spend much of his time climbing the hills on the perimeter of the land, among the few places from which he could spot heads bobbing above the brush. He was thrilled to have his patrol area used as a test for the reconnaissance planes [UASS]."[116] These systems saved Border Patrol agents from wasting "much of [their] time" by overcoming the environmental obstacles of the borderlands—from "moon dust" to the thick brush hiding unauthorized border crossers. UASS hovered over "the land," gathering data that were then shared with interested entities and archived in DHS databases for future reference. Sensors (mounted on a drone or installed on the ground) brought "the signal out of the noise."[117] As a prototyping networked platform, the system of systems was simultaneously mobile and static. And its networked sensors were designed to detect and process signals emitted by targets in the border environment. Human sensory capacity was thought to expand through the interconnection of video feeds, mapping platforms, and electromagnetic and infrared sensors. The labor of CBP agents looking over the borderlands was supplemented and multiplied by unmanning—machines that did not tire and that could "monitor the entire border," as Representative Jim Turner (a Democrat from Texas) had proposed, "24 hours a day, seven days a week."[118] Even when unmanning still required human operators to control the system, the allure of automated control kept imperial fantasies of remote control alive.

The system of systems was understood to have the advantage of height of eye because it sought to make perceptible all the objects within the enclosure of its networked operational layers. Whenever ground sensors recorded the ever-inconspicuous, unauthorized border crosser, CBP agents activated another part of the networked platform, requesting visual identification of the trigger by calling for a drone to fly over the area. The UAS sensor operator would use one or more of the sensors equipped on the drone to get a sense of who might be in the area, how many there were, and where they were headed. Figure 3.5, taken from a video produced by the CBP's Office of Public Affairs, shows the targeting function displayed on the operator screen of a Predator B. It consists of an outer square marking the center of the image while an inner square marks and follows the target. The targeting function literally "centered" the object of technical vision. It narrowed who or what had to be engaged by Border Patrol agents. With this information, the agent at sector headquarters would determine the kind of force needed and where it should be dispatched to apprehend targets. The crosshairs of the Predator B operator screen operationalized the "crossing off" of unauthorized border crossers—their removal from the borderlands.

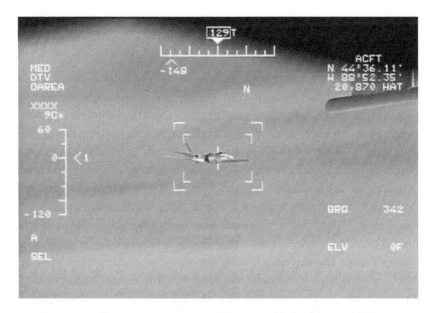

FIGURE 3.5. Predator B UAS operator/sensor screen showing targeting functions. Source: DHS, CBP, Office of Public Affairs, Visual Communications Division, "CBP UAS B-Roll," *Defense Visual Information Distribution Service*, 2012.

AUTOMATING ENMITY

What the system of systems produced, then, was what visual artist and media theorist Harun Farocki calls an "operative image." These images "do not represent an object, but rather are part of an operation."[119] They are meant to be "seen" by a machine, like the targeting square that helps keep a drone locked-in to its target (see figure 3.5) even while both are in constant movement. The value of operative images on the border resided not in their representative quality but in their capacity to shape the behaviors of entities in the cybernetic border. As a sensory regime, the cybernetic border produces an image of sorts so that those objects contained within its platform could be acted on.[120] The operative image establishes asymmetric relations between entities to make them governable. The operative image is a technical inscription of how border security operations are supposed to unfold. Like other media, drones are inscription systems that produce, register, integrate, and allocate discourses, as well as human and nonhuman entities, across surfaces. UASs discern and inscribe, as the inspector general stated, "a human form" onto the operator's screen. These forms are not actually interpreted as unidentified subjects. Instead, they are read within an institutional discourse that targets some subjects for exclusion from US national territory.

On the US border, Predator B data are integrated into CBP's information analysis efforts with the aim of granting situational awareness to participants of the security apparatus. In a scenario included in a CBP public relations video from 2014, a Predator B flown from Arizona encountered a group of twelve people crossing an area of the southern border without authorization.[121] Surveillance footage of the group taken by the drone showed how "shadowy figures wait in the cover of the underbrush," the narrator explained, "for a quick sprint and a promise of illegal entry." The "shadowy figures" were not unlike those shown in figure 3.6 or those previously described by the DHS inspector general as "a human form." The Predator B crew attempted to communicate directly with a nearby Black Hawk helicopter unit, but it was out of radio contact. The crew then reached out to CBP's Air and Marine Operations Center (AMOC) in Riverside, California. This center was responsible for helping coordinate field activities by supplying officers and agents with relevant data on their border sector areas. In this case, data were supplied by the video feed of the Predator B. AMOC alerted the Black Hawk unit of the presence of the twelve unauthorized individuals, their location and direction. As a result, they were apprehended by an air interdiction crew and by field agents.

This scenario shows how the border as a networked platform produces an operative image where different entities are automatically prescribed distinct roles. In figure 3.6, a still image from surveillance footage produced by a CBP drone, the entities of air power and information technology are the Predator B UAS and the Office of Air and Marine Operations helicopter (center-right of image) that hover over what seem to be panicking and running unauthorized border crossers (the dark dots next to trees and bushes in the center of the image). After their apprehension, deployed Border Patrol agents on the ground eventually identify and process the human form on the screen by using CBP's subject types. Unauthorized border crossers played the role of the prey hunted by a predatory assemblage. This assemblage comprised the Predator B UAS, the Black Hawk helicopter, agents at the AMOC, and Border Patrol agents. Together, they were predators seeking to capture those that DHS had named as risks and threats—populations identified by the classification schema of Mexicans, Other than Mexicans, or person from special interest country. The operative image resulting from

FIGURE 3.6. Predator B UAS operator/sensor screen during CBP operations. Source: DHS, CBP, Office of Public Affairs, Visual Communications Division, "CBP UAS B-Roll," *Defense Visual Information Distribution Service*, 2012.

Predator B operations scripts how enemies are engaged by and within the border technopolitical regime.

CBP's UASs and its BigPipe platform create a plane of perception within which unauthorized border crossers are made perceptible and knowable— that is, they are trackable and manageable. The sensors mounted on the UAS monitor the target's movements as the UAS operator screen maps out the territory for state action. The assemblage of these systems allows for the material demarcation of the racial/territorial borderlines and the exercise of imperial sovereignty. As categories, subject types inform which bodies become visible to a UAS's sensors, even if their supposed personal identity markers are unknown. In the case of the US-Mexico border, that which appears on the screen is predetermined suspect.

Subject types are associated with the category of intruder used by sensor technology researchers.[122] The notion of intruder calibrates the shifting borders of empire and the techniques through which inclusion and exclusion are performed. Thinking through how Browne understands the operations of surveillance technologies, the supposedly "disembodied gaze" of drones "do[es] the sorting work of nationalizing, and by extension racializing" the bodies displayed on the screen.[123] The experimental usage of drones on the southern border as well as the heavier presence of Border Patrol agents there, when compared to the US-Canada border, demonstrate a structural over-commitment to policing the southern borderlands.[124] UASS were designed to target "a single cluster of racialized information [i.e., the threat] that is used for remote-controlled processes of control and harm. Bodies below become things to track, monitor, apprehend, and kill, while the pilot and other allies on the network remain differentiated and proximate."[125] Similar to other surveillance technologies, the UASS combine with federal policy in the intimate stratification of space and objects into discernible, categorized matter to control. Hence, control emerges through the proliferation of racially codified "intruder" types inscribed into the prototyping operations of the border as a networked platform; the result is the targeting and removal of vulnerable populations from the body politic.

Detractors of this approach insisted early on that among its underlying effects was that unauthorized border crossers, especially migrants and *coyotes* (human smugglers), would be driven to seek entry through more remote, risky, and lethal areas.[126] In other words, similar to prevention through deterrence in the 1990s, the system of systems plays a part in the production of social death. Unauthorized border crossers are made not to matter because they are driven farther into the life-threatening geography of the border zone. The system of systems has not stopped migration or unauthorized border crossings; it has merely made them more dangerous.[127] As José Matus, director of Coalición de Derechos Humanos, told the press, "poor, harmless immigrants" would make the difficult and life-threatening trip regardless of border enforcement efforts. By making migration more difficult, "we're shoving them to their deaths."[128] Contrary to claims made by DHS officials that part of operational awareness aimed to reduce the number of border crossing deaths, according to one American Civil Liberties Union report, there was no improvement in migrant deaths on the border since pursuit of this technopolitical arrangement. A total of 1,391 deaths throughout the border region, or an average of 347.75 per year, took place during part of the experimental use of drones from 2003 to 2006.[129] Automation in the borderlands has been a mortal arrangement in the purported crisis of control.

The border as a networked platform brought together air power, unmanning, and automation. The technopolitics of this new iteration of the cybernetic border are defined by the struggle to use the aerial environment as a domain from which to exercise sovereignty on the earth's crust. When it comes to the US-Mexico border, the cybernetic border institutes a technoaesthetics that makes the territorialized boundary of the nation and unauthorized border crossing into perceptible and actionable data. Even though drone sensor data cannot "clearly identify individuals," as made evident in figure 3.6 and the statement of the DHS inspector general, they do indicate a human form. Data points sensed and computed by UASS are mapped out as patterns of a human body "rendered into mere spatial or tactical coordinates."[130] The system of systems, in other words, produces a signal—an operative image—that stands out over the noise of the borderlands. It is a signal that demarcates the US empire-nation's territorial boundaries and activates sovereign entities (e.g., Border Patrol agents, helicopters) to execute order by eliminating the presence of "foreign" bodies. Targeting the enemies of the empire-nation, the Predator hunts for its prey.

This chapter addresses the moment at the turn of the twenty-first century when the border technopolitical regime committed itself to the creation of smart borders as the means to attain the strategic goal of operational control. The logics of war and security were co-constitutive of how actors imagined border enforcement. Angie C. Marek told her readers at *US News & World Report* that the US-Mexico borderlands was considered a space of struggle were a "multifront war" was being waged between unauthorized border crossers (migrants, smugglers, drug cartels), Border Patrol agents, and nativist paramilitary groups.[131] Though Marek did not explicitly state the identities of the enemies or the friendlies, the logics of war (e.g., "targets," "front lines," "war wagons," "blitzkrieg" meetings), previously articulated during the 1970s, continued to shape how actors in the borderlands were imagined in relation to the border technopolitical regime. Where the electronic fence was concerned with the internal boundaries of the empire-nation, smart borders were concerned with the proliferation of boundaries in the articulation of US global power, which led to the securitization of the border. The productive logics of security post-9/11 posited the primacy of US governmentality over other territorialized forms of power as well as US citizens over other populations classified as racialized risk objects.

Insisting on targeting, recording, capturing, and removing risk objects, the border technopolitical regime is stuck by the inertia of smart borders. A historical focus on apprehension was transformed into an arrangement that affords the measurement of efficiency through a range of border metrics like apprehension rates. The high and low values of apprehensions were read by elected and government officials and the wider public as evidence that more resources were needed for enforcement efforts. If they were high, it was because a wave of unauthorized border crossers threatened to overwhelm Border Patrol agents. If they were low, on the other hand, it was because the Border Patrol lacked the appropriate resources to do their job. Apprehension rates, meanwhile, have been deemed by a Congressional Research Report and other researchers as unreliable measures.[132] With operational control unachieved in most border sectors, apprehension rates are constant reminders that enforcement operations are not closing the border to unauthorized border crossing. A paranoid orientation commits itself to provide further funding and resources to increase apprehension rates as a means to secure the (whiteness of the) nation from the racialized threat represented by Latina/o/es, Arabs, and Muslims.

Smart borders, and drones within them, are media infrastructures of a racializing data regime that imagines itself as clashing with enemy civilizations. They execute racializing surveillance through government practices, policies, and performances seeking to institute norms around citizenship that define who and what is in or out of place.[133] This is the kind of surveillance that Browne has shown relates to turning data subjects into sorted data aggregates of a population. The making of risk objects for a racial technopolitical order is premised on the purported purity and supremacy of the (white) nation. Though UASs are now used in both the northern and southern borders of the continental United States, their experimental testing in Arizona and their larger presence along the Mexican border expose how the brown bodies of Latina/o/es, Arabs, and Muslims are among the priorities of the border technopolitical regime.[134] The Predator B UAS with its technical vision capabilities does not hunt for white migrants from Western Europe but for brown bodies marked as risks and threats. The border as a networked platform produces an operative image that automatically prescribes how subjects within its frame relate to each other. In such framing, risk objects are inscribed as knowledge objects and objectives of the cybernetic border.

The survival of the US empire-nation is enabled at the expense of unauthorized border crossers who are pushed into remote areas of the border, vulnerable to the viciousness of the desert environment and the violence of smuggling operations. Government officials and settler nativists were not the only ones paying close attention to operational control and the fixation to produce and mark borders. Artists and immigration rights activists have sought to contest the platforms of enmity embedded in the cybernetic border. Especially their fabrication of social death, necropolitics, and necroviolence. Their techniques of dissent seek to create different imaginative pathways for solidarity and belonging in an age of paranoid anxiety.

4. TECHNOAESTHETICS OF DISSENT IN THE AGE OF THE CYBERNETIC BORDER

What if you could extract all the labor necessary to perform agricultural work but could dispense with the human bodies that had always executed it? What if you could have "all the labor without the worker?"[1] This is the central premise in Alex Rivera's "Why Cybraceros? (1997)," a short speculative and mixed-media video (see figure 4.1) that presents a retro-futuristic vision in which the US Department of Labor transformed agriculture into a subset of the information industry. In the world conjured by this short video, the Department of Labor seeks to do away with pesky issues entangled with guest worker programs such as runaway workers overstaying their visas, unauthorized border crossers hiding within the crowd of guest workers, racist vitriol leveraged against migrant workers, workers fighting for their labor and human rights, and police committing violence to suppress their efforts. The Cybracero Program, inspired by the Bracero Program (1942–1964) and the science of cybernetics, creates an infrastructure for agricultural labor through unmanning and automation. From a networked desktop computer, a Mexican worker observes a livestream of the plots that need tending, then decides which fruits are ripe and must be picked and what plants need pruning or watering. Actions are commanded by the Mexican data worker and performed by a robotic farmworker through a system of remote control, "as simple as point-and-click-to-pick." The Cybracero Program disavows the messy racial politics enrolling Mexican labor as disposable cheap labor for US industries through techniques of control

FIGURE 4.1. Collage of Alex Rivera's "Why Cybraceros? (1997)." Image courtesy of the artist.

that treated agricultural work as a technical, informational problem to solve. Four decades after the US Navy and Air Force enacted technoscientific scenes whereby pilots and their "trusted mounts" fought against drone "intruders," the Cybracero Program found a human-machine configuration that keeps Mexicans-as-intruders outside of the United States using drone farmers at home.

"Why Cybraceros?" constitutes a critical if parodic inquiry into the hegemonic technopolitical regime of the cybernetic border. It does so by centering the internet, computers, and drone technology as representatives of a racializing sociotechnical arrangement that governs the Mexican migrant agricultural proletariat, which I have shown the US government constructed as a risk object. The video repurposes footage from a historic public information campaign developed for the Council of California Growers by the Wilding-Butler Division of Wilding Inc. in 1959, as well as other journalistic footage from United Farm Workers struggles and border enforcement operations.[2] The original film and Rivera's video imagine an anxious and concerned "American" audience that is apprehensive about the presence of Mexican laborers on US soil. In both instances, (guest) worker programs are described as instruments that safely manage and administer migrant labor, all the while delivering benefits to US citizens. In the case of cybraceros, the Department of Labor "program" becomes a pun that suggests naming conventions in government and corporate initiatives as well as software applications. This generates the sense that modern "migrant" workers could be seamlessly controlled by informationalizing their work and severing them from the impacts of their embodied presence—thereby alienating them from their labor. By employing computing and other information technologies, the US government, informed by cyberutopian discourses about borderless worlds and the information superhighway, transformed agricultural work into immaterial labor—networked knowledge work.[3] Rivera's video highlights the technoliberal visions embedded within the cybernetic border. This border technopolitical regime embodies the sense that, as Neda Atanasoski and Kalindi Vora contend, "unfree and invisible labor have been the hidden source of support propping up the apparent autonomy of the liberal subject," or the citizen, "through its history."[4] Mexican drone operators, like their bracero brethren in the mid-twentieth century, are the invisible infrastructure of US citizenship. They are, the video's narrator tells her audience, "a worker who poses no threat of becoming a citizen. And that means quality products at low financial and social cost to you, the American consumer." Through the regime of the cybernetic border, US farmers and landowners have their produce picked, US consumers have access to this fresh produce, and Mexican workers have work without physically crossing the border. Differently treated and racialized populations are kept in place, their mobility controlled as their mental faculties are enrolled to perform specific kinds of unseen, informational labor. This is labor that props up and benefits US capital and US citizens, all the while excluding the supposed intruder subjects of the nation.

This chapter engages a different kind of voice in understanding the cybernetic border and its human-machine configurations. Rather than continuing to explore the ideas of technicians and military and government officials, it centers voices of dissent in the fields of art, performance, and activism. It explores works by Alex Rivera, Humane Borders, Ian Alan Paul, Ricardo Dominguez, Jane Stevens, and Josh Begley—interventions that respond to the structure of feeling in, and practices of, the cybernetic border. This group of activists and artists, most of whom were in direct conversations and even collaborated with each other, was chosen because their work interrogates the entanglements between life, death, data, and the border technopolitical regime. They are representative of the range of cultural and everyday practices that, as Simone Browne argues, constitute instances where folks live with and against as well as offer "alternatives to routinized, racializing surveillance."[5] The works discussed in this chapter date from 1997 to 2016, a period that chapter 3 shows as one of intense transformations and intensifications in border enforcement. Just as the US Border Patrol and, later, Customs and Border Protection (CBP) consolidated their enforcement strategy to rely on data from human-machine configurations, activists and artists responded by probing this regime's technoaesthetics. And in doing so, they articulate divergent relations of recognition, solidarity, knowledge making, and fugitivity.

Such inquiry led these artists and activists to identify the machine, in its literal and metaphorical dimensions, as a critical (art)ifact. Throughout the chapter, then, computers, drones, and databases are three of the "machines" that actors thought with and against. Computers, drones, and databases institute an art of the state, an infrastructural assemblage that structures the bounds of the sensible and governs the production of knowledge. The technoaesthetics of the cybernetic border are not only available to those with access to the classification regime but to a wider audience making sense of its maneuvers. An approach to technoaesthetics offers an analytical path to examine their conceptual and political meanings—its ordering of the senses, its normalization of relations of enmity, and the organization of the borderlands as a data-filled environment to govern.[6] I explore technoaesthetics in action within technoscientific scenes. In these, as chapter 1 shows, the cultural power of human-machine configurations is at play. Thick descriptions of technoscientific scenes offer an opportunity to examine interpretations of said configurations—that is, how they are understood to take place as well as what they mean. Scenes are made of actors prescribed to perform distinct roles, to comport in certain ways, and to enact relations to diverse phenomena. But where technoscientific scenes in chapter 1 were developed by government and corporate actors assembling a border technopolitical regime, the scenes in this chapter were either constructed or intervened by activists and artists.

Following a discussion of boundary technoaesthetics, I go on to analyze three scenes and the techniques deployed by actors to engage the cybernetic regime. Embedding themselves in the regime, they disrupted its operations through "disassembly" and "data haunts." The first scene dives into the works of Humane Borders and Ian Alan Paul, and how they centered border crossing deaths. The "Arizona OpenGIS Initiative for Deceased Migrants" (ca. 2004–present) and "Border Haunt" (2011), respectively, showcase how data haunts reorient conversations about intrusions by publicizing the ways that the cybernetic border was, for all intents and purposes, a killing machine. The second scene addresses the "Drone Crash Incident" (2012) by Dominguez, Paul, and Stevens as a disassembling gesture designed to trigger a brief, community-wide questioning of higher education's and people's acquiescence to and complicity with the cybernetic border. The final scene is devoted to Begley's video for Field of Vision, "Best of Luck with the Wall" (2016), and its attempt to mobilize seeing machines to understand the vastly complicated southern border. Each scene is devoted to different media assemblages: geographic information systems, web design, and livestreaming; performance art; and satellite imagery, databases, software, and video. The prominence of mixed media described and analyzed in this chapter underscores the fact that the border technopolitical regime successfully transformed the field of engagement to one dominated by the hegemony of data and the recursive loops that are so central to cybernetics. In other words, the cybernetic border dictates the conditions of critical intervention, and artists and activists have sought ways to operate within them.

I want to be careful not to fold the artistic interventions in this chapter under the banner of "border art." As visual studies scholar Claire Fox has argued, artists in the last decades of the twentieth century were often at cross-paths with those intent on naming or branding their work under this category. Fox states that border art can be hardly defined as a movement because there was no shared political orientation or aesthetic project.[7] For some, disavowing this categorization constituted a gesture for resisting US capitalism and the commodification of cultural production, while others happily or ironically welcomed it. In much of the aesthetic production post-1965, the border figured in ambivalent ways as a site or non-site of imagination and embodiment. This led to what the poet, artist, and Latina/o studies scholar Amy Sara Carroll describes as an aesthetic practice that engaged the border in material, spatial, allegorical, and symbolic dimensions.[8] And while some artists were willing to identify their practice under the category of "border art," such as the Border Art Workshop/Taller de arte fronterizo (BAW/TAF), their wide-ranging concerns, methods, and media, as well as their tenuous relationships with state and cultural institutions, destabilize the category as such.

Rivera, Dominguez, Paul, Stevens, and Begley are all interested in the border not only as a site but a regime of knowledge making, a mode of governance with distinct human-machine configurations. Their location did not define their relation to the border. Some of these artists were not born and do not live in the southern US borderlands, while others do (or did). They echo the artistic commitments of the BAW/TAF to treat the border region as their own laboratory.[9] The technoscientific scenes discussed here are concerned with interrogating the technological conditions that constitute the southern border and that the southern border makes possible. Going beyond the site of the border, these artists find in bordering a governmental assemblage to disassemble. Bordering is not limited to the geopolitical boundary between the United States and Mexico; rather, it is a distributed process enacted through relations across time and space. The promise and desire for control of the border and its peoples is subjected to critique as the regime is parodied, led astray, and questioned. The aesthetic practices of these artists also perform a self-reflexive and ambivalent move toward bordering that, drawing from tactical media, allows them to inhabit the same networked platforms they contest—from livestreams, drones, satellites, and webmapping platforms to databases and blogs. Rather than continuing to fetishize vision or the gaze, these tactical media practices highlight the importance of data to bordering in the age of the cybernetic border.

Boundary Technoaesthetic Maneuvers

Borders are not hard and sharp cutting devices but, as political theorists Sandro Mezzadra and Brett Neilson contend, instrumental articulations of "space, labor power, markets, jurisdictions, and a variety of other objects in ways that converge on the production of subjectivity."[10] They are the product of border technopolitical regimes, a dynamic assemblage devoted to establishing and operating, within sets of parameters, the channeling of flows and the articulation of exceptions. These regimes are permanently working to define the limits of bounded space and what/who can belong to such space and what/who cannot. Understanding the operations of the border technopolitical regime requires the experimental and strategic deployment of technoaesthetics. Technologies discussed in this book have often been described by government officials, engineers, and members of the public in terms of a state-of-the art—as products of the frontiers of science and of imagination. Using the work of Joseph Masco on nuclear technoaesthetics as a jumping off point, I argue that activists and artists have flipped the script to show an art of the state.[11] The border technopolitical regime is not only a project in governmentality but an aesthetic one. It is in the coproduced plane of the sensible and its structures so that meaning and knowledge of the regime are constituted and expressed.[12] Reasons that compel actors to challenge it abound when the social and human cost of such a regime includes the creation and targeting of enemies and the institution of a racializing structure of feeling that justifies the death of thousands of border crossers.

Activists and artists in the United States engaged the border technopolitical regime through techniques of disassembly and data haunts. Rather than fixate on rigid, unchanging structures like walls or fences, these actors sought to understand how the border technopolitical regime worked.[13] Entities such as machines are not stabilized objects but ensembles of relations, ideas, and practices—ways of knowing and ways of acting. Actors approached the regime as an assemblage comprising a variety of entities that themselves were made from heterogeneous components, which were material and symbolic.[14] Assemblages are not stable wholes but rather are constituted by/through ever-changing, interacting, and autonomous components. "Beneath the surface stability of any entity" one finds "discrete flows of an essentially limitless range of other phenomena."[15] To disassemble is to point toward the lack and the opposite, to pull apart that which is seemingly whole and stable. Piercing the surface stability of entities, actors find the expressive matter of historical processes. Disassembling a regime reveals that which is missing in the coming together of its elements as much as the political objectives of its entangled parts. Disassembly, as Dominguez and Paul reasoned, is about understanding how its parts relate to one another and how they work separately and in concert. The disassembly of technopolitical regimes led artists and activists to an encounter with the codes and protocols governing its operations. These include the treatment of border enforcement and elements of the borderlands as data and the fabrication of unauthorized border crosser deaths. Disassembly is about disturbing ongoing operations by pointing to its failings and contradictions. The informational and necropolitical protocols of the cybernetic border were urgent phenomena for these activists and artists to dismantle.

Doing so led them to grapple with data haunts of the cybernetic border. Data haunts name that which is segmented from what was made into data, that which exceeds the property attributed at a specific moment to signs, traces, and inscriptions. If data are the initial transformation of nature in the assembly line of knowledge, data haunts are what gets cordoned off from entering this chain of production.[16] Where data in the cybernetic border optimize the operations of the regime, haunts register the harm, the trauma, and loss produced through such optimization. Through their disassembling maneuvers, these artists identified death and data as indispensable and interconnected elements of the hegemonic regime. Data haunts were opportunities to listen, to read, and to feel the "hidden transcripts" of those unwilling to consent to the machinations of the cybernetic border.[17] Data haunts register the agency of unauthorized border crossers. Even as the regime works to redraw the bounds of territory around their movements, uncontrolled unauthorized border crossers enact a fugitivity, an unwillingness to cohere.[18] Activists and artists were compelled by the fact that at the center of this regime was a propensity to fail. I argue, then, that these actors found in failure a political opportunity to bring forth a different way of relating in the borderlands. Through their techniques of disassembly and data haunts, actors reprogrammed the historical narrative of intrusion that shaped the border technopolitical regime throughout the second half of the twentieth century. For them, intruders were the technopolitical project of the border itself and its racial investments in the fabrication of death.

The work of Dominguez and Paul, like that of Rivera, is representative of an aesthetic practice concerned with grasping the contemporary operations of border making. Intervening in the realm of understanding was not enough for them; instead, they also sought to disturb. Dominguez has been at the forefront of performance and conceptual art since the 1980s, when he cofounded the Critical Art Ensemble (CAE) in Tallahassee, Florida. As he explained in an interview, CAE was interested in reconsidering the trajectories of the Situationists and the avant-garde in the context of "new regimes" of governance particularly around "data bodies."[19] Later on, CAE and Dominguez, once he left the group, would establish critical "territories of investigation and practices" centered on what they termed "electronic civil disobedience," which was an iteration of what people today call hacktivism. Dominguez's practice of electronic civil disobedience was at the heart of the creation in 1997 of a new artistic collective called Electronic Disturbance Theater (EDT). Its work engages digital platforms to question militarism, border and immigration enforcement, and capital. Paul, on the other hand, began his formal artistic practice through his graduate education at the San Francisco Art Institute in 2011. His MA thesis at the institute was devoted to studying artists whose work engaged borders, which led him to Dominguez's practice. Paul's work mobilizes practices of defamiliarization: he takes things that appear to be normal—things that are taken for granted—and creates "situations . . . in which [things] can appear very strange, or very unnatural, or very artificial."[20] To defamiliarize is to destabilize it is to unsettle the seeming coherence of the status quo. Dominguez and Paul found in de-familiarization the basis for collaboration (more on this later).

If artists are to grasp and disturb the operations of border making, they must contend with a crucial question in contemporary aesthetics: How does one articulate resistant practices under conditions of waning agency and permanent co-optation? Activists and artists worked through dialectical lines of encounter found within the cybernetic border regime. These actors felt compelled by their situations, and by those who are more vulnerable than them, to go beyond performing a certain kind of aesthetic playfulness and to burrow themselves in the conditions of technopolitical and imperial formations. At times, especially in the "Drone Crash Incident," their practice might be understood as a kind of non-frontal or oblique resistance that American studies scholar Anna Watkins Fisher calls parasitical resistance. This is a practice whereby the parasite "successfully install[s] itself within the host system" where it "can survive the host's attempts to inoculate itself against the parasite."[21] Actors in the following technoscientific scenes hold ambivalent positions within the border technopolitical regime—some are or have been affiliated with higher education institutions—even as they push through gaps that might help disassemble it. While resistance, as Fisher correctly notes, "presupposes the structural conditions against which it struggles," these artists understand their work "cannot destroy or escape them outright."[22] Instead, their defamiliarizations befuddle, disorient, and confuse. Or, as Dominguez told me, they aim "to antagonize the machine and its protocols. You want to antagonize activists, and you want to antago-nize artists. . . . A good work of art should make everybody ill. Everybody should be going, 'That's bad.'"[23] While their work might have inadvertently cropped up in ways that left their audiences doubting their provenance or truthfulness, these artists and activists worked to trigger an affective and embodied response, "making everybody ill." This is where the ambivalent and disruptive force of parasitical resistance is traversed by a sociological and tactical media praxis.

The technoscientific scenes explored here can be understood as drawing from sociological art and a sense of the experimental. As a collectivist and activist shift to aesthetic practice, sociological art emerged in the aftermath of May 1968 and its revolutionary fervor and inspirations, its seductions, its disillusionments, and its defeats. French art critics Pierre Restany and François Pluchart proposed, for example, the need to abolish bourgeois values like beauty, skill, and material worth in favor of democratic values attentive to social and political engagement.[24] Sociological art represented a shift away from the art markets and the commodification of creative practice in exchange for an aesthetic inquiry into art and society, capitalist (re)production, technology and communication, and power relations. This reflexive and critical approach to art sought to transform artworks from isolated artifacts of contemplation into instruments for making collectivities: performances that would disrupt the ongoing conditionings of modern capitalist society. Sociological art moved from conceptual interventions, which had replaced the (art)ifact with an idea, to simultaneously interrogating the idea's ideological, social, and economic structures.[25] This aesthetic practice contended that its own conditions of production were objects of inquiry and contestation.

Such self-reflexivity can also be found in tactical media. Digital studies scholar Rita Raley describes tactical media as a mutable category, lacking fixity yet allowing for some categorical unity through rationales of disturbance.[26] Tactical media groups a range of practices such as reverse engineering, digital hijacks, contestational robotics, collaborative software, denial-of-service attacks, and hacktivism. These practices are often premised as or meant to be an "intervention and disruption of a dominant semiotic regime, the temporary creation of a situation in which signs, messages, and narratives are set into play and critical thinking becomes possible."[27] Dominguez's work with the CAE and the EDT is emblematic of this approach. Projects by these groups called into question regimes of capital accumulation, border making, and sovereignty by tending to their semiotic orderings. CAE, for example, argued in the mid-1990s that "as far as power is concerned, the streets are dead capital." As capital and the state were increasingly understood in abstract informational terms and made viable through information infrastructures, "blocking information access is the best means to disrupt any institution, whether it is military, corporate, or governmental."[28] CAE and other tactical media practitioners often integrate into their work a self-reflexivity that opens existing technopolitical regimes to critique even while inhabiting them. Tactical media does not shy away from redeploying the same sociotechnical arrangements they seek to challenge since part of their goal is to create temporary autonomous zones that would make political transformation possible.[29] This is part and parcel of tactical media's experimental mode.

In adopting an experimental mode, activists and artists conduct a permanent and self-reflexive process of understanding. Experiments, after all, are technologies "of truth-making," of producing facts with the goal of testing theories through observation.[30] Experimentation in their case reversed the practices of the border technopolitical regime to test specific human-machine configurations on unwilling subjects. Instead, they sought to render stable and continuous that which was ever-changing, the border technopolitical regime, especially because of its prototyping tendency. Its operations and entanglements became the (art)ifacts of observation and inquiry. Rivera, for example, has spoken about how his work centers processes of alienation—"all the [migrant] labor without the worker"—in order to listen to those made invisible by it. It is them, he concludes, who can imagine ways out of the ongoing dynamics of crisis.[31] In experimenting with alternate imaginings, Rivera, Dominguez, Paul, and Stevens push the operations of the regime onto the surface—its gaps, its failings, its contradictions—to compel audiences, participants, and others to contend with their role within them. This is what Ruha Benjamin calls liberatory imagination, a way to not only describe and challenge discriminatory logics that are embedded in technology but "to work with others to imagine and create alternatives to the *techno quo*." Liberatory imagination contributes to a larger struggle for "collective freedoms and flourishing."[32] In the case of "Why Cybraceros?" (and as this book demonstrates), the process of alienation and displacement is central to the cybernetic border. It abstracts apprehended people, workers, and more into data assemblages and data-producing entities that are then processed in relation to classifications (e.g., human/nonhuman, enemy, intruder, Mexican, and "Other than Mexican"). Through an experimental mode in liberatory imagination, actors expose the supposed neutrality of the regime's arrangements and its hidden features. An experimental disposition creates an opening to unexpected insights and encounters with others in order to collectively observe, interrogate, jam, and disorient the operations of the regime.

Ghosts in the Border Machine: Death and Data Haunts

The border technopolitical regime has played a critical role in the production of migrant deaths since the 1990s.[33] In their efforts to institute a semblance of control over unauthorized border crossings, US government officials, chapter 3 showed, have implemented a border enforcement strategy predicated on the idea of prevention through deterrence. But as Maria Jimenez's report for the American Civil Liberties Union (ACLU) stated, "since 1995, increased border enforcement measures have not had an impact on the ability of unauthorized migrants to enter despite increased staffing, deployment of troops, or building virtual, physical or natural barriers."[34] Worse still, "immigration policies have severely restricted legal entry, and border security policies have forced unauthorized entry through dangerous routes in perilous conditions."[35] This resulted in an estimated death toll of 3,861 to 5,607 from 1994 to 2009, the year the ACLU published its report.

The accuracy of migrant death data has been an object of debate between human rights organizations, activists, and local, state, and federal government officials. If local authorities were the first to respond to the presence of human remains, that statistic was not included in the Border Patrol's database of border deaths. This made the Border Patrol database, according to the ACLU, the least complete.[36] In its report on the *Humanitarian Crisis* on the border, the ACLU concluded that the Pima County Medical Examiner's Office (PCMEO) in Arizona generally had a significant discrepancy with the Border Patrol's statistics on the total number of unauthorized border crosser bodies recovered—from 2002 to 2004, for example, the discrepancy was of more than 30 percent per year. Neither the PCMEO nor the Border Patrol accounted for those migrants who, in their attempt to cross the border, may have been injured and returned to Mexico or, as the report continues, "who may have drowned in a river, canal, or ocean but whose corpses were deposited by currents on the Mexican side or who are classified as locals by Mexican authorities." In this sense, accurate data on migrant deaths were difficult to access.

Motivated to break the silence about border crossing deaths, various groups organized projects to document the missing and the dead. Humane Borders (Frontera Compasivas) activists and Ian Alan Paul sought ways to counter the data practices of the border technopolitical regime by foregrounding their shadowy contours and haunting dynamics. In the struggle to produce the border and control it, information technologies are simultaneously positioned as strategic components of the cybernetic border and as tools used by those who resist the detrimental impacts it has on racialized communities. Calculating logics and processes produce unauthorized border crossers as risk objects for the cybernetic border to manage. Human rights activists and artists deploy these same technoaesthetics to push back against the necropolitics of the regime. And, in the process, they create spaces of encounter and memory where new relations are forged in the recognition of the dignity of border crossers.

MAPPING NECROPOLITICS, PRODUCING SITES
OF MEMORY

Humane Borders was founded in 2000 with the mission "to save desperate people from a horrible death by dehydration and exposure and to create a just and humane environment in the borderlands."[37] Theirs was not a project to undo national borders or bring about the end of the nation-state but to transform an inhumane dynamic.[38] This led the group to maintain eighty water stations in southern Arizona and northern Mexico, each consisting of one to three 60-gallon tanks with a blue flag mounted on a 30-foot steel pole that alerted migrants of its location.[39] The organization was also interested in educating the public and government officials about the hardships migrants endured during the border crossing process. To that end, in 2002 they began mapping the locations of their water stations and of migrant deaths using a combination of Global Positioning System navigation software, Google Maps, and Adobe Photoshop, among other data visualization applications. By 2004, Humane Borders began mapping water station and migrant death data using a geographic information system (GIS). Initially, the project, spearheaded by then University of Arizona doctoral student John F. Chamblee, aimed to establish "simple relationships between migrant deaths and the natural and human environment along the Arizona border."[40] These relationships were statistically defined through spatial analysis and statistical modeling as volunteers at Humane Borders attempted to measure the impact of their water stations in preventing border crossing deaths.

Through their GIS effort, a separate migrant death mapping project soon began, formally called Arizona OpenGIS Initiative for Deceased Migrants (see figure 4.2), and its stated purpose was to remember those who lost their lives attempting to cross the border desert. The project, pursued by volunteers at Humane Borders and the PCMEO in Arizona, was grounded in the "common vision of raising awareness about migrant deaths and lessening the suffering of families by helping to provide closure through the identification of the deceased and the return of remains."[41] In other words, actors hoped their migrant death map would play a dual role in the public sphere. First, it could be employed as an instrument to "raise awareness" while people pushed for policy changes so that "continuing increases in death rates call into question the long-term sustainability of a deterrence-based approach."[42] And second, families could come to terms with their loss by having access to information on their deceased loved ones. Focusing on the migrant dead centered the precariousness of the migrant experience in the United States. Treated by the cybernetic border as risks and threats, migrants were made to bear the force of a regime committed to their elimination. For the migrant death mapping project, these were not the supposed intruders of the cybernetic border; they were its victims. These were lives that mattered and merited remembrance.

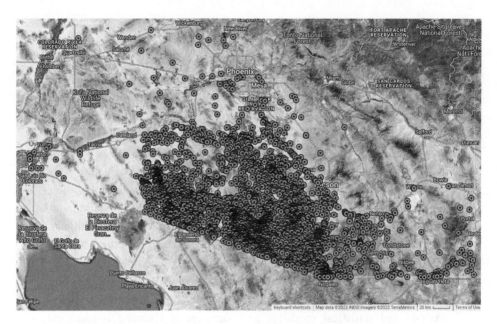

FIGURE 4.2. Screenshot from July 2022 of the Arizona OpenGIS Initiative for Deceased Migrants. Source: https://humaneborders.info/app/map.asp.

Examining how the migrant death map is accessed and how data are presented reveals its haunting power. At the time of publication of this book, the county medical examiner and the nongovernmental organization collaborated in producing a dynamic webmap using the Google Maps interface. The webmap is shared through the Humane Borders website. There, visitors can query the map's database using different data points such as name of the deceased migrant, their gender, the year or cause of death, county of discovery, land corridor used to migrate, and which sovereign entity managed the land in said corridor. If no data are entered in the search, the query pulls all entries in the database and the webmap displays all documented cases (as in figure 4.2). Visitors can also see a table below the map with all pertinent data for each visualized case. In addition to the searchable data points, the table also includes a case report number from the PCMEO, geospatial data on the location of the body, and comments on location precision. The migrant death map not only visualizes data for other internet users, but it gives them access to the actual database used to create the map itself. These gestures multiply the ways these named or anonymous bodies can circulate in public debate. "Our records," as Chamblee and the other volunteers at

Humane Borders stated, "stand as a virtual monument to those who have died."[43] The mapping efforts of Humane Borders were a means to name and remember those who had lost their lives attempting to evade the machinations of the border technopolitical regime, those who dreamed of another kind of life yet were deprived of their lives. They were no longer remains left to the ravages of the desert; they now took on a new haunting mode of existence.

The webmap by Humane Borders creates a series of associations between the Sonoran Desert, border enforcement, and migrant deaths. This is the problem of the twenty-first century laid bare for internet users to perceive: calculating logics and recursive loops draw a racial line between those allowed to live and those made to die. As the proper balance of the system of systems works toward operational control of the border, unauthorized border crossers are pushed farther into lethal terrains where they lose their lives. CBP plans and policy documents rarely mention and leave unaddressed the thousands of people who have died under the seeming all-sensing regime of the cybernetic border. The webmap offers insight into how the migrant dead exceed the border metrics developed to measure operational control. Figure 4.2 includes 3,909 light gray circles (though they are red in the original webmap) with a black dot in the center, each representing the place of death of a border crossing migrant within the territorial boundaries of the state of Arizona between 1981 and 2022. The geographical area can be seen from high above, like a kind of "eye in the sky." Instead of emulating the vision technoaesthetics of Predator B unmanned aerial systems (UASS), which naturalize the hunt for enemy intruders and are premised on a desire for mastery, the area is visualized as a constructed killing field. It is filled with so many red circles that almost the whole border between Arizona and Sonora, Mexico, is transformed into a blood line. This is a line made by draining the life of thousands of non-white migrants. Additionally, the black center in the red dots creates a visual effect through which sections of the map turn completely black, as if the geographical data beneath disappeared. There is no Arizona. There is no map. There is only a void. Perhaps presciently visualizing Gloria Anzaldúa's description of *la frontera*, the interplay between black and red summons an image of the border as an open wound. Here lies a different kind of intrusion on the border. This is the haunting trace of the cybernetic border. These red circles are its technoaesthetic remainders.

The practices of remembering and honoring those no longer present relate to the idea of haunting. The "virtual monument" of Humane Borders is, as Jacques Derrida once said of specters, an act of being-with a ghostly presence. "And this being-with specters would also be, not only but also, a *politics* of memory, of inheritance, and of generations."[44] In being-with them, the ghosts of the migrant dead summon others to transform the conditions of life in the borderlands. The ongoing gesture of recording, locating, and circulating the names of migrants who die is a technopolitical act. By mobilizing death data generated by the Border Patrol, the PCMEO, and the Mexican consulates in Arizona, Humane Borders operates within a regime of truth predicated on the value of empirical evidence and, especially, of governing the border through the sense-making value of data.[45] Yet it does so while attempting to redress the forgetfulness that arises from the border technopolitical regime's efforts to drive migrants farther into the crevices of the border environment and into the bellies of wild animals.[46] This map works as an ethical imperative against the operations of a regime that reduces unauthorized migrants to *bare life*, or "life that can be taken without apology, classified as neither homicide nor sacrifice."[47] In its careful documentation of migrants who lose their lives crossing the border, the mapping project refuses to let them go unnoticed. More starkly, the project conjures the traces of those now gone as a gesture that refuses to be complicit with and turn a blind eye to the violence of the cybernetic border.

The map by Humane Borders punctures the anonymity of the border technopolitical regime by creating a relation between the deaths of migrants and territorial sovereignty—that is, the terrain on which the regime is dictated to act by law. "Sovereignty means," according to Achille Mbembe, "the capacity to define who matters and who does not, who is *disposable* and who is not."[48] And the Humane Borders webmap contests the sovereign practices of the border technopolitical regime. To name the dead and be with them—or more accurately, to be with their traces—seeks to trigger a public debate about responsibility. The questions of how and where they died—which the data in the migrant death map attempt to answer—lead to other questions about why they died and who is accountable. After all, "the land of open graves," as Jason De León calls the vast stretches of the Sonoran Desert in Arizona, did not come about as a random result; rather, it is the product of "a killing machine that simultaneously uses and hides behind the viciousness" of the desert. It is there where "the Border Patrol disguises the impact of its current enforcement policy by mobilizing a combination of sterilized discourse, redirected blame, and 'natural' environmental processes that erase evidence of what happens in the most remote parts of southern Arizona."[49] However, this attempt to disguise and obfuscate the impacts of the border as a networked platform generates its excess.

Data haunts are the excesses that creeped into and plagued CBP's border metrics. The Border Patrol's process of accounting for the migrant dead, for example, prioritizes where bodies are found and not the fact that life is extinguished through the migratory process. Migrants who die crossing the border but whose bodies are displaced from US into Mexican territory are made statistically irrelevant. As such, they are not just a statistical excess, they are also the lingering detritus of a regime programmed to disregard them. The death webmaps made legible the limits of border metrics—recording that which is not initially documented. The ghosts in data are "the myriad forces that make up the composite multiplicities of data," the forces "that produce an excess and a beyond the purported referent."[50] In this sense, data haunts evade capture yet hover in the vicinity of the production of data, marking its limit and beckoning actors in the public sphere to contend with the forces that fabricate them. A visitor to the map is led to reflect on the fact that many names and entries included in the PCMEO databases are not included in the ones managed by the Border Patrol. The agency of the dead crosses from the "other side" into the world of the "living" to animate a demand for recognition.

To think about data haunts today has been to tackle the US-Mexico border as a problem of cybernetic governmentality—that is, of the datafied and informationalized technoaesthetics structuring and channeling the conducts of humans.[51] Contemporary governmentality on the border, as this book has shown, has rendered subjects and objects as data producing entities, as knowable and measurable quantities. Like Rivera's attempt in "Why Cybraceros?" to grapple with alienation on the borderlands and in racial capital, the migrant death map demonstrates that haunting cannot be disentangled from the border technopolitical regime. Data are the figure and the trope; that is, they are the technoaesthetic through which governmentality is operationalized.[52] In such ordering of subjects and objects through data, the stage is set for a ghostly presence—the simultaneous manifestation of being and not being there.

"BORDER HAUNT"

This haunting interplay of being and not being there was one of the dynamics explored by Ian Alan Paul in his online performance "Border Haunt" (2011). Developed in response to the thousands of migrants who had lost their lives over border enforcement efforts, "Border Haunt" echoed the critical impulse of activist organizations that, like Humane Borders, wanted to bring attention to what was and remains a human rights crisis. Paul's performance took place on July 15, 2011, and it consisted of bringing "two different databases associated with the US-Mexico border into contact with one another": a migrant death database and an anti-immigrant one. He extracted data from a border death map managed by the *Arizona Daily Star*; this map was built using the design and data from the one produced by Humane Borders.[53] He called the contact between databases a "border database collision" because it consisted of entering data from the migrant death map into a crowdsourced surveillance system known as the Virtual Community Watch (VCW) that used livestreaming cameras and sensors. His border database collision replicated the recursive logics of cybernetic control so crucial for the cybernetic border; it mobilized data of border phenomena to inform and shape the human-machine configurations of operational control. Feeding death data to the VCW both obfuscated actual border phenomena and recorded the excesses of the border technopolitical regime—the names of the dead and its mostly unaccounted necroviolence. "Border Haunt" played with the ghostly, spiritual visit of the dead and the hunt that is emblematic of the border technopolitical regime. Ultimately, Paul's performance disturbed the anti-immigrant and nativist politics embedded in the cybernetic border, the hunting after enemy-prey through crowdsourcing initiatives like VCW, by leading its constituent elements adrift.

VCW is part of a supposed autonomous civil society response to the border as a problem object. Its policing system, created and administered by the private social network company BlueServo, allowed internet users to sign up for free as "Virtual Texas Deputies" and "proactively participate in fighting border crime."[54] VCW, now branded the Virtual Border Watch, gave users access to camera feeds from various regions along the Texas border with Mexico and asked them to report via email any suspect activity. Examples of what BlueServo users were told to consider as suspect activities were people carrying backpacks or bundles. Echoing the operation of the electronic fence and the situational awareness of the system of systems, the local county sheriffs were then tasked with responding to reports, conducting investigations, and taking any other necessary actions because of sensor activations and user inputs. VCW builds on centuries of settler colonial violence promulgated and deputized by the US government that had led to the proliferation of non-state groups committed to the embodiment of imperial sovereignty and acting against those imagined as excludable from the nation. VCW continues this history of vigilante violence against Mexicans, Latina/o/es, and other migrants through what I have elsewhere termed "un-civil technoscience." Seemingly volunteer-driven, VCW articulated care for the nation

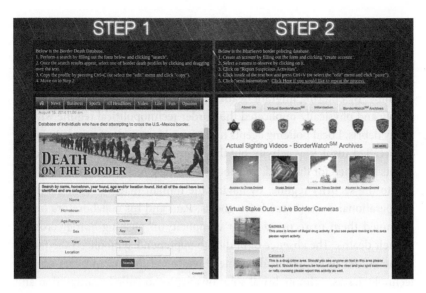

FIGURE 4.3. Screenshot of user interface in Ian Alan Paul's "Border Haunt" (2011). Image courtesy of the artist.

by normalizing and legitimizing the ensemble of human-machine configurations against a racialized Other construed as enemy or intruder.[55]

"Border Haunt" made the nativist and anti-immigrant BlueServo complicit in misdirecting the border technopolitical regime, thereby disassembling it. In "Border Haunt" (see figure 4.3), Paul's objective was to have participants "direct flows of information and collectively migrate the data from the border death database into the border policing database, haunting the servers of the border security structure."[56] The performance made the vigilante social network BlueServo responsible for leading local county sheriffs to search for the bodies of dead migrants "as if the deceased were making attempted crossings."[57] Occupied with searching for the deceased or for the zombie-like, sheriffs could not hunt for border crossers. For a day, over 600 participants reoriented the operations of a regional assemblage of the border technopolitical regime by rewriting the kinds of actionable data at their disposal. The names of the bodies of dead migrants found in Arizona were resituated and made to haunt the Texas borderlands. Police officers looked for the ghostly trace of what was there and not there. Data haunts pointed to the gap—the missing parts the regime worked hard to cast outside its assembling practices. Pulling this hanging thread disassembled the cybernetic border's imperial fantasy of mastery and control.

During our conversation, Paul described his work as a "symbolic gesture" that "animated . . . deceased migrants" by registering their agency.[58] This symbolic reanimation of dead migrant bodies was something more than the passive, anonymous detritus of the border regime; death data haunted the machine. By entering migrant death data into the policing database, actors visibly and physically implicated the border technopolitical regime with its fleshy debris. Local policing agents hit the road in search of people involved in so-called suspicious activity, but they found no one. Unknowingly, police agents searched for the dead; they looked for the ghostly traces of those lives lost to the security regime. By having the human-machine configurations of operational control search for ghosts, Paul and his collaborators reprogrammed them to recognize their complicity in pushing border crossers to their deaths. The absence of bodies to apprehend symbolized the failure of the border technopolitical regime's investment in data and data-sensing technologies as technopolitical solutions for its so-called immigration and border control problems. Ghostly data led border enforcers off their paths to apprehend and remove. The ghost in the machine pulled actors "in one direction or another . . . almost always unknowing of if, and how, [they were] exactly being pulled."[59] As Avery Gordon comments on what generally happens with ghostly matters, the moment in which actors saw data haunts was the moment they were shaken by the tangle between "lost beloveds and the force[s] that made them disposable."[60] These data haunts challenged the reduction of populations on the border to bare life. Data haunts confronted the desire for quantitative, categorical, and governmental capture with evasion and with fugitivity. The undetected movements of border crossers proved the inefficiencies of the cybernetic border to deliver its technical efficiency over the borderlands. These were resisting bodies contesting the sovereign practices of the US empire-nation. These data haunts were finally counted, but in the process, they disturbed the political project to exert control over racialized bodies and populations as disposable matters of sovereignty.

"Border Haunt" engaged the same technoaesthetics of modern governmentality—data—not only to reveal what was expelled from the cybernetic border but to obfuscate as well. Participants used real data of dead migrants to confuse or mislead the regime to search for what was not there. Data haunts helped "buy time" for others who now could "hide in the crowd of signals."[61] The obfuscating quality of data haunts contested how the US empire-nation treated individuals and populations as trace-producing entities for subjectification, objectification, and commodification. Contrary to data inputs that guide and improve the functioning of the Border Patrol's apprehension system, these data did not improve the border apparatus or any of its technological artifacts. They did not lead to apprehended subjects being processed and held in the growing network of private detention centers that extract value in the captivity of otherness.[62] "Bare life" on the border, as De León concludes, "has been reduced to shoes, shards of bone, and the 'Unknown.'"[63] "Border Haunt" recalibrated the networked platform of the border so that the only subjects that had to be accounted for—that had to be both counted and looked at—were those deceased migrants the human-machine configuration made into "bare life."

Engaging data haunts was a way to refocus debates about the border and the operations of the border technopolitical regime. The Humane Borders migrant death map and Paul's "Border Haunt" mobilized data to challenge the ghastly inhumanity of this regime because it conscripted the desert environment to threaten the lives of migrants. Intrusion was not the problem. It was the strategy of prevention through deterrence and the border metrics of operational control that tried to make border crossing migrants into the lifeless matter of remote border areas. "Routine in their occurrence," the ACLU report concluded, "these [migrant] deaths have passed unnoticed and have become invisible in the public consciousness. Both the US and Mexican governments have failed to acknowledge their responsibility in contributing to deaths of hundreds of migrants every year."[64] The agency of unauthorized border crossers, the migrant death map, and the obfuscating tactics of Paul intervened in public debate by transforming non-matter into ghostly matters. Different kinds of data—such as names, ages, places of birth, location where bodies were found—indexed the violence of a machine implicated in the production of human suffering. Data haunts helped map out the terrain and vectors of a border technopolitical regime now understood as "a killing machine."

The following section tackles drones as killing data machines; only rather than the drones being deployed in faraway lands, artists instead turned them lose at "home." Just like in Operation Top Gun and Project William Tell, drones were once again intruders in US territory.

Disassembling Complicity, Disrupting the "Eye in the Sky"

On December 4, 2012, domestic drone warfare, which had plagued the US-Mexico borderlands with minimal attention since 2004, briefly reared its head when a UAS crashed in the middle of the campus at the University of California–San Diego (UCSD). An image of the incident (see figure 4.4) circulated

FIGURE 4.4.
Ricardo Dominguez,
Ian Alan Paul, and
Jane Stevens's "Drone
Crash Incident"
(2012). Image courtesy
of the artists.

across various media outlets showing a crashed drone and a person in a hazmat suit in front of UCSD's Geisel Library. The drone, which looked like the Predator B UAS used by CBP as one of the machines in its system of net-worked platforms, created a sense of intimacy for spectators. This UAS was the product of San Diego company General Atomics (GA), whose headquar-ters were next to the UCSD campus. Members of the university community interacted with GA and multiple high-tech companies that were established along the Mesa through their funding of research projects and recruitment of graduates.[65] The image of a GA drone crashed in the middle of campus made drone warfare a matter of concern for the community. A local NBC affiliate covered the news of the crash, and press inquiries reached the uni-versity administration. The recently created UC Center for Drone Policy and Ethics (CDPE) took the lead in responding to public commotion over what became known as the "Drone Crash Incident." Guerne N. Ka, a principal investigator at the CDPE, declared that even though "drone crashes [were] rare and another malfunction [would be] extremely unlikely," the center wanted to take the opportunity to "teach basic drone safety techniques that [could] be practiced on a daily basis to keep ourselves and others safe."[66] Ka did not address why the malfunctioning drone was initially flying over the university's campus. Instead, the CDPE normalized the fact that the public needed to learn how to be safe in a "dronified" environment. In keeping with its role as a public educator, the center announced it would host a town hall to discuss the incident with students, faculty, and staff at Calit2's Gallery. University of California officials quickly sought to disavow any drone crash as well as the existence of the CDPE. The center repudiated the denials. Confusion and disorientation reigned. A few days later, people finally figured out that the crash was an "art hoax" created by a trio of performance artists, Ricardo Dominguez, Ian Alan Paul, and Jane Stevens.[67]

A statement announcing the appointment of Dominguez as the lead researcher for the CDPE described him as a recognized artist "in the field of social code disassembly."[68] The announcement was, in fact, a statement of intent and method. Dominguez and his fellow conspirators would disassemble/critique the different social codes/discourses that made drones into political entities. Social code disassembly opens technopolitical regimes like the cybernetic border to scrutiny. Designed and developed in San Diego, a technopolitical frontier of the US empire-nation, drones are the point of contact of various relations and political objectives of the cybernetic border. Drones are among the emblematic technologies of modern biopolitical governmentality because they are involved in the fabrication of individuals, populations, and territories. The Predator B UAS is strategic in producing operative images that shape how Border Patrol agents on the southern border engage border crossers. The aim of Dominguez, Paul, and Stevens was to disassemble the entities and codes involved in drone production by troubling the role of higher education. This might have been why they chose an image of a crashed drone that resembled the "homegrown" Predator B. Designed and developed by GA, the Predator B epitomizes drone warfare abroad and at home; it is a symbol of the border technopolitical regime.

When Dominguez, Paul, and Stevens simulated the crash of a drone in UCSD, they echoed those who approached machines as entanglements of technopolitical regimes. Universities in the United States, for example, are programmed to play a role in the production of technical knowledge and expertise to be leveraged by industry and the military. A crashed drone in front of a campus library symbolizes these entanglements between university research or knowledge making and the manufacture of killing machines. In other words, regimes create, implement, and follow certain codes that govern how entities and their components relate with one another. These codes are sets of modulating instructions, rules, protocols, instruments, and bodies executing given roles. The regime in the "Drone Crash Incident" was not a given whole but a programmable machine that had to be reassembled by tracing messy relations and associations between phenomena and processes.

The "Drone Crash Incident" sets the border technopolitical regime as a problem object. That the incident was the "creation" of the CDPE within UCSD highlights this site as a critical element in the production of knowledge and the constitution of a regime of truth. Academics are identified as managers in the administration of said regime but also as managers of normative desire (i.e., how the public ought to feel about military technologies operating above them). The crash of a drone on the UCSD campus exposed the assembling of knowledge for empire and border making; after all, this campus was founded in part through the investments of defense contractors like General Dynamics—the founder of GA.[69] This is an empire that, since the early twentieth century, identified San Diego as its settler gateway for territorial expansion and overreach into the Pacific frontier. Such an identification led to the growth of an expansive network of military settlements in the region of San Diego that cast their glance both within and beyond US territory. Drones researched and manufactured in and around the UCSD campus are implicated in the territorial expansion of US power abroad and at home through their use in wars in Vietnam, Iraq, Afghanistan, Pakistan, and in the US southern borderlands. By conjuring the CDPE, Dominguez, Paul, and Stevens simulate or re(a)ssemble the collaborative relationship between the university and the military. Their collaboration creates and produces drones as machines of governance—machines designed to subject entities to the will of US imperial sovereignty.

The artists' enactment of social code disassembly exposed the openness of higher education and its complicity with border technopolitical regimes.[70] This is a relationship that, after the creation of the Department of Homeland Security (DHS) in 2002, was formalized through the DHS Science & Technology Directorate and its Homeland Security Advanced Research Projects Agency, which funds universities and research institutes as centers of excellence (COEs).[71] In performing their existing roles at UCSD—Dominguez was at the time an associate professor of visual arts at Calit2, and Paul was a lecturer in interdisciplinary computing and arts—both artists passed as nonthreatening, perhaps even sympathetic figures of the regime. Paul told me how, when he started his lecturer position, he used to walk the halls of Calit2's building and notice offices for DARPA (Defense Advanced Research

Project Agency). Despite the purported openness of this information, Paul asked his students and other faculty about UCSD's relation to military research only to be told that they had not heard about it.[72] During the public meeting, Paul told the audience about aerodynamic research conducted on campus in the Structural and Materials Engineering building thanks to contracts with Northrop Grumman and other drone manufacturers. He also highlighted the work of GA in the university's neighborhood. Meanwhile, Stevens's role as the head archivist for the CDPE allowed her to comment on the fact that, historically, drone development was bound to "spectacular crashes" and experimental deployment in policing practices on colonial spaces.[73] Even when dispersed and subjected to the obfuscating practices of the classification regime, archives, particularly those documenting military and governmental actors, constituted the material traces of settler colonial and imperial violence. Reassembling archival traces was a necessary intervention in flipping the anonymity of the border technopolitical regime. Rather than continuing to function black-boxed and unnoticed, entanglements between industry, higher education, and the military were subjected to open debate. The effects of these entanglements, linked to the outgrowth of drone warfare and imperial formations, were questioned at UCSD after the simulated crash incident.

By folding themselves into this assemblage as researchers concerned with ethical drone operations and public policy, the artists ran a kind of parasitical interference with the regime. Their disassembling practice was parasitical in the sense that they transformed "their complicity with hegemonic structures into a counterintuitive resource for undermining them in plain sight."[74] The press releases of the CDPE called attention to the university's role in maintaining, developing, and legitimizing drone research—which was already a central component in CBP's networked platforms for operational control. If regimes like air power and atomic power were predicated on instilling fear in target populations, universities were enrolled not only to conduct the technical research to make it happen but to negotiate how populations came to imagine, live with, and acquiesce them. Dominguez commented, during the group's public meeting, that the CDPE might be understood as a university initiative in the administration of fear—a brief block on fear as a constitutive feature of the regime. In disavowing the existence of the CDPE and attempting to shut down the conversation, UCSD disregarded the need for ethical and public debate on the institution's complicity. Thanks to the disassembling, parasitical work of the group of artists, the university unsettled its own standing as a paragon of frank openness.

What Dominguez proposed through his expertise in social code disassembly was to reassemble the social by resembling it—or, as he described the performance, to operate through "minor simulations." Minor simulations are those events that are "difficult to understand as either real or not real."[75] Emphasis on minor simulations, as a performative gesture, triggers disorientation or confusion; it blurs the boundaries of the real. They are minor because they do not involve any virtuous or masterful use of technology. To perform minor simulations such as the "Drone Crash Incident" involves playing with how regimes of truth fabricate subjects and objects through their technoaesthetics. This simulation began through the mundane circulation of an email announcing the appointment of Dominguez as the lead researcher of the CDPE. It continued with press releases posted on the center's blog online, and it ended with a town hall meeting so that community members could meet, learn, and discuss why a drone had "crashed" on the UCSD campus.[76] Aside from the supposed drone crash, there were no oddities in this sequence of mundane events in a university setting. The performance hid within the assemblage of the border technopolitical regime by replicating its protocols and weaving together different stages that produced an aura of verisimilitude around the disorienting notion that drones were operating overhead.

The minor simulation assigned drones the role of intruder. To imagine life beneath the shadow of drones that could fail and crash was the truly disturbing notion that haunted members of the UCSD community. Drones were made to interrupt the safe environs of university life. The power of minor simulations like the "Drone Crash Incident" is, Dominguez argued, in the gesture's "symbolic efficacy" and not in its "technological efficiency."[77] There was no need to fly drones over the UCSD campus; it was enough to imagine them. This simulation sought to generalize the feeling of dread that surveilled populations experienced when drones flew overhead and delivered mortal payloads. After all, just one year before the drone "crashed" at UCSD, the US military used a drone for the first time to kill US citizens in Yemen.[78] When Dominguez, Paul, and Stevens embarked on their performance, the US public was growing anxious about the idea of drones flying above them. By simulating such dread, these artists hoped to prompt spectators to reflect on their relationship to these kinds of operations, and perhaps oppose them.[79]

If the public was unsettled and concerned with the mere simulation of a drone crash, how should it respond to ongoing drone operations in the Middle East, northern Africa, Southeast Asia, and the US-Mexico border? If UCSD was integral to drone research and development, how should the institution and the community hold each other accountable for drone strikes overseas and migrant deaths in the desert? In the context of a border imagined as a networked platform, glitches offered a generative opportunity to consider its trappings and deadly repercussions. Dominguez argued that efforts to solve the so-called border and immigration problem through technological means, which permeated much public debate and policymaking, were a dead end. "The solution to holes, or gaps, ruptures, glitches, [was] another machine." Imagining how a government official would respond, he said, "'The sensors on the ground can't tell the difference between a cow, a human, and a rabbit, and rolling bushes? Well, let's try to add another layer by flying automated elements.'"[80] Machines were the solutions for the problems left unaddressed by other machines, and UCSD was one of the many institutions involved in developing new technologies but also improving existing machines. In simulating the failure of a drone and its crash on campus, Dominguez, Paul, and Stevens opened space for a dissident politics to challenge the status quo. Their tactical media practice foregrounded the experiential dimension of performance to transform the moral morass of acquiescing university members.[81] Students and faculty encountered one another as constituents of an institution and an artistic intervention to call into question drone algorithm and defense research at UCSD. The border technopolitical regime could no longer continue to function in relative anonymity.

Most worryingly of all, however, was that the biggest ethical flaw or glitch in the border regime and the drones operating within it was the programmed political objective of driving migrants into treacherous and life-threatening areas of the border—and that this flaw was never considered as such. On the contrary, government officials like Asa Hutchinson, DHS under secretary in 2004, argued that enforcement efforts on the border were meant "to save lives but also to enforce the law."[82] But whose lives were being "saved"? Humane Borders documented hundreds of border crossing deaths yearly, so there was significant evidence that these enforcement efforts were not saving the lives of migrants but rather transforming them into disposable subjects, into data haunts of a killing machine. The cybernetic border combined the threat of death and its actualization to produce a regime of fear. The anxious response by the press and members of the community to the simulated drone crash demonstrated that domestic drone operations were widely imagined through the prism of danger and threat. Rather than normalize these operations, the social code disassembly work of Dominguez, Paul, and Stevens interrupted the regime's pretenses from within and called into question its unethical politics of fear.

The "Drone Crash Incident," the cybracero video, and "Border Haunts" all operate through sociological inquiry, tactical media, and speculation. The aesthetic practices of the artists and activists cannot to be collected and commodified. Instead, they study the operations of the border technopolitical regime through simulation and mimicry. In replicating the maneuvers of the regime, they also call into question the values embedded in its practices. These artists and activists exploit openings in its everyday operation to disrupt and disorient the regime. They document and build on historical and actual technopolitical arrangements to invite us to imagine another world. What if agricultural migrant labor could be automated and controlled through information technology? What if the ghosts in the machine, the data of border enforcement, could haunt it? And what if we debated the justice of drone operations and the knowledge infrastructures that make them possible rather than proceeding with dutiful complicity? Rigorous attention to actual operations creates pathways to a different life elsewhere.

Of Seeing Machines and "Living Elsewhere"

Imagine you could watch the entirety of the US-Mexico border without having to leave where you are. What would capturing and reproducing the almost 2,000 miles of international boundary look like? "Best of Luck with the Wall" (2016) was created to insist on the geography and materiality of the southern border and to convey to viewers "a sense of the enormity of it all." Digital artist Josh Begley's six-minute video was produced in collaboration with Laura Poitras and her team at Field of Vision, a filmmaker-driven documentary unit that commissions short-form nonfiction films about ongoing world issues.[83] His video, also shared through *The Intercept*'s website, was meant as a sarcastic and critical response to then presidential candidate Donald Trump's anti-immigrant rhetoric and his drive to build a border wall. "Best of Luck with the Wall" operates within the speculative framework of ghostly matters; as Gordon describes it, "We need to know where we live in order to imagine living elsewhere."[84] Begley hoped the video got viewers to "imagine what it would mean to be a political subject of that [border] terrain" and, through this process perhaps, to imagine a different way of relating to and in the borderlands.[85] In the end, the political subject that emerges from this work is one overwhelmed by the breathtaking flows of geography and the speed of operative images that suture and condense time and space. In a sense, the video succeeds in showcasing the sublime immensity of the southern border.

"Best of Luck with the Wall" was created using a variety of digital technologies, some of which are also part of the cybernetic border itself. First among them were about 200,000 geolocated satellite images of "the entire southern border." These images were originally collected by a small computer script. Begley then employed a command-line tool called *ffmpeg* to "programmatically stitch the images together," like different threads of fabric. The result of this process was a collection of vertical images of the US-Mexico border that flow swiftly from one to the next. Even though the video is in fact a kind of collage of images, Begley generates a sense of movement by sequencing them rather than leaving them on the screen. In summary, the video was only possible through the entangled production of machines and technologies: the satellite camera and its information networks, the database storing border images, the computer script that collected images, the program that stitched them together, the server that stores the video and makes it accessible on Field of Vision's website, and the viewer's computer, which accesses it. The immensity of the border (see figure 4.5), to put it another way, is imagined to be communicable by the power of an assemblage of machines that transform natural and urban geography into visual data points. Assembling machines and data, the video disrupts the regime's claims of mastery and control. Drawing on the same technoaesthetics of the cybernetic border, Begley's video shows us a different sense of the regime, one where failure to achieve and institute control haunts it and where such haunting might help disassemble its objectives.

The video starts with an empty black space followed by the sound of the sea that grows in its presence. The ebbs and flows of the waves can be felt reaching the shore when suddenly noise echoes as if bouncing off the walls of a gorge. The sound of the sea feels like gasps for air. Big block letters in the middle of the screen read: "The US-Mexico border is 1,954 miles long." Behind the video's opening statement, a sequence of satellite images of the Pacific Ocean appear. Playas de Tijuana enters the frame and, with it, the border wall/fence separating Southern California from northern Baja California. What was initially the sound of waves crashing on the shore now turns into a clanking noise accompanied with chirping birds and the slow plucking of guitar strings. The geopolitical boundary occupies the center of each image while "the camera" pans over the border between the United States and Mexico. Each muted guitar strum hangs over the aural plane. Together with the sound of a howling wind, they fill the visual landscape with a hurried pace. Sonic lethargy counters the quick tempo of the satellite images. Starting on the southwestern section of the border and moving east, the

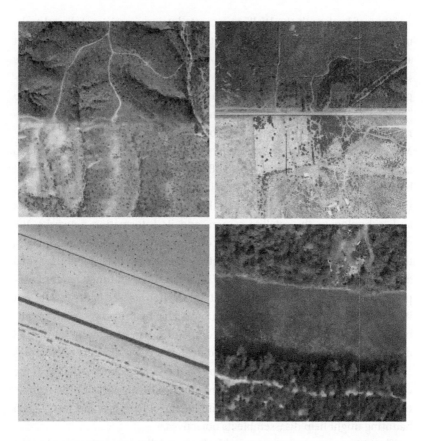

FIGURE 4.5. Collage of still images from Josh Begley's "Best of Luck with the Wall" (2016). Images courtesy of the artist and Field of Vision.

images follow each other at greater speeds (see figure 4.5). Shifts on the geography are displayed in quick succession: border urban spaces give way to deserts, to mountains, to valleys, to farmlands, to more urban spaces, to more deserts, and to the Rio Grande until it reaches the Gulf of Mexico. An eerie, haunting ambience emanates from the audiovisual experience. It feels as if the southern border was the scene of a terrifying crime.

The video conjures aesthetic work by other artists who have long thought and studied the border through critical and poetic lenses. Louis Hock's *Southern California: A Cinemural* (1979) immediately comes to mind for its representation of the geopolitical boundary as a rectangular and horizontal partitioning made through an assemblage of spatiotemporal cuts.[86] Hock ran his 16-millimeter film through three projectors set one next to the other. The single film was staggered in 20-second increments, creating a visual triptych and literary poem whereby images and text worked together in imagining Southern California as a mythological space—a technopolitical frontier for capital, a frontier articulated in and through moving infrastructures. First screened on the side of a shipping container attached to a truck at the Los Angeles Institute of Contemporary Art, the film calls to mind the border technopolitical regime's focus on differential mobility—the commodities entering US markets, the haunting presence of the migrant labor necessary to pick and make such commodities, and the social capital of those curating and visiting the museum. The images of the borderlands move across the screen, attempting and failing to capture the layered complexities of the landscape. The assembling and assembled border technopolitical regime in *Southern California* can only be engaged in its aftermath, like a colonial crime we learn after the fact.

Where Hock operates primarily on the conceptual and symbolic dimensions of the border and borderlands, Begley concerns himself with the technoaesthetics of the cybernetic border—its structuring of time, space, objects, and subjects through data networks. His video mimics the operations of the border as a networked platform with data capture and processing techniques, with databases and computers attempting to order the borderlands environment. Though not exclusively bound to the domain of vision, these technologies were premised on the idea that, as Begley states in his description of the video, the border landscape can be translated into sensible patterns of order to be governed by "seeing machines."[87] Visual artist Trevor Paglen defines seeing machines as the ways humans use technology to "see" as well as "the ways machines see the world for other machines." Seeing machines are imaging devices and systems such as photographic cameras, iPhones, airport security backscatter-imaging devices, electro-optical reconnaissance satellites, and drones, among others, that capture, circulate, and store data.[88] In the case of "Best of Luck with the Wall," the video is "an attempt to linger on that idea [of seeing machines] for a moment, and to explore ways of using those technologies—in this case satellites—to better visualize some of the spaces they are enforcing."[89] Begley's work mobilizes seeing machines as a way to reenvision the boundary line by improving general understandings of what the border is, what its characteristics are, and how it traverses diverse landscapes. This way of conceptualizing seeing machines echoes the discourse of technical efficacy espoused by officials at the DHS who have trusted combining humans with electronic and digital technologies like drones, ground sensors, and computers to produce a system of systems that records and circulates data on border intrusions. Officials crave having an "eye in the sky" to hover over the border. This mixture of human-machine configurations comprises a sensory regime that, not unlike Begley's objective, was brought together "to better visualize" the border.

Aiming to better visualize, Begley's video redeployed the imperial control fantasy of technological mastery by sidelining that which was unseen and, consequently, out of control. Whereas Paul's intervention offers a critique of what remains hidden within seeing machines—their data haunts—and Dominguez argues for an aesthetics of symbolic efficacy, "Best of Luck with the Wall" operates through the logics of technological efficiency. It reproduces the belief that seeing machines, like drones and satellites, can transparently reveal the inner truths of the border.[90] Begley's video is a technically complex artifact convinced of what data assemblages can make plain. This is the same technopolitical imaginary embodied by the electronic fence and the system of systems. Without these human-machine configurations, according to this logic, the totality of the US-Mexico border would not be visible and, consequently, remains incomprehensible. These machines, however, are part of a logic of efficiency and a desire for hypervisibility that seeks to master subjects and objects. The drive for hypervisibility, Gordon contends, is "a kind of obscenity of accuracy that abolishes the distinctions" it makes between what it allows to be seen and what it prohibits, between what it deems as knowable and not.[91] In other words, the human-machine configurations of seeing machines are blind to their obfuscations and the ways that they govern the kinds of subjects/objects they produce. Seeing machines hide their political objectives within their purported objectivity of just recording what is in front of them. They are designed to record and capture certain kinds of beings while ignoring or erasing others. Their political orientations are, in short, black-boxed.

"Best of Luck with the Wall" attempts to criticize the racist, nativist, and anti-immigrant zeal of the Trump administration, yet it did so by reproducing the cyberutopian hubris of digital mastery. Like the work by Humane Borders and Ian Alan Paul, the video conceded the hegemony of data in the operations of the technopolitical regime. But instead of data mastering the landscape, stitched data made evident the impossibility of this imperial desire. Satellite imagery, at times used in actual border enforcement operations, documents historical instances of the geopolitical boundary between the United States and Mexico—a line where urban spaces give way to massive geological features stubbornly resisting human control. By assembling satellite data, Begley's video resembles the imperial desire for control without questioning the limits of data. An insistence on seeing similarly disaggregates images from the wider set of informational processes at the heart of the cybernetic border. Satellite and drone feeds are not merely visual cues for their observers; data in aggregate shape the operations of a far more complex regime. Sensor data (visual and nonvisual), for example, are currently processed by artificial intelligence and machine learning algorithms that determine the nature of the entities represented in the data. Understanding that the cybernetic border operates beyond the visual field creates an opportunity to disassemble the regime and account for its hauntings and its investments. The roughness and expansiveness of the landscape haunted and still haunts the cybernetic border, reminding it of its unruly nature.

Rather than articulate a clear vision of the border, "Best of Luck with the Wall" operates in the realm of opacity. More succinctly, the border it re(a)ssembles is incomprehensible and incoherent. The border, as this book has shown at length, does not exist "out there" but is constructed through a regime of data assemblages. At times, the boundary line in the video is clearly visible; at other times, it disappears, as if blurred out of sight by the breakneck speed of the seeing machines attempting to visualize the border. No image stayed on-screen for longer than a few milliseconds. It was as artist Hito Steyerl suggests when writing about perception as "a sea of data." "Not seeing anything intelligible is the new normal. Information is passed on as a set of signals that cannot be picked up by human senses."[92] And as a result, the border seen in "Best of Luck with the Wall," though not fully grasped, is the product of a machinic perception. This is a perception that renders sutured data points opaque, unrecognizable if not for the title of the video at the beginning. The video's technoaesthetics offers a vision of the border as a disjointed imaginary line splintered by quick-moving images and sharp shifts in the terrain. Signals sent from machine to machine were devoid of any human bodies. Human presence in each satellite image was only visible epiphenomenally, through interventions in the natural landscape—in buildings, roads, parks, and so on. The absence of human bodies, like the "human forms" captured by Predator B UAS video feeds, haunted this visualization of the border. They were spectral figures that, by "not" being there, beckoned so many people and institutions to act. In this way, perhaps, Begley's video succeeded in imagining what it meant "to be a political subject of that [border] terrain." "Best of Luck with the Wall" offers viewers a glimpse into the arbitrariness and the opacity of national borders and the technological foundations from which territory and populations are made. In knowing the boundary line as a capricious project in an expansive and overwhelming landscape, the video generates Gordon's "elsewhere." His video pushes viewers to relate beyond the construction of infrastructures of blockage.

The artists and activists written about in the previous pages helped push conversations about border enforcement by critically examining what technologies did, how they came about, and what their limits were. To do this, they employed a series of techniques, at times the same technoaesthetics deployed by the cybernetic border, to disassemble the regime's operations. The interventions of Alex Rivera, Humane Borders, Ian Alan Paul, Ricardo Dominguez, Jane Stevens, and Josh Begley question this regime as a desiring apparatus of control and mastery. Their challenges were not frontal attacks at the heart of the regime but rather strategic maneuvers reorienting its operations through confusion and disruption. Actors enacted a technoaesthetics of dissent whereby the cybernetic border was contested through the same structures of the sensible that it instituted. Rivera summoned the ghosts of futures past to invite audiences to imagine another world. Rivera's ghosts were those that historically and consistently sought to commodify migrant labor as the means to allow the US economy to thrive; US abundance depended on the dispossession of migrant labor and the management of their mobility through techniques of unmanning and automation. Humane Borders and Paul, meanwhile, set their sights on contesting the necropolitics and data politics of the border technopolitical regime. They did so by calling attention to the metrics of migrant border deaths, a metric that is absent from the regime's emphasis on data as vectors for controlling the border. Data haunted the border technopolitical regime by foregrounding its paradoxical failures—succeeding in making border crossers die and failing to keep them alive. Dominguez, Paul, and Stevens's tactical media intervention disassembled the social codes organizing the border technopolitical regime by pushing members of the community at UCSD to reflect on their complicity with the regime itself. Drawing on their existing roles as researchers and teachers in higher education, these artists rehearsed their complicity in the administration of fear while pushing the UCSD administration to be accountable for its actions. In doing so, the collaborations between higher education and the regime were contested from within. Lastly, Begley's work repurposed seeing machines—satellite imagery and mapping platforms—to have viewers imagine what it meant "to be a political subject" of the southern border and "to better visualize" the entirety of the boundary line. Yet, in attempting to show this, the video embodied the potential for data assemblages to be opaque. Hoping to cast its masterful gaze into the deep and hidden crevices of the borderlands landscape, networked platforms quickly overwhelm and overrun a human user's capacity to grasp what they record, process, store, and communicate.

The artists and activists discussed here respond to the actual operations of the border technopolitical regime by recognizing that the cybernetic border has set the conditions from which actors must interrogate the regime. Rather than limit themselves to the establishing shot of the border—the wall/fence—activists and artists identify, study, and test the human-machine configurations that make and enforce the border. These actors employed racialized drone workers, data haunts, drone crashes, higher education's complicity, and seeing machines to articulate lines of flight and identify exploits for an exit.

Digital technology and art were approached by mobilizing a conceptual apparatus produced by (or in collaboration with) actors themselves. The terms they used (e.g., social code assembly, disassembling, haunts, gestures, disruptions) and their practices "highlighted the limitations of many of our prevalent modes of inquiry and the assumptions they make about the social world."[93] The interventions by Humane Borders and by Paul, for example, suggested the importance of being with those no longer there, the haunting presence of the border crossing dead. Data haunts became a means of reorienting the privileged position afforded to data in modern governmentality. Instead of gestures to effect control over populations, data haunts were a way to name, to place, and to remember the lost. There was no way to quantify or document all the migrant dead, but activists and artists redeployed data to demand responsibility. The conceptual work of these actors offers an opportunity to redraw the boundaries of the laboratory for technology. How technologies are engaged in the field is as important as how they were designed, imagined, and constructed by "experts." This approach expands the actor network by listening to actors beyond the bounds of purported expertise. In the language of Dominguez, technical efficiency is not the only realm requiring critical understanding, and artists are excellent interlocutors for processes of symbolic efficacy. This is of special significance when the bounds of imagination are those of the empire-nation and the unbearable endurance of enmity.

EPILOGUE

The Unbearable Endurance of
Data Technopolitics and Enmity

Assembled at the annual Border Security Expo in San Antonio, Texas, in March 2022, industry officials listened to the chief of US Border Patrol, Raul Ortiz, announce that the agency was looking to "capitalize on both the fusion of technology, the fusion of information, and making sure that those front-line agents have the resources that they need."[1] Border Patrol was looking for proposals from folks in the defense and homeland security industries for consolidated tower and surveillance equipment that would integrate the various systems used by the agency and manufactured by Anduril Industries, Elbit Systems of America, and General Dynamics. The organization's priority was to have data feeds from this integrated network of platforms processed through artificial intelligence and machine learning. After "autonomously sort[ing] out items of interest," the system will "alert operators and dismiss innocuous activity such as that of animals."[2] The command-and-control platform can then deliver a common operating picture to agents in border sectors and in central command.

The technopolitical regime that Ortiz and the Border Patrol sought to articulate has been a matter of concern for the US government since the second half of the twentieth century. Conceiving intrusion as a problem object of the border and, consequently, the nation, the US government and its military as well as industry and academia have been hard at work designing different human-machine configurations to manage and administer the boundaries of the imagined community. From drones as targets for the aerial defense of the nation to the data assemblages of the border as a networked platform, the regime has assembled diverse configurations to produce territory and populations as much as to govern them. Emphasis on a command-and-control platform is a testament to the enduring management of intrusion through the racial logics of enmity and the prominence of a cybernetics imaginary to make sense of "the border." In the context of the southern US border, communication and control is the hegemonic organization of practices, ideas, and human-machine arrangements responsible for making and administering territory and populations.

The geopolitical lines of territorial sovereignty in the United States follow W. E. B. Du Bois's dictum that "the problem of the twentieth century is the color line."[3] And this book shows that the color line cannot be understood without a meticulous account of technology. Tending to race and/as technology, the book scrutinized how actors instituted associations between techniques of control and racial imaginaries. When actors like Ortiz call for better resources for the Border Patrol, they often describe them in neutral terms as if new technologies, funding, and training merely correct some technical deficiency. But artifacts and sociotechnical arrangements are, as Gabrielle Hecht contends, material implements that negotiate relations. They are embedded with political objectives that are revealed through the uses they foment, dissuade, and make possible as much as by how diverse actors interpret them. Artifacts like Anduril's Sentry towers, discussed in the book's introduction, are meant to represent, according to the company's founder Palmer Luckey, the "flame of the West . . . the best technology that Western democracy has to offer."[4] In imagining itself as a protector of "the West," Anduril produces human-machine configurations designed with an adversary in mind. An enemy to ward off and keep at bay. Caught up in a white supremacist fantasy where non-white monstrous Others besiege (white) humanity, Sentry towers are the products and producers of a technopolitical regime meant to maintain the racial line on the southern border. Another prototype in the forever-beta testing of the border as an infrastructure of enmity.

The Cybernetic Border explored the place of drones, electronic technology, computing, and data in the emergence of a regime programmed to manage, administer, and police intruders to the US empire-nation. Studying the thoughts of government and military officials, technicians, and journalists, the book shows how the border technopolitical regime is invested in mobilizing sets of rules, methods, and devices that prescribe what/who belongs and what/who does not, between what/who is internal and external to the United States. These human-machine configurations favor the translation of border subjects and objects into data-producing entities. The cybernetic border that emerged out of long periods of experimentation is a programmable assemblage bound to racialized targets that, despite attempts to construe its processes as mere technique, is steeped in the ebb and flow of politics. Responding to ongoing border conditions, the cybernetic border works through routines that adjust to existing intruder behaviors and Border Patrol resources. Consequently, the sociotechnical arrangements of border enforcement function in a permanent beta-model. Even when the border is but a prototype of human-machine configurations of enmity, it requires constant inquiry and challenge.

The hegemonic border technopolitical regime should not be understood as the simplification or the reduction of the situation of borders to an uncomplicated solution: data. Instead, it is an example of the vast and ever-growing apparatus necessary for the production of borders and the enactments of sovereignty. Data in this regime are not a singular element but an outwardly expanding amalgam connected to multiplying practices and procedures, people, organizations, technologies, and funding rationales. The cybernetic border is an assemblage of data and racial feedback loops that rather than reducing labor, multiply it. It requires ongoing research and development, recursive tinkering, testing, and redesign. Different senses like vision and touch are folded into the cybernetic border as data sources in the making of a sensory regime of control. Data here are not an end goal but an animating vector, a pulsating entity producing and being produced by sovereignty. Even when the cybernetic border fails to fulfill expectations set up by logics of cost-effectiveness or to supply reliable data for analyses of border metrics, the allure of its imperial promise permeates in the discourse of those who endorse, promote, fund, and constitute it. The flip side to the glare and presumed neatness of control emerging out of cybernetic routines is the actual disorder of things that are sovereign practices. In the networks of inscriptions discussed in this book, we do not find masterful and exhaustive understandings of matters of concern but impressionistic accounts animated by fear and hostility.

When I began preliminary research for this book in 2014, Barack Obama was president of the United States. Donald J. Trump was not yet a candidate for the presidency, and if he was ever mentioned, it was to be widely ridiculed as a fringe, racist character who demanded President Obama's birth certificate.[5] It was hard to foresee then where the country was collectively headed. On June 16, 2015, Trump formally announced his candidacy to become the 45th president of the United States. He spoke to followers, campaign officials, and the press about what soon became the staples of Trump's candidacy. Chief among these was representing border and immigration enforcement as fraught with problems. They were fraught because Trump imagined them as failing to "protect" the country. They failed to keep out and remove those he portrayed as constituting a threat. Though Trump expressed his animosity toward many other nationalities and regions, he reserved a particular vitriol against Mexicans in his announcement speech. He did not call them "enemies" outright, but it was hard to imagine that Trump saw them as something else if, as he told the US public, "they are not our friend, believe me." Marked as the opposite of "friend," migrating Mexicans were quickly characterized as "bringing drugs," "bringing crime," and being "rapists."[6] These familiar and racist tropes, among many others, have been historically mobilized to brand non-white populations in the United States as menaces to the nation.[7] During Trump's presidential bid announcement, Mexicans were quickly joined by people "coming from all over South and Latin America" as well as "from the Middle East." These varied populations not only were the targets of Trump's racist venom, but they continued to be treated as "enemies" to be managed.

In the process of branding Latina/o/es, Arabs, and Muslims as enemies, actors asked themselves why and how such a threat ought to be addressed. Trump's response in the campaign trail became an enduring and bonding leitmotif for conservatives and white supremacists alike: "We are going to take our country back."[8] In his statement, there was a sense of entitlement to a country that was slipping away from an imagined community. Control was lost to the unfriendly presence of an Other, implied here for its opposition to "us." "They" took away what belonged to "us." Such carefully vicious phrasing was coded language for how white "America" imagined itself losing its grip on the nation to non-white populations. To bring back control, Trump's administration would "build a great wall along the southern border," pursue a "total and complete shutdown of Muslims entering the United States," and deport millions of "undocumented immigrants."[9] Blockage, exclusion, and removal of the Other were the paradigms through which a Trump presidency would function. These were the promises Trump offered not just to his followers but to the wider US electorate. They became the foundational premises of a political project invested in enmity.

The Cybernetic Border helps understand the Trump presidency's animosity toward Latina/o/es, Arabs, and Muslims as part of longer historical and political maneuvers in the construction of the US empire-nation. The project traces how discourses of enmity, which were entangled with ideas about intrusion, have intensified across time. These discourses have fueled as well as relied on the design, development, and use of technologies that were thought to bring enemies under control. For Trump, the wall was the chief infrastructural device that would protect the nation. When the obduracy of nearly 2,000 miles of southern border became evident to Trump's campaign, his advocates transformed the promise of blocking structures into a "digital wall"—a network of devices that would "track and . . . prevent illegal immigration."[10] Anduril's Lattice system and its network of Sentry towers and unmanned aerial systems (UASs), funded by the Trump administration as much as by President Joe Biden, are but the latest iteration of the data-focused electronic fence. Theirs is a networked platform of enmity, a human-machine arrangement managing populations sorted as enemies of the nation.

To write about contemporary drones generally raises questions about vision—especially when engaging those UASs used by military and intelligence forces for combat and reconnaissance missions. The vision techniques programmed into Predator B drones were inexorably bound to the machine's design as an instrument of war.[11] It was meant to segment space into manageable quantities while fixing the system's sights—its "eyes" and its crosshairs—on pre-inscribed targets. In the context of the US-Mexico border, drone vision is fixated on types of subjects. "Mexicans," "other-than-Mexicans," and "persons from a special interest country" must be "seen" to be known so that they can be captured and removed from the United States. More succinctly, drones seek to invert the plane of the visible. Those who are imagined to be hidden from the border technopolitical regime—intruders—are now supposed to be visible to Border Patrol actors who hide themselves in the work done by drones flying high above the southern Arizona desert. The surveilled cannot watch the watchers. With drone manufacturers promising a persistent stare over targets, this kind of vertical vision hinges on relations of domination from "nowhere."[12]

Rather than continuing to emphasize the optics of drone warfare and its kill box, this book argues for an approach to drones and the border technopolitical regime as an infrastructural and epistemological organization of sovereignty.[13] We grasp their roles as sovereignty- and data-assembling entities when we situate drones as part of wider human-machine configurations that enact operational control and situational awareness. Drones are not a unified, stable whole. They draw together human operators, organizations, knowledge practices, assorted sensors and communications systems, and imaginaries. This arrangement, which I theorize as a regime, privileges data as its strategic vector of power. By insisting on describing sovereign practices as dominated through an ocular politics, we fail to grasp its networked and networking abstractions. Translating environments, subjects, and objects into data, drones and the cybernetic border are emblematic articulations of our digital present, which is also to say our digital past.

As networked platforms, drones and the cybernetic border tie together a vast web of entities, times, and spaces that ought to also be examined as matters of concern. Tending to their colonial persistence and their imperial obduracies creates openings to understand their situated enactments of racial formations. *The Cybernetic Border* troubles public understandings that thought US military and intelligence drone operations were limited to northern Africa, the Middle East, and South Asia. The US-Mexico border and the southern borderlands have figured prominently in the history of drone design, development, and use. And, contrary to claims about the militarization of the border, they show how military logics are integral to the empire-nation and its territorialized sovereignties. The same can be said of cybernetics and the intricacies of the closed world of computing. Often described and imagined in terms of World War II and the Cold War, there are unexplored histories about cybernetics and computing with regard to race and nation making. This book contributes to these conversations by examining the bounds of the US empire-nation where the cybernetic border has sought to institute and perpetuate a sensory regime anchored in relations of enmity.

And yet, not all drone vision is necessarily an imperial formation. Hobbyist and commercial UAS design, development, and use are a growing sphere of interest for drone scholars inside and outside the United States.[14] Similar to the works of Alex Rivera, Ian Alan Paul, Ricardo Dominguez, Jane Stevens, and Josh Begley, the art collective Postcommodity has sought to insert itself in existing human-machine configurations to imagine a different set of political valorizations. The collective offered an intriguing instance during which drone vision (see figure E.1) and border technopolitical regimes were mobilized in ways that ran counter to the machinations of empire and its investments in enmity.

The group, originally founded in 2007 in the US Southwest, has had a revolving cast of members devoted to exploring Indigenous representations. "While their largescale installations certainly involve the positionality and representation of Native peoples," Matthew Irwin's work documents, "they also tend to critique colonial structures—such as capitalism, globalism, and neoliberalism rather than lament the poor or sad Indian that has appeared in countless renderings."[15] In early October 2015, Postcommodity installed

FIGURE E.1. Postcommodity's "Repellent Fence" (2015). Image courtesy of the Postcommodity art collective.

twenty-six helium-filled balloons on the desert grounds of Douglas, Arizona, and Agua Prieta, Sonora. The balloons floated fifty feet over the ground in a display that offered a different articulation to the domineering inclinations of air power. These balloons did not search for "intruders" as did the Predator B UAS. Instead, they helped link the lands south and north of the US-Mexico border in visual and conceptual terms. As Postcommodity stated in the video of the land-art installation, the balloons were "a suture that stitches the peoples of the Americas together—symbolically demonstrating the interconnected-ness of the Western Hemisphere by recognizing the land, indigenous peoples, history, relationships, movement and communication."[16] These balloons produced together a new imagined community that spanned across the national boundary line and its structural manifestation: the border fence.

"Repellent Fence" (2015), as the installation was called, played around with the construction and use of technologies that would contest the operations of the US-Mexico border. The repellent fence was made from yellow balloons, each with a diameter of ten feet, that floated along a north/south axis for two miles. More importantly, they were anchored to the ground but were only connected to each other symbolically, by their similar designs. Only their uniformity and their relative proximity allowed spectators to symbolically connect the dots (or balloons). Each balloon had four sets of concentric circles that were red, blue, black, and gray with a black center. The balloon graphic design was inspired by "scare eye" balloons used to repel birds from fruit trees, gardens, or any area where they were not wanted. But what did this new repellent fence push away? The fact that the original scare-eye balloon was used to fend off birds and that Postcommodity's balloons floated fifty feet over the desert makes me think of "Repellent Fence" in relation to aerial surveillance. First, airplanes have been commonly called "birds" across history. Second, drone aircraft have been in use to patrol and surveil the border. But by enlarging the "scare eye" in these inflatable devices, Postcommodity produced balloons that could be imagined to repel the "birds" of the Border Patrol. In this sense, "Repellent Fence" speculated about the possibility of scaring away those entities involved in making national borders that separate people from each other.

The association between "Repellent Fence" and UASs was strengthened using drones that filmed the installation itself. The kind of drone vision articulated by Postcommodity sought to break away from, or perhaps scare away, its entanglements with empire and air power. The images were not of targeted subjects. They were not produced in anticipation that a feared "intruder" might cross the national boundary without authorization. There was no "God trick"; neither was there an appetite for a prey down below. Instead, drone vision here helped visualize the connections between the balloons across the border. In a gesture of its symbolic efficacy, it visualized connections between groups of people kept apart by the operation of the border technopolitical regime. This iteration of drone vision coincided with the way Irwin interpreted the colors of the "scare eye" on the balloons. Relying on interviews with the members of Postcommodity, Irwin concludes that, even though the idea of an "eye" had an implied sense of surveillance in much "Western" culture, "a 'scare eye' . . . has been recognized by Indigenous people all over the world as an 'open eye' or an eye of consciousness." The four colors in Navajo culture represented the emergence of four worlds into the present world. They represented an encounter. The video of the installation is now a historical document that chronicles this conceptual encounter. Hence, the drone eye as well as the balloons' scare eye are wide open. They produce a different past as they convene a turn toward another way of being and relating in the borderlands. In other words, these balloons, drones, and drone vision represented the making of a new consciousness, an autonomous sovereignty undoing the strictures of settler colonial and imperial formations.[17] Drone vision, as an Indigenous technology, offered spectators a glance into the possibility of undoing the persistence of the southern racial line and the unbearable endurance of enmity.

INTRODUCTION

1 Levy, "Inside Palmer Luckey's Bid."

2 Turner, "Reasons for Liking Tolkien."

3 Quoted in Levy, "Inside Palmer Luckey's Bid."

4 The usage of the category of "unauthorized border crosser" is not without its limitations and drawbacks. It names groups of people who traversed the borderlands beyond ports of entry. In stressing their lack of authorization to cross, I am inevitably acknowledging a sovereign power that grants access and permits people to move from one territorialized sovereign assemblage to another. Yet this should not be understood as if these actors themselves acknowledged such sovereign power; rather, it is the scholarly voice exerting its role in naming, recording, and analyzing their actions. Unauthorized border crossers were and continue to be part of the social reality of the United States, even when their inclusion, as Mae Ngai argues, "was also a legal impossibility." It is the insistence to maintain their legal impossibility that animates the machinations of the border's technological and political regime. Ngai, "Strange Career of the Illegal Alien," 89–90.

5 John Cheney-Lippold analyzes a similar dynamic in the production of what he calls algorithmic citizenship. Cheney-Lippold, "*Jus algoritmi.*"

6 Border walls and fences do not meet this boundary test and, as a result, fall outside the scope of this book, even if they underscore the ways that borders, as geopolitical demarcation lines, constitute the media of contemporary politics. This is what social scientist Peter Andreas calls "border games": the performative and audience-directed nature of border policing. Border games are not only coercive practices but communicative ones that prop up state claims to territorial authority and reaffirm the symbolic boundaries of the nation. Andreas, *Border Games*, xiv, 11, 143.

7 See, for example, Alvarez, *Border Land, Border Water*; Brown, *Walled States, Waning Sovereignties*; Díaz-Barriga and Dorsey, *Fencing in Democracy*; Fox, *Fence and the River*.

8 Many immigration enforcement techniques like identification cards or the use of artificial intelligence to monitor the profiles of migrants on social network sites confirm the hegemonic role assigned to information technologies. However, they all have their own distinct institutional practices and fall outside the duties and

responsibilities of Border Patrol agents. Instead, they are part of Immigration and Customs Enforcement. For more, see Amoore, "Biometric Borders"; Amoore and Hall, "Taking People Apart"; Biddle and Devereaux, "Peter Thiel's Palantir"; Browne, *Dark Matters* , chap. 4; Chaar López, "Alien Data"; Funk, "How ICE Picks Its Targets"; Haggerty and Ericson, "Surveillant Assemblage"; Horton and Heyman, *Paper Trails*; Magnet, *When Biometrics Fail*; Vukov and Sheller, "Border Work."

9 Mbembe, "Society of Enmity."

10 Mbembe, *Critique of Black Reason*, 55.

11 Kaplan, *Anarchy of Empire*, 13–15, 28.

12 St. John, *Line in the Sand*, 17.

13 De Lara, "Race, Algorithms, and the Work of Border Enforcement," 155; Molina, *Fit to Be Citizens?*; Ngai, *Impossible Subjects*, esp. chap. 1; and Stern, *Eugenic Nation*.

14 Bousquet, *Eye of War*, 64–65; Churchland, Ramachandran, and Sejnowski, "A Critique of Pure Vision"; Haraway, *Simians, Cyborgs, and Women*, 188–89.

15 Ostrow, "Bell Says Immigration Service Is 'Drowning'"; Sterba, "Electronic Vigil Fails."

16 Simpson, *Mohawk Interrupted*, 22.

17 Chávez-García, *States of Delinquency*; Lee, *At America's Gates*; Molina, *Fit to Be Citizens?*; Molina, *How Race Is Made in America*; Ngai, *Impossible Subjects*; Ramírez, "Making of Mexican Illegality"; Shah, *Contagious Divides*; Stern, *Eugenic Nation*.

18 Barnett, "Policing Peyote Country in the Early Twentieth Century"; Chavez, *Latino Threat*; Ettinger, *Imaginary Lines*; Hernández, *Migra!*; Inda, *Targeting Immigrants*; Jacoby, *Shadows at Dawn*; Lee, "Enforcing the Borders"; Massey, Durand, and Pren, "Why Border Enforcement Backfired"; Rosas, *Barrio Libre*.

19 Stern, "Buildings, Boundaries, and Blood."

20 Stern, "Buildings, Boundaries, and Blood," 52 (emphasis in original).

21 Stern, "Buildings, Boundaries, and Blood," 81.

22 Shah, *Contagious Divides*, 6–7.

23 Inda, *Targeting Immigrants*, 3, 5–8.

24 Cacho, *Social Death*, 6, 8, 17.

25 Inda, *Targeting Immigrants*, 25.

26 Hacking, "Biopower."

27 Hecht, *Radiance of France*, 16.

28 Hecht, *Radiance of France*, 17.

29 Foucault, *Birth of Biopolitics*, 19–20.

30 Weheliye, *Habeas Viscus*, 12–15.

31 Stoler, "On Degrees of Imperial Sovereignty," 128.

32 Benjamin, "Introduction," 5.

33 In the United States, "race" is inexorably entangled with the settler colonial project whereby Indigenous populations, imagined as uncivilized non-white populations, are dispossessed and displaced with the aims of establishing colonial and, subsequently, postcolonial sovereignty. It is also tethered to the violent system of

chattel slavery that treated Black bodies as nonhuman, commodity-producing commodities—simultaneously disposable and exploitable. Byrd, *Transit of Empire*; Day, "Being or Nothingness"; Goldstein, "Where the Nation Takes Place"; Johnson, *Soul by Soul*; Robinson, *Black Marxism*; Smallwood, *Saltwater Slavery*; Wang, *Carceral Capitalism*; Wolfe, "Land, Labor, and Difference."

34 Chun, "Introduction," 10.

35 Omi and Winant, *Racial Formation in the United States*, 107–8, 125.

36 Chun, "Introduction," 8 (emphasis in original); Coleman, "Race as Technology."

37 Fojas, *Border Optics*, 94–121; Paredes, *"With His Pistol in His Hand."*

38 Nakamura, *Digitizing Race*, 11.

39 Sharma, *Home Rule*, 3–4.

40 Stoler, *Duress*, 177–78.

41 Bratton, *The Stack*, 20.

42 The work of surveillance scholars Tamara Vukov and Mimi Sheller informs my understanding of border enforcement as relying on technological forms of mediation. They described border enforcement in the early 2000s as made through rationales of logistics, or the securitization of flows rather than a single borderline. In that sense, twenty-first-century border enforcement is modular—an ever-shifting and mobile regime of control attendant to the movements of its objects (e.g., bodies, populations, and data assemblages). Vukov and Sheller, "Border Work."

43 Bousquet, *Eye of War*, 8.

44 Bratton, *The Stack*, 97.

45 My understanding of "infrastructures" is indebted to the work of Geoffrey Bowker and Susan Leigh Star, who posit that infrastructures consist of both static and dynamic elements of equal importance in the functioning of a system. They are the underlying features of a system that allow it to work—its practices, people, institutions, ideas, artifacts, and relations. They are situated sociotechnical entanglements designed and configured with prescribed objectives. Infrastructures are sets of pervasive and enabling resources brought together through a series of relations around objects and subjects. Bowker et al., "Toward Information Infrastructure Studies," 98–99; Star and Ruhleder, "Steps towards an Ecology of Infrastructure," 253.

46 Andreas, *Border Games*; Dunn, *Militarization of the US-Mexico Border*; Brownell, "Border Militarization"; Fojas, *Border Optics*, 68–69; Nevins, *Operation Gatekeeper and Beyond*.

47 For Operation Wetback, see Hernández, *Migra!*, 184–91. For militarization in the early twentieth century, see Alvarez, *Border Land, Border Water*, 54–62; Levario, *Militarizing the Border*; St. John, *Line in the Sand*, 119–47. For militarization through US fortifications and military appropriation of Indigenous knowledge-making practices, see Schaeffer, *Unsettled Borders*.

48 Fojas, *Border Optics*, 95.

49 Levario, *Militarizing the Border*, 2–3.

50 Neocleous, *A Critical Theory of Police Power*.

51 Blackhawk, *Violence over the Land*; Jacoby, *Shadows at Dawn*; St. John, *Line in the Sand*, 39–62.

52 Scholars that study contemporary border making stress the role of the politics of death. The necropolitics of border enforcement create the conditions whereby unauthorized border crossers, disposed of their rights and protections, become killable during their attempt to enter US territory. De León, *Land of Open Graves*, 68. For more on this topic, see Boyce and Chambers, "Corral Apparatus"; Chambers et al., "Mortality, Surveillance, and the Tertiary 'Funnel Effect'"; Díaz-Barriga and Dorsey, *Fencing in Democracy*; Doty, "Bare Life"; Rosas, "Necro-Subjection."

53 Edwards, *Closed World*, 239–73.

54 Beniger, *Control Revolution*.

55 Franklin, *Control*, xviii.

56 Heims, *Constructing a Social Science*; Kline, *Cybernetics Moment*; Leslie, *Cold War and American Science*.

57 Galison, "Ontology of the Enemy," 232.

58 Galison, "Ontology of the Enemy," 233.

59 Galison, "Ontology of the Enemy," 264.

60 Galison, "Ontology of the Enemy," 230.

61 Haraway, *Simians, Cyborgs, and Women*, 149–81; Hayles, *How We Became Posthuman*.

62 Campbell-Kelly et al., *Computer*; Ceruzzi, *History of Modern Computing*; Edwards, *Closed World*.

63 Halpern, *Beautiful Data*; Light, *From Warfare to Welfare*; Medina, *Cybernetic Revolutionaries*.

64 Chandler, *Unmanning*, 60–80; Wagner, *Lightning Bugs and Other Reconnaissance Drones*.

65 Chandler, *Unmanning*, 39, 134.

66 DHS is also using small UASs after President Donald Trump escalated the fabrication of enmity by the border technopolitical regime in 2017. These small drones used in border enforcement, however, are still on an experimental basis. Fang and Biddle, "Google AI Tech"; Levy, "Inside Palmer Luckey's Bid."

67 DHS, "Privacy Impact Assessment for the Aircraft Systems."

68 The US CBP has considered arming Predator B UASs with nonlethal weapons, though they have not yet moved forward with it. Lynch, "Customs and Border Protection Considered Weaponizing Drones." UASs are part of the Border Patrol strategy of "prevention through deterrence," which human rights reports and scholarly research shows is linked with the deaths of unauthorized border crossers. Chambers et al., "Mortality, Surveillance, and the Tertiary 'Funnel Effect'"; De León, *Land of Open Graves*; Jimenez, *Humanitarian Crisis*.

69 Chamayou, *A Theory of the Drone*.

70 Delmont, "Drone Encounters"; Gregory, "Drone Geographies"; Pugliese, *State Violence and the Execution of Law*; Shaw, *Predator Empire*.

71 Chandler, *Unmanning*, 5.

72 Antoine Bousquet's *Eye of War* also engages drones as part of a larger information infrastructure that he calls the logistics of perception.

73 DOJ, INS, *Annual Report of the Immigration and Naturalization Service for 1973*, 9; Chapman, "Illegal Aliens.

74 Rachel St. John writes in *Line in the Sand* about "how a line in the sand became a conditional barrier between two nations and their people." Analyzing their hegemonic genres sheds light on their distinct sociotechnical entanglements and the politics they made possible.

75 The border technopolitical regime might seem similar to what those in the social sciences call the homeland security–industrial complex (HSIC). After the attacks of 9/11, a partnership between government, the military, and private interests in the United States set the course for state policy in national security and public safety. This complex, according to sociologist Michael Welch, was created in "response to growing concern and anxiety over the threat of terrorism." Some of the actors involved in the operations of the complex are border wall contractors, electronic surveillance contractors, private detention center operators, and the Border Patrol. This partnership can be said to be a variation on a theme that political scientists like Gordon Adams have long described as an "iron triangle." Like in the iron triangle, participants in the HSIC share common values, interests, and perceptions about the threats to the nation and what is needed for its defense. The outcome is a blurring of distinctions between private and public interests that leads to a sector of the defense industry appropriating government authority.

There are two key differences between the HSIC and the border technopolitical regime. First is that the former is a post-9/11 political formation, whereas the latter helps explain broader historical processes associated with border making in the United States. The organizing ideas, techniques, and styles of border technopolitical regimes shift; at times, multiple regimes might overlap, reinforce, or contradict one another. One could speak, for example, of the hegemony of the medicalized regime of the late nineteenth and early twentieth centuries, which treated Chinese and Mexicans as sources of racial impurity for the US nation. The HSIC cannot offer insight into the heterogeneous set of social practices, discourses, actors, and techniques enacting and enforcing the boundaries of the nation—on land and bodies—during these periods.

The second difference is that the border technopolitical regime does not presume to speak a priori of a unity; it requires the rigorous tracing of relations and conditions that change in time. Here is where the association of the border technopolitical regime to the metaphor of a "regime"—that which produces, orders, and governs regularities—expands its concerns beyond HSIC's privileging of political economic ones. In this sense, the border technopolitical regime allows for an examination that is not limited by time period or the profit motive. Instead, it sheds light on how government and military officials, technicians, and the broader public engaged ideas, technological artifacts, and institutions in the creation of territory and social space in different moments in time. Perhaps more importantly, the concept stresses an analysis of the construction of subjects and objects of knowledge (e.g., people, categories, ideas), of infrastructural and economic arrangements, and of sociopolitical visions in the making of the nation. For more, see Adams, *Politics of Defense Contracting*; Chaar López, "Alien Data"; Heyman, "Capitalism and US Policy at the Mexican Border"; Rana, "Racial Infrastructure of the Terror-Industrial Complex"; Risen, *Pay Any Price*, xiv–xvi; Uchitelle and Markoff, "Terrorbusters, Inc."; Welch, "Seeking a Safer Society."

76 Masco, *Nuclear Borderlands*, 14, 44, 345.

77 Law, *Aircraft Stories*, 2–3.

78 Heyman, "Putting Power in the Anthropology of Bureaucracy," 262. For more on the anthropology of bureaucracy, see Ackleson, "Securing through Technology?"; Ackleson, "Border Security in Risk Society" and "Constructing Security"; Heyman, "United States Surveillance over Mexican Lives," "US Ports of Entry," and "Constructing a Virtual Wall."

79 Stoler, *Along the Archival Grain*, 29.

80 Galison, "Removing Knowledge," 231.

81 Pandya, "Vanishing Act," 105.

82 Law, *Aircraft Stories*, 21–35.

83 Latour and Johnson, "Mixing Humans and Nonhumans Together," 304–5.

84 Latour and Johnson, "Mixing Humans and Nonhumans Together," 307.

85 Weheliye, *Habeas Viscus*, 4.

86 Stoler, *Along the Archival Grain*, 29; Weld, *Paper Cadavers*, 6.

87 I am grateful here for the work of Kirsten Weld and what she calls archival thinking as a way to grapple with how archives were and continue to be tools of/for political action, enablers of gaze and desire, and sites of social struggle. See Weld, *Paper Cadavers*.

88 Stoler, *Along the Archival Grain*, 53.

89 Gordon, *Ghostly Matters*, 17.

90 Net discretionary funding data can be found in "Budget-in-Brief" statements published yearly by the DHS. DHS, "Budget-in-Brief Fiscal Year 2006," and "FY 2022 Budget-in-Brief."

1. SCRIPTING THE FRONTIER

1 DOD, Office of Public Affairs, "Navy's 4th Annual Air Weapons Meet."

2 Chandler, *Unmanning*, 7.

3 Joseph Masco makes a similar argument about the atomic bomb's materiality and semiotic dimensions; it was and continues to be a "world-making and world-breaking" artifact. See Masco, *Nuclear Borderlands*.

4 Chandler demonstrates this point masterfully in her book on *Unmanning*. Lucy Suchman makes a parallel, though different, argument about how the drone target is constructed through the boundary distinction between friend and enemy, as if it is merely a technical operation and not a political decision. See Suchman, "Situational Awareness."

5 Latour and Johnson, "Mixing Humans and Nonhumans Together," 304–5.

6   Hall, "Encoding and Decoding."
7   Suchman, *Human-Machine Reconfigurations*, 187.
8   Cited in Chandler, *Unmanning*, 42.
9   Chandler, *Unmanning*, 21.
10 Chandler, *Unmanning*, 17.
11 New York Times, "Another Attempt to Solve Aerial Navigation Problem";
    New York Times, "Flying Machine."
12 Kaplan, *Aerial Aftermaths*, 11.
13 For diverse explorations of air power and aerospace by historians, anthropolo-
    gists, and STS scholars, see Boyer, *By the Bomb's Early Light*; Call, *Selling Air
    Power*; Ceruzzi, *Beyond the Limits*; Hippler, *Bombing the People*; Mets, *Air
    Campaign*; Law, *Aircraft Stories*; Mindell, *Digital Apollo*; Sherry, *Rise of American
    Air Power*; Warner, "Douhet, Mitchell, Seversky"; Westwick, *Blue Sky Metropolis*.
14 Douhet, *Command of the Air*, 23.
15 Masco, *Nuclear Borderlands*, 45.
16 Kaplan, *Anarchy of Empire*; Stoler, "On Degrees of Imperial Sovereignty."
17 Mitchell, *Winged Defense*, 4.
18 Nurick, "Distinction between Combatant and Noncombatant," 680.
19 Mitchell, *Winged Defense*, 4, 19; Mitchell, "Give America Airplanes," LOC.
20 Mitchell, "Give America Airplanes," LOC.
21 Shah, *Contagious Divides*, 12, 119.
22 Ngai, *Impossible Subjects*, 7.
23 Lee, "Enforcing the Borders," 62–63.
24 Mitchell, "Give America Airplanes," LOC.
25 Kaplan, *Aerial Aftermaths*, 14.
26 Lefebvre, "Space and the State," 224.
27 State Department document, cited in New York Times, "Rumor of Recall of
    Troops False."
28 Atlanta Constitution, "Hard Flying for Aviators with Pershing Expedition";
    Keehr, "Air Power in Mexico"; Washington Post, "Need of Aeroplanes."
29 Chávez-García, *States of Delinquency*; Lira, *Laboratory of Deficiency*; Molina, *Fit
    to Be Citizens?*, 46–74; Stern, "Buildings, Boundaries, and Blood."
30 Cited in Bokovoy, *San Diego World's Fairs*, 23.
31 San Diego Chamber of Commerce, *Aviation Industry Looks to San Diego!*
32 Carpio, *Collisions at the Crossroads*, 22–23.
33 This argument builds on Jackie Wang's claim that Black racialization follows a
    double logic of disposability and exploitability to contend with processes bound
    to the profit motive as much as beyond it. Wang, *Carceral Capitalism*, 88.
34 I mobilize "structure of feeling" as articulated by Raymond Williams, who defines
    it as a set of social experiences through which meanings and values were actively
    felt as they were simultaneously related to systematic beliefs and forms of mean-
    ing making. Williams, "Structures of Feeling," 128–35.
35 Wolfe, "Land, Labor, and Difference," 868.
36 Casanovas, *Bread or Bullets*; Martínez, "Settler Colonialism in New Spain."

37 Day, *Alien Capital*, 25.

38 The subject position of ethnic Mexicans in the borderlands and in relation to settler colonialism merits clarification. Their presence in the northern states of Mexico was part of ongoing settler colonial projects displacing, dispossessing, and exploiting Indigenous communities. Continuing the practices of Spanish settler colonialism, Indigenous labor was exploited, Wolfe shows, "in spite of rather than as a result of the primary tendency of settler-colonial policy" to replace "natives on their land." Native surplus labor was integral to Spanish and Mexican settler colonialism. The logics of exclusion and elimination were complicated by encounters between competing settler colonial projects in the nineteenth century in the southern borderlands. The newly independent state of Mexico struggled, just as the previous Spanish colonial territories did, to defend its parsed-out land claims from the actions of Indigenous communities that fought for their survival and against the logic of elimination. The Mexican state enrolled the help of US settlers to enforce the boundaries of the nation—which, paradoxically, were undone when Texas independence was proclaimed in 1836 and in the aftermath of the US-Mexican War. Decades later, even as Indigenous peoples took up arms within the Mexican revolutionary ranks, Rosaura Sánchez and Beatrice Pita argue, settler colonial practices persisted as settlers on both sides of the border fought for the preservation of their sovereign rule. The intellectual class (lettered and artisan) during the Mexican Revolution did, however, promote an ethnicized vision of the Mexican nation-state that integrated Indigeneity into its national identity formation. Yet, as Rick López's work demonstrates, enduring struggles over land and political rights in postrevolutionary Mexico did not undo but rather reified the nation-state's settler colonialism. See Carpio, *Collisions at the Crossroads*; López, *Crafting Mexico*; Sánchez and Pita, "Rethinking Settler Colonialism," 1046–50; Wolfe, "Land, Labor, and Difference," 868.

39 M'Groarty, "History Is Repeated."

40 Davis, Mayhew, and Miller, *Under the Perfect Sun*.

41 Los Angeles Times, "Harkness Flies over the Line."

42 See, for example, Estades Font, *Presencia militar de Estados Unidos*; Joseph, LeGrand, and Donato Salvatore, *Close Encounters of Empire*; Kramer, *Blood of Government*; LaFeber, *Inevitable Revolutions*.

43 Los Angeles Times, "San Diego."

44 Los Angeles Times, "Curtiss to Conduct Aerial Experiments"; Kurutz, "Only Safe and Sane Method."

45 "Learn to Fly," SDASM.

46 "Learn to Fly," SDASM.

47 Los Angeles Times, "Uncle Sam's Aviation Experts"; Los Angeles Times, "Feat Solves Difficult Problem."

48 Leslie, "Spaces for the Space Age"; Rainger, "Constructing a Landscape for Postwar Science"; Davis, Mayhew, and Miller, *Under the Perfect Sun*, 46–47; Shragge, "'A New Federal City,'" 339.

49 Morin, "Lindbergh Winging His Way."

50 Among the factors contributing to the growth of aviation in Southern California: the amenable climate, the open shop movement, the vast network of key military bases, and the establishment in Los Angeles of the western terminals for all the transcontinental airlines. Crowe, "March of Finance"; Scott, "Aerospace-Electronics Industrial Complex," 441.

51 Allen and Schneider, *Industrial Relations in the California Aircraft Industry*, 5; Ryan Reporter, "R&D," 43; Ryan Reporter, "Fledgling Wings."

52 New York Times, "Explosion!"; Call, *Selling Air Power*, esp. chap. 2.

53 Ryan Reporter, "Birthplace of the Atomic Age."

54 Department of the Army, "Push-Button Warfare," 2.

55 Plotnick, "Predicting Push-Button Warfare," 658.

56 Hine, *Populuxe*, 128.

57 Plotnick, "Predicting Push-Button Warfare," 658–61.

58 New York Times, "Penalty of Weakness."

59 Los Angeles Times, "Only 10 Years to Push-Button Warfare."

60 Edwards, *Closed World*, 70–71.

61 Edwards, *Closed World*, 65.

62 Ryan Aeronautical, "Target Plane," SDASM.

63 Wright-Patterson Air Force Base, "XQ-2 Aerial Target," SDASM.

64 For pre-1948 drones, see Chandler, *Unmanning*, chap. 1 and 2; Newcome, *Unmanned Aviation*; Rothstein, *Drone*, chap. 2.

65 The Firebee went through multiple variations and modifications throughout its development and use. The descriptions included here are meant to give the reader a sense of the dimensions of this semiautonomous aircraft more than offer a fixed set of characteristics. Warren, "History of the Q-2," SDASM; Ryan Reporter, "Drone Design," 1.

66 New York Times, "Jet to Power Targets"; New York Times, "Ryan to Make Pilotless Jets"; Wall Street Journal, "New Ryan Aeronautical Order"; Los Angeles Times, "$3.9 Million in Orders to Ryan."

67 Los Angeles Times, "Robot Plane for Target Use Unveiled"; New York Times, "Jet to Power Targets."

68 Hale, "Equipment, Facilities, and Techniques," SDASM; Ryan Reporter, "Jet Bull's-Eye," 22.

69 Ryan Reporter, "Bee with the Electronic Brain," 13.

70 Edwards, *Closed World*; Turner, *From Counterculture to Cyberculture*.

71 Chandler, *Unmanning*, 61.

72 Chandler, *Unmanning*, 64.

73 Sands, "Guided Missile Development," 24.

74 Atanasoski and Vora, *Surrogate Humanity*, 90–91.

75 Ryan Reporter, "Under Arrest," 4–5; Ryan Reporter, "Q-2 Away"; Ryan Reporter, "Bee with the Electronic Brain"; Ryan Reporter, "Birthplace of the Atomic Age," 2–5; Ryan Reporter, "Ryan High-Speed Targets."

76 Aune, "Euthanasia Politics and the Indian Wars"; Chandler, *Unmanning*, 88–89; Edgington, *Range Wars*, 24–30. On US military settlements and practices in

New Mexico and their relation to Indigenous peoples, see Genay, *Land of Nuclear Enchantment*; Huggins, "Terrorism on the Great Plains"; Masco, *Nuclear Borderlands*; Myers, "Military Establishments in Southwestern New Mexico." On settler colonial logics, see Wolfe, "Land, Labor, and Difference."

77   Ryan Reporter, "Firebee Tops New Building," 11.

78   My understanding of plans and situations builds on the work of Suchman, *Human-Machine Reconfigurations*, 31, 52.

79   Callander, "Ground Observer Corps."

80   Wilson, "Tyndall Story," 12.

81   General Curtis E. LeMay, cited in Ryan Aeronautical, "Ryan Firebee at Project William Tell," SDASM.

82   Ryan Aeronautical, "Ryan Firebee," SDASM; Los Angeles Times, "Robot Plane for Target Use Unveiled."

83   Deloria, *Playing Indian*, 105.

84   DOD, Joint Chiefs of Staff, *A Dictionary*, 116.

85   Ryan Reporter, "Ryan Firebee at Project William Tell."

86   Ryan Reporter, "Pushbutton Targets," 4.

87   Ryan Reporter, "Firebee: 'Enemy' Jet."

88   Hale, "Equipment, Facilities and Techniques," SDASM; Ryan Reporter, "Drone Design."

89   Ryan Reporter, "Ryan Firebee at Project William Tell."

90   Ryan Reporter, "Ryan Firebee at Project William Tell."

91   Curry, "4756th Drone Squadron," SDASM.

92   Edwards, *Closed World*, 75.

93   Brotherton, "Firebees Test America's Defense Shield," 24; Ryan Reporter, "Big Apple," 5.

94   "F 2666 Operation Top Gun," YouTube video.

95   See, for example, Ryan Reporter, "Q-2 Away," cover, 14–15; Ryan Reporter, "Drone Design," 1; Ryan Reporter, "Fast and Versatile"; Ryan Reporter, "Nikes Fired at Ryan Firebee," 3; Ryan Reporter, "Another Reason," back cover; Ryan Reporter, "Ryan Firebee Sets New Records"; Mallan, "Firebee Chase," cover, 1; Ryan Reporter, "Another Example," back cover.

96   Schaeffer, *Unsettled Borders*, 57.

97   Law, *Aircraft Stories*, 121–25.

98   Chandler, *Unmanning*, 88–89.

99   Brown, "Logic of Settler Colonialism."

100 Naval Aviation News, "Navy's Pioneer Aviators Meet on the Forrestal"; Air Force, "Pioneer in Supersonic Flight," 16; Ryan Reporter, "Pioneering Ten"; Ryan Reporter, "This Is the Airplane Division," 5; Van Wyen, "Pioneer Airmen at Pensacola."

101 Guidotti-Hernández, *Unspeakable Violence*.

102 "F 2666 Operation Top Gun," YouTube video.

103 Ryan Reporter, "Operation 'Top Gun.'"

104 "F 2666 Operation Top Gun," YouTube video.

105 Mindell, *Between Human and Machine*, 22–23.

106 "William Tell (1965)," YouTube video.

107 Hämäläinen and Truett, "On Borderlands," 342.

108 There are a variety of versions of the William Tell story that qualify or modify each character's role, place of residence, and relation to each other. The complexity of these stories, however, is beyond the focus of this chapter. For more information, see Lerner, "William Tell's Atlantic Travels."

109 "William Tell (1965)," YouTube video.

110 Ward, "Meaning of Lindbergh's Flight," 9.

111 For more on the history of the Texas Rangers, see Hernández, *Migra!*; Johnson, *Revolution in Texas*; and St. John, *Line in the Sand*.

112 Fitzgerald, "White Savior and His Junior Partner," 98.

113 "Lone Ranger 1949–1957," YouTube video.

114 Schaeffer, *Unsettled Borders*, 8, 35.

115 Ngai, *Impossible Subjects*, 128.

116 Hernández, "Crimes and Consequences of Illegal Immigration," 423, 430. For more information on earlier manifestations of air power on the US-Mexico border, see Vanderwood and Samponaro, *Border Fury*.

117 Immigration and Nationality Act of 1952.

118 See, for example, Lee, *At America's Gates*; Ngai, "Strange Career of the Illegal Alien"; Plascencia, "'Undocumented' Mexican Migrant Question."

119 Ngai, *Impossible Subjects*, 127–66; De Genova, "Legal Production of Mexican/Migrant 'Illegality,'" 161. See also Ramírez, "Making of Mexican Illegality."

120 Suchman, *Human-Machine Reconfigurations*, 15–16.

121 Atanasoski and Vora, *Surrogate Humanity*, 9–10.

122 For a universal description of the posthuman, see Hayles, *How We Became Posthuman*. For the posthuman figure of the cyborg as a situated arrangement, see Haraway, "A Cyborg Manifesto" in *Simians, Cyborgs, and Women*.

123 See Hecht and Edwards, *The Technopolitics of Cold War* , in which the authors invite STS scholars and historians to go beyond geopolitical paradigms to understand Cold War technoscience.

2. AUTOMATING BOUNDARIES

1 Sterba, "Electronic Vigil."

2 I and N Reporter, "First Fifty Years," 2.

3 Salazar, "Thousands Cross Border."

4 DOJ, INS, *Annual Report of the Immigration and Naturalization Service for 1973*, 8–9.

5 "Border Patrol," USCIS.

6 Seitz, "Border Patrol at Work," 36.

7 McLuhan, *Understanding Media*, 56–60.

8 Hacking, "Making Up People."

9 Beller, *World Computer*, 13.

10   Clawson, "US Testing Sensors."

11   Galison, "Removing Knowledge."

12   Ngai, *Impossible Subjects*, 27.

13   Ngai, *Impossible Subjects*, 6.

14   Molina, "Constructing Mexicans as Deportable Immigrants."

15   Immigration Act of 1882, sec. 2.

16   DOJ, INS, *Annual Report of the Immigration and Naturalization Service for 1973*, 9.

17   Molina, "Constructing Mexicans as Deportable Immigrants," 659.

18   David Montejano sheds light on the negotiations between class segments of the Anglo community that led to the increasing presence of Mexicans as farm labor during the 1920s and 1940s. Montejano, *Anglos and Mexicans in the Making of Texas*, 179–96.

19   Hacking, "Biopower," 280.

20   Bowker and Star, *Sorting Things Out*, 10.

21   Bowker and Star, *Sorting Things Out*, 41.

22   Inda, *Targeting Immigrants*, 25.

23   Inda, *Targeting Immigrants*, 80.

24   Cohen, *Braceros*, 6.

25   Hernández, *Migra!*, 103, 222.

26   DOJ, INS, *Annual Report of the Immigration and Naturalization Service for the Year Ended June 30, 1949*, 38.

27   Kang, *INS on the Line*, 105. Kitty Calavitta previously made a similar argument while Deborah Cohen shows how the Border Patrol effectively opened the border to satisfy grower demands and reduce agricultural labor costs. See Calavitta, *Inside the State*; Cohen, *Braceros*, 203–5.

28   DOJ, INS, *Annual Report of the Immigration and Naturalization Service for the Fiscal Year Ended June 30, 1947*, 24.

29   DOJ, INS, *Annual Report of the Immigration and Naturalization Service 1966*, 12.

30   Cohen, *Braceros*, 45–46. Alexandra Minna Stern shows an earlier racialization and bordering of Mexicans as neither white nor Black through public health discourses. Stern, "Buildings, Boundaries, and Blood."

31   Lassiter, "Pushers, Victims, and the Lost Innocence."

32   Treviño, "Mexican Americans and the War on Narcotics."

33   Inda, *Targeting Immigrants*, 175.

34   For the biopolitical management of Mexican life in the United States, see Marez, *Drug Wars*; Stern, *Eugenic Nation*; Molina, *Fit to Be Citizens?*; Hernández, *Migra!*; and Chávez-García, *States of Delinquency*.

35   For more on the war on drugs and migration, see Gootenberg, *Andean Cocaine*; Marez, *Drug Wars*; Timmons, "Trump's Wall at Nixon's Border."

36   Alexander, *New Jim Crow*; Lassiter, "Impossible Criminals." Processes of racial criminalization have significantly longer histories. See Muhammad, *Condemnation of Blackness*.

37   The Globe and Mail, "Nixon Declares Electronic War on Drug-Smuggling from Mexico"; Anderson and Whitten, "US Losing Drug-Smuggling War";

New York Times, "Immigration Head Voices Alarm"; Holles, "Hundreds of Mexican Children Cross Border."

38 Cohen, *Braceros*. Others show that, despite border enforcement efforts, Mexican migrations during and after the end of the Bracero Program were circular; see Massey, Durand, and Pren, "Why Border Enforcement Backfired." For more on the Bracero Program, see Calavitta, *Inside the State*; Loza, *Defiant Braceros*; Rosas, *Abrazando el espíritu*; Kang, *INS on the Line*.

39 Williams, "Illegal Aliens Win a Beachhead."

40 Chapman, "Illegal Aliens," 188.

41 Chavez, *Latino Threat*.

42 I and N Reporter, "Introducing Leonard F. Chapman."

43 Tichenor, *Dividing Lines*, 29.

44 "Biography," USCIS.

45 Rosenblueth, Wiener, and Bigelow, "Behavior, Purpose, Teleology," 19; Wiener, "Cybernetics," 14; Wiener, *Cybernetics*, 6–7.

46 Turner, *From Counterculture to Cyberculture*, 22.

47 Rosenblueth, Wiener, and Bigelow, "Behavior, Purpose, Teleology," 18.

48 Halpern, *Beautiful Data*, 46.

49 Wiener, *Human Use of Human Beings*, 12; Chaar López, "Latina/o/e Technoscience."

50 For more on the Macy Foundation conference, see Heims, *Constructing a Social Science*.

51 Wiener, *Cybernetics*, 18.

52 Heims, *Constructing a Social Science*, 22; Shannon, "A Mathematical Theory of Communication." For a nuanced account of the relation between Norbert Wiener and Claude Shannon's work, see Kline, *Cybernetics Moment*.

53 See, for example, Bateson, *Steps to an Ecology of Mind*; Colomina, "Enclosed by Images"; Halpern, *Beautiful Data*; Heims, *Constructing a Social Science*; Kline, *Cybernetics Moment*.

54 Bateson, *Steps to an Ecology of Mind*, 276.

55 Halpern, *Beautiful Data*, 61.

56 Roney, "Memorandum for Marian Smith, Historian," USCIS.

57 Aplin and Schoderbek, "A Cybernetic Model of the MBO Process," 19.

58 DOJ, INS, *Annual Report of the Immigration and Naturalization Service 1976*, 3.

59 Colomina, "Enclosed by Images," 18.

60 Haraway, *Simians, Cyborgs, and Women*, 188.

61 For more on the performance of loops in system diagrams, see Law, *Aircraft Stories*, 26–29.

62 Halpern, *Beautiful Data*, 24.

63 Ali, "Race," 100.

64 Omi and Winant, *Racial Formation in the United States*.

65 Ali, "Race," 100.

66 Ali, "Race," 93.

67 Royal, "In-Service Training Programs," 17.

68 Turner, "Signcutting and Aerial Observation," USCIS.

69 I and N Reporter, "First Fifty Years," 12.

70 Deloria, *Playing Indian*.

71 Schaeffer, *Unsettled Borders*, 6–7.

72 Schaeffer, *Unsettled Borders*, 38–42, 54.

73 Aune, *Indian Wars Everywhere*, 4.

74 Niebuhr, "False Claims to United States Citizenship"; Merkel, "Mobile Operational Communications"; Vandersall, "Steps to a Better Records System"; Clawson, "US Testing Sensors"; Meyer, "Aliens Hard to Count"; New York Times, "Immigration Head Voices Alarm"; Hunter, "Immigration Agency Engulfed in Trouble"; Jones, "Border Patrol"; Ostrow, "Bell Says Immigration Service Is 'Drowning.'"

75 Klemcke, "Role of the Communications Operator," 29.

76 Edwards, *Closed World*, 131.

77 "Records Administration and Information Branch," February 4, 1969, in DOJ, INS, "Authorization and Budget Request for the Congress" [for FY 1974], USCIS. For more on "alien files," see Chaar López, "Alien Data."

78 Williams, "Illegal Aliens Win a Beachhead"; Reston, "'Silent Invasion.'"

79 Time, "Technology: The Cybernated Generation," 85.

80 Edwards, *Closed World*, 72.

81 On the links between cybernetics, computers, governmentality, and biopolitics, see Halpern, *Beautiful Data*.

82 Interventionism, though contested, has persisted since the nineteenth century; see Joseph, LeGrand, and Salvatore, *Close Encounters of Empire*; Kramer, *Blood of Government*.

83 New York Times, "Escalation"; Sheehan, "Infiltration Rise Seen If Raids End"; Blumenthal, "'69 Infiltration to South Vietnam." For research on this topic, see Edwards, *Closed World*, 3–5, 113–45.

84 Hartt, "McNamara's Viet Wall."

85 *Investigation into Electronic Battlefield Program*; Edwards, *Closed World*, 3, 65; Comptroller General of the United States, "Cost and Effectiveness of Electronic Sensor and Surveillance Systems"; Mitgang, "Sensors Don't Bleed."

86 *Investigation into Electronic Battlefield Program*, 11.

87 Mitgang, "Sensors Don't Bleed."

88 Mitgang, "Sensors Don't Bleed."

89 Edwards, *Closed World*, 114.

90 Hartt, "McNamara's Viet Wall."

91 Schaeffer, *Unsettled Borders*, 4.

92 Smith, *Fort Huachuca*, 318–19; *Department of Defense Appropriations for 1961*.

93 Hartt, "McNamara's Viet Wall."

94 Sterba, "Close-Up of the Grunt"; Lifton, "'Gook Syndrome' and 'Numbed Warfare.'"

95 Chong, *Oriental Obscene*, 98.

96 Beecher, "Sensor 'Seal' around Vietnam Studied."

97 "Border Patrol," USCIS; *Investigation into Electronic Battlefield Program,* 3–14.

98 McLucas, *Reflections of a Technocrat,* 55–56; Stodola, *Line Intrusion Detector.*

99 Freeman, *MIT Lincoln Laboratory.*

100 DOJ, INS, "Authorization and Budget Request for the Congress" [for FY 1976], USCIS. The budget for INS in 1962 was around $62 million; in 1970, it was $104 million; and by 1978, it was $275 million. Congressional Budget Office, "Trends in Federal Spending," 9.

101 Cited in Clawson, "US Testing Sensors."

102 Shaw, *Predator Empire,* 89–90. For an account of MITRE Corporation's diversification in the civilian sector during the period of escalation and de-escalation in Vietnam, see Meisel, Jacobs, and MITRE Corporation, *MITRE, The First Twenty Years,* 120–29.

103 DOJ, INS, *Annual Report of the Immigration and Naturalization Service 1976,* 2.

104 I and N Reporter, "First Fifty Years."

105 Frankel, "INS Research and Development Programs," 33.

106 Frankel, "INS Research and Development Programs," 33.

107 DHS, *Department of Homeland Security Border Security Metrics Report,* 12.

108 Seitz, "Border Patrol at Work," 34.

109 GAO, "Problems and Options in Estimating the Size"; DHS, CBP, *Holding the Line in the 21st Century.*

110 DOJ, INS, *Annual Report of the Immigration and Naturalization Service for 1973,* 8, 10.

111 I and N Reporter, "Fifty First Years," 17.

112 DOJ, INS, "Authorization and Budget Request for the Congress" [for FY 1974], USCIS, addenda from March 2, 1972.

113 Hernández, *Migra!,* 222.

114 Edwards, *Closed World,* 1, 7–8.

115 "Border Patrol," USCIS.

116 Steinbergs, Friedman, and Rothschild, *Wide Area Remote Surveillance.*

117 Andelman, "US Implanting an Electronic 'Fence.'"

118 Los Angeles Times, "Let's Put Local People to Work."

119 Henneberger, "Electronics Support Program of INS."

120 DOJ, INS, "Program Objectives and Budget FY 1976," 15.

121 Hunter, "Immigration Agency Engulfed in Trouble"; DOJ, INS, "Program Objectives and Budget FY 1976," 14–15.

122 DOJ, INS, *Annual Report of the Immigration and Naturalization Service 1977,* 20–21.

123 DOJ, INS, Office of Planning and Evaluation, "Research and Development Plan," 2, USCIS.

124 DOJ, INS, *Annual Report of the Immigration and Naturalization Service 1975,* 16.

125 GAO, "Problems and Options in Estimating the Size," 9–11.

126 Sterba, "Electronic Vigil."

127 Henneberger, "Electronics Support Program of INS," 55.

128 DOJ, INS, Office of Planning & Evaluation, "Research and Development Plan"; Frankel, "INS R and D Development."

129 Henneberger, "Electronics Support Program of INS," 59.

130 DOJ, INS, "Authorization and Budget Request for the Congress" [for FY 1975], USCIS.

131 Lin and Jackson, "From Bias to Repair."

132 Henneberger, "Electronics Support Program of INS," 59.

133 Coronil, "Foreword," xii.

3. PLATFORMS OF ENMITY AND THE CONSOLIDATION
OF THE NETWORKED INFORMATION REGIME

1 *Strengthening Border Security* (statement of Kirk Evans, Director, Mission Support Office, Homeland Security Advanced Research Projects Agency, Science & Technology Directorate, DHS).

2 DHS, CBP, Office of the Border Patrol, *2012–2016 Border Patrol Strategic Plan*, 14.

3 Suchman, Trigg, and Blomberg, "Working Artefacts," 175.

4 Andreas, *Border Games*, 8–11.

5 Gillespie, "Politics of 'Platforms,'" 349–50.

6 Vukov and Sheller, "Border Work," 225–26.

7 National Commission on Terrorist Attacks, *9/11 Commission Report*, 362.

8 Howie and Campbell, *Crisis and Terror*; Leland, "United States of Anxiety"; Moses, *Anxious Experts*.

9 For more recent examples on the consolidation of the cybernetic border through the Automated Virtual Agent for Truth Assessments in Real-Time, see Schaeffer, "Automated Border Control"; De Lara, "Race, Algorithms, and the Work of Border Enforcement."

10 Andreas, *Border Games*; Nevins, *Operation Gatekeeper and Beyond*.

11 Ackleson, "Directions in Border Security Research," 575.

12 De Genova, *Working the Boundaries*, 6, 61–62, 91, 229.

13 Carpio, *Collisions at the Crossroads*, 23–24.

14 DHS, *Performance and Accountability Report, Fiscal Year 2003*, 6; New York Times, "Farewell to the INS."

15 Chun, *Control and Freedom*, 3.

16 Ackleson, "Constructing Security," 168.

17 Cadava, *Hispanic Republican*, 284–322.

18 Huntington, "Clash of Civilizations?" 48.

19 Huntington's thesis underwent multiple rounds of critique in the 1990s and in the 2000s. A common criticism was that his understanding of civilizations was quite devoid of significant anthropological, sociological, or historical nuance. Civilizations were cultural entities spanning across villages, regions, ethnic and religious groups, and nationalities. Such lumping inevitably leads to an understanding of culture as an immutable essence and a racial ordering of the world. Edward Said wrote one of the sharpest responses to Huntington's

conceptualization, which he argued is representative of a vision that casts "civilizations" into "shut-down, sealed-off entities that have been purged of the myriad currents and countercurrents that animate human history, and that over centuries have made it possible for that history not only to contain wars of religion and imperial conquest but also to be one of exchange, cross-fertilization and sharing" (Said, "Clash of Ignorance").

20 See, for example, Behr, "Opposition to NAFTA"; Bernstein, "Clinton Faces Hurdles"; Darling, "NAFTA Worries"; Fuentes, "Mexicans Fear 'Giant Crunching Sound'"; Rusk, "Dump NAFTA, Coalition Urges."

21 Buchanan, "America First, NAFTA Never."

22 Buchanan, "America First, NAFTA Never."

23 Travis B. Franks builds on the work of Indigenous studies scholars Eve Tuck and K. Wayne Yang to elaborate this understanding of settler nativism. Franks, "Non-Natives and Nativists," 6–8.

24 Anzaldúa, *Borderlands/La Frontera*, 25.

25 Cited in Cadava, *Hispanic Republican*, 295.

26 Spivak, "Wilson Blames Budget Woes on Unchecked Immigration."

27 Wilson, "California Won't Reward Lawbreakers."

28 For more on anti-immigrant sentiments in the 1990s, see, for example, Andreas, *Border Games*; Nevins, *Operation Gatekeeper and Beyond*; Purcell and Nevins, "Pushing the Boundary."

29 Chacón, "Security Myth," 83.

30 Cadava, *Hispanic Republican*, 309–10, 315. Geraldo Cadava also argues that Clinton won the 1996 presidential election in part because the electorate believed the Republican-led Congress "catered too much to the conservative wing of the party."

31 Ackleson, "Directions in Border Security Research," 574.

32 DHS, CBP, Office of Border Patrol and Office of Policy and Planning, *National Border Patrol Strategy*, 3.

33 DOJ, INS, *Building a Comprehensive Southwest Border*, 3.

34 Schaeffer, *Unsettled Borders*, 56–57.

35 De León, *Land of Open Graves*, 31, 29–30.

36 Government Accountability Office, "INS' Southwest Border Strategy," 24.

37 Cacho, *Social Death*, 6–7.

38 Fred Moten cited in Harney and Moten, *Undercommons*, 137–40.

39 My engagement of "assemblage" draws much from Deleuze and Guattari, *A Thousand Plateaus*; Weheliye, *Habeas Viscus*.

40 Chapter 2 examines the history of how Mexican migrants were imagined as "intruders" and "threats" to the nation. This was made manifest in anti-narcotics (the "war on drugs") and border and immigration enforcement operations that grew in intensity since the Cold War era. For the precarity and insecurity of border crossings and of life on the borderlands, see Alonso Meneses, *Desierto de los sueños rotos*; De Genova, "Migrant 'Illegality' and Deportability"; Lugo, *Fragmented Lives, Assembled Parts*; Gaspar de Alba and Guzmán, *Making a*

Killing; Massey, Durand, and Pren, "Why Border Enforcement Backfired"; Rosas, *Barrio Libre*; Rosas, "Managed Violences of the Borderlands"; Spener, *Clandestine Crossings*.

41 Harney and Moten, *Undercommons*, 137.

42 Rana, "Language of Terror," 213–14.

43 Journalists and academics alike paid particular attention to the idea that the United States was hated, and that hatred was at the root of the 9/11 attacks. See, for example, Kamber, "Why They Hate Us"; Rollins, Fradkin, and Wurmser, "Why They Hate Us"; Sunstein, "Why They Hate Us"; Caputo, "Why They Hate Us."

44 Welch, *Scapegoats of September 11th*, 4.

45 Alsultany, *Arabs and Muslims in the Media*, 6–7.

46 Alsultany, *Arabs and Muslims in the Media*, 5.

47 Cacho, *Social Death*, 98.

48 National Commission on Terrorist Attacks, *9/11 Commission Report*, 364.

49 Office of the President of the United States, Office of Homeland Security, *National Strategy for Homeland Security* (my emphasis).

50 National Commission on Terrorist Attacks, *9/11 Commission Report*, 362.

51 Rana, "9/11 of Our Imaginations," 513.

52 Kaplan, *Anarchy of Empire*; Stoler, *Duress*.

53 Canaday, *Straight State*; Ngai, *Impossible Subjects*; Shah, *Contagious Divides*.

54 In 2002 and as part of the federal government's reorganization in response to the attacks of 9/11, the US Customs Service and the INS were combined with twenty other agencies into the Department of Homeland Security. CBP was tasked with controlling the nation's borders and, within this agency, the Border Patrol became the chief conduit of border enforcement.

55 For more on the practice of field processing, see Nuñez-Neto, Siskin, and Viña, *Border Security*, 1–4. Processing apprehended people was an essential practice of the border security assemblage because it allowed the activation of its different components and their attendant procedures. For example, Mexican aliens without a "criminal history" were allowed to "voluntarily return" to Mexico after processing. Meanwhile, non-Mexicans lacking a criminal history were sent, whenever possible, to a detention facility administered by Immigration and Customs Enforcement (ICE) and from there would be deported.

56 Nuñez-Neto, Siskin, and Viña, *Border Security*, 1.

57 Senator John Cornyn seeks to clarify what OTM means during Chief David Aguilar's testimony. *Strengthening Border Security* (statement of David Aguilar, Chief of Office of Border Patrol, CBP, DHS), 12.

58 *Strengthening Border Security* (statement of David Aguilar), 13.

59 Bowker, and Star, *Sorting Things Out*, 10.

60 Browne, *Dark Matters*, 16.

61 Massey, Durand, and Pren, "Why Border Enforcement Backfired," 1563.

62 For more on transgressions and the law, see Foucault, "A Preface to Transgression."

63 Cited in Strohm, "Wild, Wild Southwest," 3017.

64 DHS, CBP, Office of Border Patrol and Office of Policy and Planning, *National Border Patrol Strategy*.

65 Edwards, *Closed World*, 110.

66 DOD, Office of the Secretary of Defense, *Defense Strategy for the 1990s*; Office of the President of the United States, *A National Security Strategy*, 5–6; Kolet, "Asymmetric Threats to the United States."

67 National Commission on Terrorist Attacks, *9/11 Commission Report*, 416–19.

68 Kennedy, ". . . S.: Fighting an Elusive Enemy."

69 Dowd, "Modernity of Evil."

70 Anxiety about "elusive foes" crossing the border was not limited to Mexico, as government officials in Republican and Democratic administrations also claimed attackers in 9/11 crossed from Canada. Such paranoia fed efforts to police ports of entry through failing biometric technologies. Magnet, *When Biometrics Fail*, 91–126.

71 DOJ, INS, *Annual Report of the Immigration and Naturalization Service for 1973*, 1–2, 8–9.

72 Office of the President of the United States, Office of Homeland Security, *National Strategy for Homeland Security*, 22.

73 DHS, CBP, *Performance and Annual Report*, 7–8.

74 Suchman, *Human-Machine Reconfigurations*, 13.

75 Suchman, *Human-Machine Reconfigurations*, 19.

76 "Message from the Commissioner," in DHS, CBP, Office of the Border Patrol and Office of Policy and Planning, *National Border Patrol Strategy*.

77 DHS, CBP, Office of Border Patrol and Office of Policy and Planning, *National Border Patrol Strategy*, 2.

78 Alberts, Garstka, and Stein, *Network Centric Warfare*, 2, 88.

79 Alberts, Garstka, and Stein, *Network Centric Warfare*, 240.

80 Cebrowski and Garstka, "Network-Centric Warfare," 35.

81 The closed world discourse associated with situational awareness produces (and is the product of) forms of systemic ignorance that imagine war fighting can be conducted rationally through a seamless web of human-machine configurations. Suchman, "Imaginaries of Omniscience."

82 "Message from the Commissioner," in DHS, CBP, Office of the Border Patrol and Office of Policy and Planning, *National Border Patrol Strategy*.

83 Government Accountability Office, "Border Security" (GAO-11-374T), 2.

84 Government Accountability Office, "Border Security" (GAO-11-374T), 8, 12.

85 DHS, CBP, Office of the Border Patrol, *2012–2016 Border Patrol*, 6.

86 Washington Post Staff, "Full Text: Donald Trump Announces a Presidential Bid."

87 Exec. Order No. 13767 C.F.R. 8793 (Jan. 25, 2017).

88 DHS, CBP, Office of the Border Patrol, *2020 US Border Patrol Strategy*.

89 DHS, Office of Strategy, Policy, and Plans, Office of Immigration Statistics, *Efforts by DHS*, 18.

90 DHS, CBP, Office of the Border Patrol, *2022–2026 US Border Patrol Strategy*, 3.

91 DHS, CBP, Office of the Border Patrol, *2022–2026 US Border Patrol Strategy*, 8–9.

92 Cited in DHS, Office of Strategy, Policy, and Plans, Office of Immigration Statistics, *Efforts by DHS*, 1.

93 Technoaesthetics are the evaluative aesthetic categories embedded in expert practices. Masco, "Nuclear Technoaesthetics," 350.

94 Hudspeth, "Measuring the Effectiveness of Surveillance Technology," 15.

95 DHS, Office of Strategy, Policy, and Plans, Office of Immigration Statistics, *Department of Homeland Security Border Security Metrics Report*, 8.

96 Alden, "Measuring the Effectiveness of Border Enforcement"; DHS, CBP, *Holding the Line*; Hudspeth, "Measuring the Effectiveness of Surveillance Technology"; Roberts, *Measuring the Metrics*.

97 Inda, *Targeting Immigrants*, 175.

98 DHS, CBP, Office of the Border Patrol and Office of Policy and Planning, *National Border Patrol Strategy*, 3.

99 Weintraub, "Wilson Calls for Stronger Policing."

100 Bush, "No Cheap Shots at Mexico."

101 Harris, "Clinton Talks Border Line."

102 Boyce, "Rugged Border," 246, 250–51.

103 *Strengthening Border Security* (statement of Kirk Evans).

104 Government Accountability Office, "Secure Border Initiative" (GAO-08-1086), 1.

105 Government Accountability Office, "Border Security" (GAO-06-295), 1–2. For more on the Secure Border Initiative network, see Boyce, "Rugged Border"; De Lara, "Race, Algorithms, and the Work of Border Enforcement"; Fojas, *Border Optic*; Vukov and Sheller, "Border Work."

106 Government Accountability Office, "Secure Border Initiative" (GAO-08-131T), 4n3.

107 DHS, CBP, *Performance and Annual Report*, 30–31; DHS, CBP, *Performance and Accountability Report: Fiscal Year 2005*, 11; DHS, CBP, *Performance and Accountability Report: Fiscal Year 2006*, 8; Morris, "Southern Border Patrol Flights."

108 Government Accountability Office, "Secure Border Initiative" (GAO-08-1086), 7–8.

109 *Testimony of Director* (statement of John S. Beutlich, Director, Northern Region, Office of Air and Marine, CBP).

110 DHS, CBP, "Fact Sheet—BigPipe."

111 *Strengthening Border Security* (statement of Kirk Evans), 70.

112 DHS, "Privacy Impact Assessment for the Aircraft Systems," 4–8.

113 DHS, "Privacy Impact Assessment for the Aircraft Systems," 7, 12.

114 Whittle, *Predator*, 82.

115 Whittle, *Predator*, 83.

116 Marek, "Desert Cat and Mouse," 34.

117 *Strengthening Border Security* (statement of Kirk Evans), 9–10, 33.

118 Turner, *Transforming the Southern Border*, ii.

119 Farocki, "Phantom Images," 17.

120 Grégoire Chamayou makes a similar argument regarding operative images and drones, yet he limits his point to linking vision to sighting, where the function of the eye is similar to that of a weapon. My claim here is to broaden such understanding to the ways that (digital) technology—in this case drones, sensors, and algorithms—create sensory regimes that rely on operative images that are not limited to sight. Chamayou, *A Theory of the Drone*, 114.

121 "24 Hours on the Line," YouTube video.

122 *Strengthening Border Security* (statement of Henry F. Taylor, Distinguished Professor of Electrical Engineering, Texas A&M University), 90–93.

123 Browne, "Digital Epidermalization," 142.

124 In 2003, as an example, 1,000 Border Patrol agents worked in enforcement operations along the US-Canada border, which is over 4,000 miles long. Meanwhile, 10,408 Border Patrol were stationed on the southern border to secure the over 2,000-mile-long border between the United States and Mexico. Border data are from Bolkcom, *Homeland Security*, 1.

125 Wall and Monahan, "Surveillance and Violence from Afar," 246.

126 Marizco, "US Beefing Up Border Force."

127 Jimenez, *Humanitarian Crisis*.

128 Matus quoted in Marek, "Desert Cat and Mouse," 34.

129 Jimenez, *Humanitarian Crisis*, 17.

130 Wall and Monahan, "Surveillance and Violence from Afar," 247.

131 Marek, "Border Wars," 46.

132 Rosenblum, "Border Security"; Hudspeth, "Measuring the Effectiveness of Surveillance Technology," 15.

133 Browne, *Dark Matters*, 16.

134 By 2013, there were a total of eight UASs being used on the southern border (counting two drones flown from Florida over the region of the Caribbean), while two were operated along the northern border area close to Canada. DHS, "Privacy Impact Assessment for the Aircraft Systems," 4.

4. TECHNOAESTHETICS OF DISSENT IN THE AGE OF THE CYBERNETIC BORDER

1 "Why Cybraceros?," Vimeo video.

2 "Why Braceros?," Archive.org video.

3 Lisa Nakamura argues, in an unpublished manuscript, that Rivera's "Why Cybraceros?" constituted a prescient critique of digital racial capitalism, the differential and differentiating distribution of digital labor that powers the internet. For more on immaterial labor, see Lazzarato, "Immaterial Labor"; Terranova, "Free Labor."

4 Atanasoski and Vora, *Surrogate Humanity*, 7.

5 Browne, *Dark Matters*, 82.

6 For more on technoaesthetics, see Masco, *Nuclear Borderlands*, esp. chap. 2.

7   Fox, "Fence and the River," 58.

8   Carroll, REMEX, 31, 33, 38. Carroll seems to be more in agreement with Jo-
    Anne Berelowitz's description of border art as both of a space and an embodied
    experience. Berelowitz periodizes "border art" as work concerned with issues of
    "identity politics" (1968–1980), "multiculturalism" (1984–1992), and "globaliza-
    tion" (1992–present). Berelowitz, "Border Art since 1965," 143–45.

9   Carroll, REMEX, 222.

10 Mezzadra and Neilson, *Border as Method*, 280.

11 Masco, *Nuclear Borderlands*, 54.

12 Masco, *Nuclear Borderlands*, 44.

13 Some examples of work attending to the wall/fence and river include Border Art
    Workshop/Taller de arte fronterizo, "End of the Line" (1986); Marcos Ramírez
    ERRE, "Toy and Horse" (1997); Julio Romero, "How to Dismantle an Interna-
    tional Border" (2012); JR, "Giants, Kikito, US-Mexico Border" (2017); Ronald
    Rael and Virginia San Fratello, "Teeter-Totter Wall" (2019).

14 De Landa, *A New Philosophy of Society*.

15 Haggerty and Ericson, "Surveillant Assemblage," 608.

16 Strasser and Edwards, "Big Data Is the Answer," 329.

17 Kelley, "'We Are Not What We Seem,'" 76–77, 94.

18 Harney and Moten, *Undercommons*, 93–94.

19 Ricardo Dominguez, interview by the author, June 20, 2016, interview 1, pt. 1.

20 Ian Alan Paul, interview by the author, July 20, 2016, interview 8.

21 Fisher, *Play in the System*, 12–13.

22 Fisher, *Play in the System*, 5.

23 Dominguez, interview 1, pt. 1.

24 Erickson, "Assembling Social Forms," 42. In the Latin American context, the
    work of Juan Acha, Teresa Burga, Marie-France Cathelat, Grupo Março, and
    Hervé Fischer, to name a few, pushed the boundaries of conceptual art through
    a sociological lens. Dominguez's interest in critical theory, radical politics, and
    art such as his love for Semiotext(e) publications suggest a potential cross-
    pollination bringing sociological art ideas into his purview early in his career.
    For more on Latin American sociological art see Museo Universitario Arte
    Contemporáneo, *Juan Acha*. For more on the confluence between radical politics
    and artistic approaches like sociological art see Woodruff, *Dis-Ordering the
    Establishment*.

25 Erickson, "Assembling Social Forms," 89.

26 Raley, *Tactical Media*, 6.

27 Raley, *Tactical Media*, 6.

28 Critical Art Ensemble, *Electronic Civil Disobedience*, 11, 13.

29 Raley, *Tactical Media*, 27.

30 Towghi and Vora, "Bodies, Markets, and the Experimental," 2.

31 "Alex Rivera, Filmmaker," YouTube video.

32 Benjamin, "Introduction," 12.

33 De León, *Land of Open Graves*.

34 Jimenez, *Humanitarian Crisis*, 13–14. This is also the conclusion in Massey, Durand, and Pren, "Why Border Enforcement Backfired," though the authors also show that by cutting the circular flow of labor migration, enforcement policies have had the unintended consequence of increasing the rate of undocumented population growth and turning labor migrants into a settled population.

35 Jimenez, *Humanitarian Crisis*, 12.

36 Jimenez, *Humanitarian Crisis*, 15–16; Chamblee et al., "Mapping Migrant Deaths," 10.

37 Humane Borders, "Our Mission."

38 This practice was heavily persecuted during Donald Trump's administration. Phillips, "They Left Food and Water."

39 Chamblee et al., "Mapping Migrant Deaths," 6.

40 Chamblee et al., "Mapping Migrant Deaths," 17.

41 Arizona OpenGIS Initiative.

42 Chamblee et al., "Mapping Migrant Deaths," 29.

43 Chamblee et al., "Mapping Migrant Deaths," 10.

44 Derrida, *Specters of Marx*, xix.

45 With regime of truth, I draw on Michel Foucault's understanding of that moment "marked by the articulation of a particular type of discourse and a set of practices, a discourse that, on the one hand, constitutes these practices as a set bound together by an intelligible connection and, on the other hand, legislates and can legislate on these practices in terms of true and false." Foucault, *Birth of Biopolitics*, 18.

46 For evidence of the processes of "the Sonoran Desert hybrid collectif," see De León, *Land of Open Graves*, ch. 3.

47 The original concept of *bare life* was proposed by Giorgio Agamben, but it was Roxanne Doty who applied it to unauthorized immigrants on the US-Mexico border. Agamben, *Homo Sacer*; Doty, "Bare Life," 601. See also Doty, "Fronteras Compasivas."

48 Mbembe, "Necropolitics," 27 (emphasis in original).

49 De León, *Land of Open Graves*, 3–4.

50 Dixon-Román, "Toward a Hauntology on Data," 46.

51 Foucault, *Birth of Biopolitics*, 186. For more on cybernetic governmentality see Bratton, *The Stack*; Tiqqun, *Cybernetic Hypothesis*.

52 Bowker and Star, *Sorting Things Out*; Rose, *Politics of Life Itself*; Halpern, *Beautiful Data*.

53 Arizona Daily Star, "Arizona Border Deaths, 1999–2009."

54 Virtual Community Watch.

55 Chaar López, "Un-civil Technoscience."

56 Paul, "Border Haunt: Index."

57 Paul, "Border Haunt: Live."

58 Paul, interview 8.

59 Cheney-Lippold, *We Are Data*, 259.

60 Gordon, *Ghostly Matters*, 205.

61 Brunton and Nissenbaum, *Obfuscation*, 1–2.

62 For more on immigration, carcerality, and the prison-industrial complex, see Escobar, *Captivity beyond Prisons*; Hernández, *City of Inmates*; Ordaz, *Shadow of El Centro*; Welch, "Role of the Immigration and Naturalization Service."

63 De León, *Land of Open Graves*, 29.

64 Jimenez, *Humanitarian Crisis*, 13.

65 Veltman, "Genesis of a High-Tech Hub"; Wesoff, "Return of Fed-Funded Algae Fuel Research."

66 CDPE, "Statement Regarding Campus Drone Incident."

67 This sequence of events was reconstructed from my interviews with Ricardo Dominguez and Ian Alan Paul and from materials published by the CDPE. It was later revealed that Jane Stevens was a pseudonym for drone scholar Katherine Chandler, currently an assistant professor at Georgetown University.

68 CDPE, "Statement Regarding Campus Drone Incident."

69 Leslie, "Spaces for the Space Age," 139.

70 For more on higher education complicities with the border technopolitical regime, see Miller, *More than a Wall*.

71 Homeland Security Act of 2002.

72 Paul, interview 8.

73 "Public Meeting, UCSD," YouTube video.

74 Fisher, *Play in the System*, 30.

75 Steussy, "Source of Mystery."

76 Paul, interview 8.

77 Dominguez, interview 1, pt. 1.

78 Anwar al-Awlaki, Samir Khan, and Abdulrahman al-Awlaki were executed without being granted due process required by the US Constitution and afforded by their US citizenship. For more, see American Civil Liberties Union, "Al-Aulaqi v. Panetta."

79 Paul, interview 8.

80 Ricardo Dominguez, interview by the author, August 11, 2016, interview 1, pt. 2.

81 For a reflection on tactical media's approach to performance as an experiential aesthetic practice meant to covertly foment political critique, see Raley, *Tactical Media*, 13–15.

82 Marizco, "US Beefing Up Border Force."

83 Begley, "Best of Luck with the Wall."

84 Gordon, *Ghostly Matters*, 5.

85 Begley, "Best of Luck with the Wall."

86 Another example is Romero, "How to Dismantle an International Border."

87 Begley, "Best of Luck with the Wall."

88 Paglen, "Seeing Machines."

89 Begley, "Best of Luck with the Wall."

90 In "Fatal Migrations" (2016), produced for *The Intercept*, Begley offers a different take on border making than he did in "Best of Luck with the Wall." An interactive array of circles contains different kinds of data relating to migrant deaths. When

you click on some circles you can see the location (Begley used satellite images) and the name and date of death of migrants who lost their lives attempting to cross the border. Other circles, lacking the location of where that specific migrant lost their life, contain the word "UNKNOWN" in big block letters. This juxtaposition of what was there and not there, of what was known and not known, differs from reproducing the belief of what Donna Haraway calls the "unregulated gluttony" of technical vision. Begley, "Fatal Migrations."

91   Gordon, *Ghostly Matters*, 16.
92   Steyerl, "A Sea of Data."
93   Gordon, *Ghostly Matters*, 8.

EPILOGUE
1   Biesecker, "Border Patrol Chief."
2   Biesecker, "Border Patrol Chief."
3   Du Bois, *Souls of Black Folks*, 16. Neil Foley argues that the color line was drawn at the Rio Grande in the nineteenth century when the US government sought to "take as much and as few Mexicans as possible" (Foley, *White Scourge*, 22).
4   Cited in Dean, "A 26-Year-Old Billionaire."
5   Gopnik, "Trump and Obama."
6   Washington Post Staff, "Full Text."
7   Hernández, *City of Inmates*; Molina, *How Race Is Made in America*; Puar, *Terrorist Assemblages*; Rosas, *Barrio Libre*; Shah, *Stranger Intimacy*.
8   Carroll, "'No Amnesty.'"
9   Corasanti, "A Look at Trump's Immigration Plan."
10   Corasanti, "A Look at Trump's Immigration Plan."
11   Bousquet, *Eye of War*; Kaplan, *Aerial Aftermaths*.
12   Haffner, *View from Above*.
13   For a similar argument about drone optics and sovereignty, see Chandler, "Apartheid Drones."
14   Braun, Friedewald, and Valkenburg, "Civilizing Drones"; Crampton, "Assemblage of the Vertical"; McNeil and Burrington, "Droneism."
15   Irwin, "Suturing the Borderlands."
16   "Postcommodity: Repellent Fence," YouTube video.
17   Postcommodity's work recuperates drone vision's emergence as what Felicity Amaya Schaffer calls "Nativision," or tracking of signs of presence across the land as a way of making kin. For more on "Nativision" and the making of Indigenous autonomous sovereignties, see Schaeffer, *Unsettled Borders,* esp. chaps. 1 and 4.

Bibliography

ARCHIVAL MATERIALS
HathiTrust Digital Library (HathiTrust)
Homeland Security Digital Library (HSDL)
Manuscript Reading Room, Library of Congress (LOC)
National Technical Reports Library (NTRL)
San Diego Air and Space Museum (SDASM)
United States Citizenship and Immigration Services History Reference Library (USCIS)

GOVERNMENT, CORPORATE, AND THINK TANK
PUBLICATIONS AND REPORTS
Air Force. "Pioneer in Supersonic Flight, the Bell X-1." Air Research and Development Command, Baltimore, 1953, HathiTrust.
Alden, Edward. "Measuring the Effectiveness of Border Enforcement." *Council on Foreign Relations*, March 14, 2013. https://www.cfr.org/report/measuring-effectiveness-border-enforcement.
American Civil Liberties Union. "Al-Aulaqi v. Panetta—Constitutional Challenge to Killing of Three US Citizens." *ACLU*, June 4, 2014. https://www.aclu.org/cases/al-aulaqi-v-panetta-constitutional-challenge-killing-three-us-citizens.
"Biography." Vertical File, "Chapman, Leonard Fielding, Jr.," n.d., USCIS.
Bolkcom, Christopher. *Homeland Security: Unmanned Aerial Vehicles and Border Surveillance.* CRS Report No. RS21698. Washington, DC: Congressional Research Service, 2004.
"Border Patrol." Folder 1, Vertical File, "United States, Immigration and Naturalization Service, Office of Planning and Evaluation," n.d., USCIS.
Comptroller General of the United States. "Cost and Effectiveness of Electronic Sensor and Surveillance Systems." Report No. B-163074. Washington, DC: US Government Printing Office, 1971.
Congressional Budget Office. "Trends in Federal Spending for the Administration of Justice." Washington, DC: Congressional Budget Office, 1996.
Curry, Benjamin P., ed. "The 4756th Drone Squadron and the Firebee Drone." Gunter AFB, AL: Air Defense Command, US Air Force, ca. 1966. Album 109, "Ryan Library Albums," SDASM.

Department of Defense Appropriations for 1961. Part 5 Procurement: Hearings before the Subcommittee on Department of Defense Appropriations of the Committee on Appropriations, 86th Cong. 84 (1960) (statement of Major General Robert J. Wood, Office of Research and Development, US Army).

DHS. "Budget-in-Brief Fiscal Year 2006," n.d., accessed August 1, 2022. https://www.dhs.gov/publication/budget-brief-fiscal-year-2006.

DHS. *Department of Homeland Security Border Security Metrics Report*. Washington, DC: US Department of Homeland Security, 2020, HSDL.

DHS. "FY 2022 Budget-in-Brief," May 28, 2021, accessed August 1, 2022. https://www.dhs.gov/publication/fy-2022-budget-brief.

DHS. *Performance and Accountability Report, Fiscal Year 2003*. Washington, DC: US Department of Homeland Security 2004, HSDL.

DHS. "Privacy Impact Assessment for the Aircraft Systems." DHS/CBP/PIA-018, September 9, 2013. http://www.dhs.gov/sites/default/files/publications/privacy-pia-cbp-aircraft-systems-20130926.pdf.

DHS, CBP. "Fact Sheet—BigPipe: A Collaborative Effort." 2101–1015, accessed March 8, 2023. https://www.cbp.gov/sites/default/files/documents/FS_2015_BigPipe_FINAL.pdf.

DHS, CBP. *Holding the Line in the 21st Century*. Washington, DC: Customs and Border Protection, 2012, HSDL.

DHS, CBP. *Performance and Accountability Report: Fiscal Year 2005*. Washington, DC: Customs and Border Protection, 2005, HSDL.

DHS, CBP. *Performance and Accountability Report: Fiscal Year 2006*. Washington, DC: Customs and Border Protection, 2006, HSDL.

DHS, CBP. *Performance and Annual Report: Fiscal Year 2004*. Washington, DC: Customs and Border Protection, 2004, HSDL.

DHS, CBP. *Protecting America: US Customs and Border Protection 2005–2010 Strategic Plan*. Washington, DC: Customs and Border Protection, 2005, HSDL.

DHS, CBP, Office of the Border Patrol. *2012–2016 Border Patrol Strategic Plan*. Washington, DC: Customs and Border Protection, 2012, HSDL.

DHS, CBP, Office of the Border Patrol. *2020 US Border Patrol Strategy*. Washington, DC: Customs and Border Protection, 2019, HSDL.

DHS, CBP, Office of the Border Patrol. *2022–2026 US Border Patrol Strategy*. Washington, DC: Customs and Border Protection, 2022, HSDL.

DHS, CBP, Office of the Border Patrol and Office of Policy and Planning. *National Border Patrol Strategy*. Washington, DC: Customs and Border Protection, September 2004, HSDL.

DHS, Office of Strategy, Policy, and Plans, Office of Immigration Statistics. *Efforts by DHS to Estimate Southwest Border Security between Ports of Entry*. Washington, DC: Department of Homeland Security, 2017, HSDL.

DHS, Office of Strategy, Policy, and Plans, Office of Immigration Statistics. *Department of Homeland Security Border Security Metrics Report*. Washington, DC: Department of Homeland Security, 2020, HSDL.

DOD, Joint Chiefs of Staff. *A Dictionary of United States Military Terms, Prepared for the Joint Usage of the Armed Forces*. Washington, DC: Public Affairs Press, 1963, HathiTrust.

DOD, Office of Public Affairs, "Navy's 4th Annual Air Weapons Meet 'Operation Top Gun' Starts Nov. 30," news release Nov. 2–30, 1959, 39, Harvard Law Library.

DOD, Office of the Secretary of Defense. *Defense Strategy for the 1990s: The Regional Defense Strategy.* January 1993, Defense Technical Information Center.

DOJ, INS. *Annual Report of the Immigration and Naturalization Service 1966.* Washington, DC: US Government Printing Office, 1966, HathiTrust.

DOJ, INS. *Annual Report of the Immigration and Naturalization Service for 1973.* Washington, DC: US Government Printing Office, 1973, HathiTrust.

DOJ, INS. *Annual Report of the Immigration and Naturalization Service 1975.* Washington, DC: US Government Printing Office, 1975, HathiTrust.

DOJ, INS. *Annual Report of the Immigration and Naturalization Service 1976.* Washington, DC: US Government Printing Office, 1976, HathiTrust.

DOJ, INS. *Annual Report of the Immigration and Naturalization Service 1977.* Washington, DC: US Government Printing Office, 1977, HathiTrust.

DOJ, INS. *Annual Report of the Immigration and Naturalization Service for the Fiscal Year Ended June 30, 1947.* Philadelphia: US Department of Justice, 1947, HathiTrust.

DOJ, INS. *Annual Report of the Immigration and Naturalization Service for the Year Ended June 30, 1949.* Washington, DC: US Government Printing Office, 1949, HathiTrust.

DOJ, INS. "Authorization and Budget Request for the Congress" [for FY 1974] (1973), USCIS.

DOJ, INS. "Authorization and Budget Request for the Congress" [for FY 1975] (1974), USCIS.

DOJ, INS. "Authorization and Budget Request for the Congress" [for FY 1976] (1975), USCIS.

DOJ, INS. *Building a Comprehensive Southwest Border Enforcement Strategy.* Washington, DC: US Government Printing Office, 1996, HathiTrust.

DOJ, INS. Office of Planning and Evaluation. "Research and Development Plan: Draft," Washington, DC, 1976, USCIS.

DOJ, INS. "Program Objectives and Budget FY 1976" (1974), USCIS.

Department of the Army. "Push-Button Warfare." *Armed Forces Talk* 202 (1947). Exec. Order No. 13767, C.F.R. 8793 (2017).

General Accounting Office. "Problems and Options in Estimating the Size of the Illegal Alien Population." Report No. B-209064. Washington, DC: US Government Printing Office, 1982.

Government Accountability Office. "Border Security: Key Unresolved Issues Justify Reevaluation of Border Surveillance Technology Program." GAO-06-295. Washington, DC: Government Accountability Office, 2006.

Government Accountability Office. "Border Security: Preliminary Observations on Border Control Measures for the Southwest Border." GAO-11-374T. Washington, DC: Government Accountability Office, 2011.

Government Accountability Office. "INS' Southwest Border Strategy: Resource and Impact Issues Remain after Seven Years." GAO-01-842. Washington, DC: Government Accountability Office, 2001.

Government Accountability Office. "Secure Border Initiative: DHS Needs to Address Significant Risks in Delivering Key Technology Investment." GAO-08-1086. Washington, DC: Government Accountability Office, 2008.

Government Accounting Office. "Secure Border Initiative: Observations on Selected Aspects of SBI*net* Program Implementation." GAO-08-131T. Washington, DC: Government Accountability Office, 2008.

Hale, Bert, Jr. "Equipment, Facilities and Techniques in Use for Firebee Operation." In *Firebee . . . Symposium*, Report No. G-60-3. San Diego: Ryan Aeronautical Company, 1958. Boxes Ryan Collection—RPV, SDASM.

Homeland Security Act of 2002 (Pub. L. No. 107-296).

Immigration Act of 1882, 47th Cong., Sess. I (22 Statutes-at-Large 214).

Immigration and Nationality Act of 1952 (Pub. L. No. 82-414).

Investigation into Electronic Battlefield Program: Hearings before the Electronic Battlefield Subcommittee of the Committee on Armed Services, 91st Cong. (1971).

Jimenez, Maria. *Humanitarian Crisis: Migrant Deaths at the US-Mexico Border.* New York: American Civil Liberties Union of San Diego and Imperial Counties and Mexico's National Commission of Human Rights, 2009.

Meisel, Robert C., John F. Jacobs, and MITRE Corporation. *MITRE, The First Twenty Years: A History of the MITRE Corporation, 1958–1978.* Bedford, MA: MITRE Corp., 1979.

National Commission on Terrorist Attacks upon the United States. *The 9/11 Commission Report.* Washington, DC: US Government Printing Office, 2004.

Nuñez-Neto, Blas, Alison Siskin, and Stephen Viña. *Border Security: Apprehensions of 'Other Than Mexican' Unauthorized Aliens.* CRS Report No. RL33097. Washington, DC: Congressional Research Service, 2005.

Office of the President of the United States. *A National Security Strategy for a Global Age.* Washington, DC: Office of the President of the United States, 2000, HathiTrust.

Office of the President of the United States, Office of Homeland Security. *National Strategy for Homeland Security.* Washington, DC: Executive Office of the President, 2002, HSDL.

Roberts, Bryan. *Measuring the Metrics: Grading the Government on Immigration Enforcement.* Washington, DC: Bipartisan Policy Center, 2015.

Roney, Lisa S. "Memorandum for Marian Smith, Historian," June 20, 2003. Folder 1, Vertical File, "United States, Immigration and Naturalization Service, Office of Planning and Evaluation," USCIS.

Rosenblum, Marc R. "Border Security: Immigration Enforcement between Ports of Entry." CRS Report for Congress. Washington, DC: Congressional Research Service, 2013.

Ryan Aeronautical. "Ryan Firebee at Project William Tell," c. 1958. Album 109, "Ryan Library Albums," SDASM.

Ryan Aeronautical. "Ryan Firebee: Pilotless Jet Plane," 1955. Album 109, "Ryan Library Albums," SDASM.

Ryan Aeronautical. "Target Plane," August 10, 1949. Album 108, "Ryan Library Albums," SDASM.

Strengthening Border Security between the Ports of Entry: The Use of Technology to Protect the Borders: Joint Hearing before the Subcommittee on Immigration, Border Security and Citizenship and the Subcommittee on Terrorism, Technology and Homeland Security of the Committee on the Judiciary, 109th Cong. 70 (2005).

Testimony of Director, Northern Region Office of Air and Marine, John S. Beutlich, before Subcommittee on Emergency Preparedness, Response, and Communications of the Comm. On Homeland Security, 112th Cong. 7 (2011).

Turner, Jim. *Transforming the Southern Border: Providing Security and Prosperity in the Post-9/11 World.* Washington, DC: House Select Committee on Homeland Security, 2004.

Turner, William. "Signcutting and Aerial Observation," n.d., USCIS.

Warren, F. "History of the Q-2." In *Firebee . . . Symposium*, Report No. G-60-3. San Diego: Ryan Aeronautical Company, 1958. Boxes Ryan Collection—RPV, SDASM.

Wright-Patterson Air Force Base. "XQ-2 Aerial Target—Project MX-873," March 25, 1952. Album 108, "Ryan Library Albums," SDASM.

NEWSPAPERS, MAGAZINES, AND OTHER PERIODICALS

Andelman, David A. "US Implanting an Electronic 'Fence' to Shut Mexican Border to Smuggling." *New York Times*, July 14, 1973.

Anderson, Jack, and Les Whitten. "US Losing Drug-Smuggling War." *Washington Post*, August 24, 1973.

Atlanta Constitution. "Hard Flying for Aviators with Pershing Expedition." *Atlanta Constitution*, March 28, 1916.

Beecher, William. "Sensor 'Seal' around Vietnam Studied." *New York Times*, February 13, 1970.

Behr, Peter. "Opposition to NAFTA Unites Activist Groups." *Chicago Sun-Times*, September 5, 1993.

Bernstein, Harry. "Clinton Faces Hurdles on NAFTA." *Los Angeles Times*, February 16, 1993.

Biddle, Sam, and Ryan Devereaux. "Peter Thiel's Palantir Was Used to Bust Relatives of Migrant Children, New Documents Show." *The Intercept*, May 2, 2019. https://theintercept.com/2019/05/02/peter-thiels-palantir-was-used-to-bust-hundreds-of-relatives-of-migrant-children-new-documents-show/.

Biesecker, Cal. "Border Patrol Chief Expects RFP Soon for New Sensor Tower Program, followed by Centralized Command and Control Platform." *Defense Daily*, March 30, 2022. https://www.defensedaily.com/border-patrol-chief-expects-rfp-soon-for-new-sensor-tower-program-followed-by-centralized-cop/homeland-security/.

Blumenthal, Ralph. "'69 Infiltration to South Vietnam Is Put at 100,000." *New York Times*, January 7, 1970.

Brotherton, William. "Firebees Test America's Defense Shield." *Ryan Reporter* 23, no. 1 (February 1962): 19–21, 24, SDASM.

Buchanan, Patrick. "America First, NAFTA Never." *Washington Post*, November 7, 1993.

Bush, George W. "No Cheap Shots at Mexico, Please." *New York Times*, August 20, 1995.

Callander, Bruce D. "The Ground Observer Corps." *Air & Space Forces Magazine*, February 1, 2006. https://www.airandspaceforces.com/article/0206goc/.

Caputo, Philip. "Why They Hate Us: A Journalist's Travels through the Muslim World." *New York Times*, July 17, 2005.

Carroll, Rory. "'No Amnesty': Trump Vows to Deport Millions during 'First Hour in Office.'" *Guardian*, September 1, 2016. https://www.theguardian.com/us-news/2016/sep/01/donald-trump-vows-to-deport-millions-during-first-hour-in-office-in-hardline-speech.

CDPE. "Statement regarding Campus Drone Incident." *UC Center for Drone Policy and Ethics*, December 4, 2012. https://uccenterfordrones.wordpress.com/regarding-recent-drone-malfunction/.

Chapman, Leonard F., Jr. "Illegal Aliens: Time to Call a Halt!" *Reader's Digest* (October 1976): 188–92.

Clawson, Ken W. "US Testing Sensors along Mexican Border." *Washington Post*, July 18, 1970.

Corasanti, Nick. "A Look at Trump's Immigration Plan, Then and Now." *New York Times*, August 31, 2016.

Crowe, Earle E. "The March of Finance: Work on New North American Aviation Plant Expected to Begin Soon." *Los Angeles Times*, May 17, 1935.

Darling, Juanita. "NAFTA Worries." *Los Angeles Times*, October 17, 1993.

Dean, Sam. "A 26-Year-Old Billionaire Is Building Virtual Border Walls—and the Federal Government Is Buying." *Los Angeles Times*, July 26, 2019.

Dowd, Maureen. "The Modernity of Evil." *New York Times*, September 16, 2001.

Fang, Lee, and Sam Biddle. "Google AI Tech Will Be Used for Virtual Border Wall, CBP Contract Shows." *The Intercept*, October 21, 2020. https://theintercept.com/2020/10/21/google-cbp-border-contract-anduril/.

Frankel, Harry D. "INS Research and Development Programs." *INS Reporter* 26, no. 3 (Winter 1977–1978): 33–40, HathiTrust.

Fuentes, Carlos. "Mexicans Fear 'Giant Crunching Sound' of NAFTA." *Chicago Sun-Times*, November 14, 1993.

Funk, McKenzie. "How ICE Picks Its Targets in the Surveillance Age." *New York Times*, October 2, 2019.

Globe and Mail. "Nixon Declares Electronic War on Drug-Smuggling from Mexico." *Globe and Mail*, September 9, 1969.

Gopnik, Adam. "Trump and Obama: A Night to Remember." *The New Yorker*, September 15, 2015.

Harris, John F. "Clinton Talks Border Line in California." *Washington Post*, June 11, 1996.

Hartt, Julian. "McNamara's Viet Wall Being Built in Arizona." *Los Angeles Times*, October 15, 1967.

Henneberger, Thomas C., Jr. "The Electronics Support Program of INS." *INS Reporter* 26, no. 4 (Spring 1978): 55–59, HathiTrust.

Holles, Everett R. "Hundreds of Mexican Children Cross Border to Engage in Crime." *New York Times*, March 27, 1977.

Hunter, Marjorie. "Immigration Agency Engulfed in Trouble." *New York Times*, May 13, 1977.

I and N Reporter. "First Fifty Years." *I and N Reporter* 23, no. 1 (Summer 1974): 1–20, HathiTrust.

I and N Reporter. "Introducing Leonard F. Chapman, Jr. Our New Commissioner." *I and N Reporter* 22, no. 4 (Spring 1974): 43, HathiTrust.

Jones, Jack. "Border Patrol: More Fingers in the Dike." *Los Angeles Times*, August 9, 1978.

Kamber, Michael. "Why They Hate Us: Voices from Pakistan." *Village Voice*, October 16, 2001.

Kennedy, David M. ". . . S.: Fighting an Elusive Enemy." *New York Times*, September 16, 2001.

Klemcke, George F. "Role of the Communications Operator." *I and N Reporter* 15, no. 4 (January 1967): 29–33, HathiTrust.

"Learn to Fly." 1912 Curtiss ad, Naval Aviation in San Diego and North Island Collection, SDASM.

Leland, John. "United States of Anxiety." *New York Times*, January 29, 2006.

Levy, Steven. "Inside Palmer Luckey's Bid to Build a Border Wall." *Wired*, June 11, 2018.

Lifton, Robert Jay. "The 'Gook Syndrome' and 'Numbed Warfare.'" *Saturday Review* (December 1972): 66–72.

Los Angeles Times. "$3.9 Million in Orders to Ryan," June 7, 1959.

Los Angeles Times. "Curtiss to Conduct Aerial Experiments at San Diego," January 4, 1911.

Los Angeles Times. "Feat Solves Difficult Problem for Navy," January 27, 1911.

Los Angeles Times. "Harkness Flies Over the Line," February 8, 1911.

Los Angeles Times. "Let's Put Local People to Work," February 6, 1968.

Los Angeles Times. "Only 10 Years to Push-Button Warfare," November 9, 1946.

Los Angeles Times. "Robot Plane for Target Use Unveiled," February 22, 1953.

Los Angeles Times. "San Diego: Navy Site Prospect," February 17, 1906.

Los Angeles Times. "Uncle Sam's Aviation Experts Are Beginning at the Bottom," February 4, 1911.

Lynch, Jennifer. "Customs and Border Protection Considered Weaponizing Drones." *Electronic Frontier Foundation*, July 2, 2013. https://www.eff.org/deeplinks/2013/07/customs-border-protection-considered-weaponizing-drones.

Mallan, Lloyd. "Firebee Chase." *Ryan Reporter* 18, no. 5 (December 1957): 1–3, 25, SDASM.

Marek, Angie C. "Border Wars." *US News & World Report* 139, no. 20 (November 28, 2005): 46–56.

Marek, Angie C. "Desert Cat and Mouse: Border Effort Aims to Shut Down Arizona's Deadly Smuggling Corridor." *US News & World Report* 136, no. 19 (May 31, 2004): 32–34.

Marizco, Michael. "US Beefing Up Border Force." *Arizona Daily Star*, March 17, 2004.

Merkel, Harrison H. "Mobile Operational Communications." *I and N Reporter* 9, no. 3 (January 1961): 35–37, HathiTrust.

Meyer, Lawrence. "Aliens Hard to Count." *Washington Post*, February 2, 1975.

M'Groarty, John S. "History Is Repeated: Franciscan Fathers at San Diego." *Los Angeles Times*, July 20, 1911.

Mitchell, William. "Give America Airplanes or We Shall Perish as a Nation," 1934. Box 27, Folder 1, General William Mitchell papers, Manuscript Reading Room, LOC.

Mitgang, Herbert. "Sensors Don't Bleed." *New York Times*, December 20, 1971.

Morin, Howard. "Lindbergh Winging His Way from San Diego to Paris." *San Diego Union*, May 11, 1927.

Morris, Jefferson. "Southern Border Patrol Flights under Way with Predator B UAV." *Aerospace Daily & Defense Report* 216, no. 19 (October 27, 2005).

Naval Aviation News. "Navy's Pioneer Aviators Meet on the Forrestal." *Naval Aviation News* (November 1956): 20–21, HathiTrust.

New York Times. "Another Attempt to Solve Aerial Navigation Problem," January 7, 1906.

New York Times. "The Escalation," December 5, 1965.

New York Times. "Explosion!" September 25, 1949.

New York Times. "Farewell to the INS," April 27, 2002.

New York Times. "The Flying Machine," March 2, 1906.

New York Times. "Immigration Head Voices Alarm over the Problem of Illegal Aliens," December 21, 1975.

New York Times. "Jet to Power Targets," February 22, 1953.

New York Times. "The Penalty of Weakness," March 17, 1948.

New York Times. "Rumor of Recall of Troops False," April 9, 1916.

New York Times. "Ryan to Make Pilotless Jets," July 7, 1954.

Niebuhr, Edgar C. "False Claims to United States Citizenship by Mexican Aliens." *I and N Reporter* 9, no. 1 (July 1960): 1–3, HathiTrust.

Ostrow, Ronald J. "Bell Says Immigration Service Is 'Drowning' in Paper, Plans Effort to Systematize It." *Los Angeles Times*, January 31, 1979.

Phillips, Kristine. "They Left Food and Water for Migrants in the Desert. Now They Might Go to Prison." *Washington Post*, January 20, 2019.

Reston, James. "'The Silent Invasion.'" *New York Times*, May 4, 1977.

Rollins, Karina, Hillel Fradkin, and David Wurmser. "Why They Hate Us." *American Enterprise* 12, no. 8 (December 2001): 26–29.

Royal, Frank R. "In-Service Training Programs." *I and N Reporter* 9, no. 2 (October 1960): 17–18, HathiTrust.

Rusk, James. "Dump NAFTA, Coalition Urges." *Globe and Mail*, May 6, 1993.

Ryan Reporter. "Another Example of How Ryan Builds Better." *Ryan Reporter* 19, no. 2 (May 1958): back cover, SDASM.

Ryan Reporter. "Another Reason Why Ryan Builds Better." *Ryan Reporter* 17, no. 3 (June 1956): back cover, SDASM.

Ryan Reporter. "The Bee with the Electronic Brain." *Ryan Reporter* 14, no. 2 (March 1953): 12–14, 22, SDASM.

Ryan Reporter. "The Big Apple." *Ryan Reporter* 24, no. 4 (November-December 1963): 3–5, SDASM.

Ryan Reporter. "Birthplace of the Atomic Age." *Ryan Reporter* 14, no. 4 (July 1953): 2–5, 27, SDASM.

Ryan Reporter. "Drone Design." *Ryan Reporter* 15, no. 2 (April 1954): 0–1, 24, SDASM.

Ryan Reporter. "Fast and Versatile." *Ryan Reporter* 16, no. 2 (April 1955): 6–7, SDASM.

Ryan Reporter. "Firebee: 'Enemy' Jet over America." *Ryan Reporter* 19, no. 2 (May 1958): back cover, SDASM.

Ryan Reporter. "Firebee Tops New Building." *Ryan Reporter* 20, no. 1 (March 1959): 11, 23, SDASM.

Ryan Reporter. "Fledgling Wings." *Ryan Reporter* 13, no. 6 (1952): 53–55, SDASM.

Ryan Reporter. "Jet Bull's-Eye." *Ryan Reporter* 19, no. 1 (March 7, 1958): 20–22, 26, SDASM.

Ryan Reporter. "Nikes Fired at Ryan Firebee." *Ryan Reporter* 17, no. 3 (June 1956): 2–3, 29–30, SDASM.

Ryan Reporter. "Operation 'Top Gun.'" *Ryan Reporter* 20, no. 3 (August 5, 1959): 3, SDASM.

Ryan Reporter. "The Pioneering Ten." *Ryan Reporter* 13, no. 6 (1952): 56, SDASM.

Ryan Reporter. "Pushbutton Targets." *Ryan Reporter* 20, no. 3 (August 5, 1959): 4–7, 35–36, SDASM.

Ryan Reporter. "Q-2 Away: Tracking the Ryan Pilotless Jet Plane Takes High-Speed Testwork." *Ryan Reporter* 14, no. 1 (February 1953): 14–15, 24, SDASM.

Ryan Reporter. "R&D." *Ryan Reporter* 13, no. 6 (1952): 42–46, SDASM.

Ryan Reporter. "Ryan Firebee at Project William Tell." *Ryan Reporter* 19, no. 4 (October 1958): 0–3, SDASM.

Ryan Reporter. "Ryan Firebee Sets New Records." *Ryan Reporter* 18, no. 1 (March 1957): 29, SDASM.

Ryan Reporter. "Ryan High-Speed Targets to Help Train Gun, Guided Missile Crews." *Ryan Reporter* 14, no. 5 (September 1953): 5, SDASM.

Ryan Reporter. "This Is the Airplane Division." *Ryan Reporter* 1, no. 1 (January 1949): 5–6, 18, SDASM.

Ryan Reporter. "Under Arrest." *Ryan Reporter* 14, no. 1 (February 1953): 4–5, 26, SDASM.

Said, Edward. "The Clash of Ignorance." *The Nation*, October 4, 2001.

Salazar, Ruben. "Thousands Cross Border." *Los Angeles Times*, August 31, 1969.

Sands, Colonel Harry J., Jr. "Guided Missile Development." *Ryan Reporter* 11, no. 3 (May 1950): 3–5, 24, SDASM.

Seitz, Robert J. "Border Patrol at Work: Frontier Beat." *I and N Reporter* 18, no. 3 (January 1970): 34–41, HathiTrust.

Sheehan, Neil. "Infiltration Rise Seen If Raids End." *New York Times*, May 16, 1968.

Spivak, Sharon. "Wilson Blames Budget Woes on Unchecked Immigration." *San Diego Tribune*, April 12, 1991.

Sterba, James P. "Close-Up of the Grunt." *New York Times*, February 8, 1970.

Sterba, James P. "Electronic Vigil Fails to Stem Mexican Alien Influx." *New York Times*, July 22, 1973.

Steussy, Lauren. "Source of Mystery Drone Crash Revealed." *NBC San Diego*, December 6, 2012. https://www.nbcsandiego.com/news/local/-Source-of-Mystery-Drone-Crash-Revealed-182407811.html.

Strohm, Chris. "The Wild, Wild Southwest." *National Journal* 37, no. 40 (October 1, 2005): 3016–17.

Time. "Technology: The Cybernated Generation." *Time* 85, no. 14 (April 2, 1965): 84–91.

Turner, Jenny. "Reasons for Liking Tolkien." *London Review of Books* 23, no. 22 (November 15, 2001).

Uchitelle, Louis, and John Markoff. "Terrorbusters, Inc." *New York Times*, October 17, 2004.

Vandersall, David V. "Steps to a Better Records System." *I and N Reporter* 20, no. 4 (April 1972): 51–54, HathiTrust.

Van Wyen, A. O. "Pioneer Airmen at Pensacola." *Naval Aviation News* (May 1958): 20, HathiTrust.

Wall Street Journal. "New Ryan Aeronautical Order," February 27, 1957.

Washington Post. "The Need of Aeroplanes," March 27, 1916.

Washington Post Staff. "Full Text: Donald Trump Announces a Presidential Bid." *Washington Post*, June 16, 2015. https://www.washingtonpost.com/news/post -politics/wp/2015/06/16/full-text-donald-trump-announces-a-presidential-bid/.

Weintraub, Daniel W. "Wilson Calls for Stronger Policing on State's Borders." *Los Angeles Times*, April 22, 1994.

Wesoff, Eric. "The Return of Fed-Funded Algae Fuel Research." *Green Tech Media*, July 7, 2010. https://www.greentechmedia.com/articles/read/the-return-of-fed -funded-algae-fuels.

Williams, Bob. "Illegal Aliens Win a Beachhead for the Third World." *Los Angeles Times*, June 4, 1978.

Wilson, Jeff. "The Tyndall Story." *The Aircraft Flash* 7, no. 3 (January 1959): 10–12, HathiTrust.

Wilson, Pete. "California Won't Reward Lawbreakers." *Wall Street Journal*, November 7, 1994.

MULTIMEDIA (ART, VIDEOS, WEBMAPS)

"Alex Rivera, Filmmaker and Media Artist | 2021 MacArthur Fellow (Extended)." You-Tube video, 4:36. Published by macfound, December 7, 2021. https://www.youtube .com/watch?v=L-K4NJe172E&t=26s.

Arizona Daily Star. "Arizona Border Deaths, 1999–2009." *Arizona Daily Star*, August 26, 2010.

Arizona OpenGIS Initiative for Deceased Migrants, accessed March 7, 2023. https://

Begley, Josh. "Best of Luck with the Wall." Field of Vision, October 26, 2016, https:// fieldofvision.org/shorts/best-of-luck-with-the-wall.

Begley, Josh. "Fatal Migrations, 2001–2016." *The Intercept*, June 4, 2016. https:// projects.theintercept.com/fatal-migrations/.

DHS, CBP, Office of Public Affairs, Visual Communications Division. "CBP UAS B-Roll," *Defense Visual Information Distribution Service*, 2012. https://www.dvidshub .net/video/142871/cbp-uas-b-roll.

"F 2666 Operation Top Gun A-4 Skyhawk, Douglas AD-7, A3D Sky Warrior, F3H Demon, F4D Skyray." YouTube video, 19:16. Published by San Diego Air and Space Museum Archives, November 30, 2016. https://www.youtube.com/watch?v=RBeXuuqXzpo.

"The Lone Ranger 1949–1957 Opening and Closing Theme." YouTube video, 2:01. Published by TeeVees Greatest, February 23, 2016. https://www.youtube.com/watch?v=p9lf76xOA5k.

Paul, Ian Alan. "Border Haunt: Index (2011)." *Ian Alan Paul*, accessed February 22, 2018. http://www.ianalanpaul.com/projectbackups/borderhaunt/index2.html.

Paul, Ian Alan. "Border Haunt: Live (2011)." *Ian Alan Paul*, accessed February 22, 2018. http://www.ianalanpaul.com/projectbackups/borderhaunt/live.html.

"Postcommodity: Repellent Fence/Valla Repelente—2015." YouTube video, 6:41. Published by Postcommodity Collective, February 13, 2016. https://www.youtube.com/watch?v=SZBNqwNMkQE.

"Public Meeting, UCSD Center for Drone Policy and Ethics, Thursday, December 6, 2012." YouTube video, 53:59. Published by The Qualcomm Institute, February 20, 2013. https://www.youtube.com/watch?v=OLlnoUasx5g.

Romero, Julio M. "How to Dismantle an International Border (2012)." *Julio M. Romero*, accessed March 15, 2023. http://juliomromero.com/en/projects/how-to-dismantle-an-international-border.

"24 Hours on the Line." YouTube video, 8:45. Published by US CBP, Office of Public Affairs, Visual Communications Division, May 21, 2014. https://www.youtube.com/watch?v=OkZABNL3tPo.

Virtual Community Watch, accessed February 22, 2023. http://blueservo.com/vcw.php.

"Why Braceros?" Archive.org video, 18:53. Published by Wilding-Butler Division of Wilding, Inc., July 16, 2002. https://archive.org/details/WhyBrace1959.

"Why Cybraceros? (1997)." Vimeo video, 4:53. Published by Alex Rivera, July 14, 2021. https://vimeo.com/574948774.

"William Tell (1965)." YouTube video, 27:42. Published by AIRBOYD, June 10, 2011. Accessed August 18, 2023. https://www.youtube.com/watch?v=oTc7G66urnM.

ARTICLES, BOOKS, AND DISSERTATIONS

Ackleson, Jason. "Border Security in Risk Society." *Journal of Borderland Studies* 20, no. 1 (2005): 1–22.

Ackleson, Jason. "Constructing Security on the US–Mexico Border." *Political Geography* 24, no. 2 (2005): 165–84.

Ackleson, Jason. "Directions in Border Security Research." *Social Science Journal* 40 (2003): 573–81.

Ackleson, Jason. "Securing through Technology? 'Smart Borders' after September 11th." *Knowledge, Technology & Policy* 16, no. 1 (2003): 56–74.

Adams, Gordon. *The Politics of Defense Contracting: The Iron Triangle.* New Brunswick, NJ: Transaction Books, 1982.

Agamben, Giorgio. *Homo Sacer: Sovereign Power and Bare Life*. Stanford, CA: Stanford University Press, 1998.

Alberts, David S., John J. Garstka, and Frederick P. Stein. *Network Centric Warfare: Developing and Leveraging Information Superiority*. 2nd ed. Washington, DC: CCRP, 2000. First published 1999.

Alexander, Michelle. *The New Jim Crow: Mass Incarceration in the Age of Colorblindness*. New York: New Press, 2010.

Ali, Syed Mustafa. "Race: The Difference That Makes a Difference." *tripleC* 11, no. 1 (2013): 93–106. https://doi.org/10.31269/triplec.v11i1.324.

Allen, Arthur P., and Betty V. H. Schneider. *Industrial Relations in the California Aircraft Industry*. Berkeley: Institute of Industrial Relations, University of California, 1956.

Alonso Meneses, Guillermo. *El desierto de los sueños rotos: detenciones y muertes de migrantes en la frontera México-Estados Unidos 1993–2013*. Tijuana: Colegio de la Frontera Norte, 2013.

Alsultany, Evelyn. *Arabs and Muslims in the Media: Race and Representation after 9/11*. New York: NYU Press, 2012.

Alvarez, CJ. *Border Land, Border Water: A History of Construction on the US-Mexico Divide*. Austin: University of Texas Press, 2019.

Amoore, Louise. "Biometric Borders: Governing Mobilities in the War on Terror." *Political Geography* 25, no. 3 (March 2006): 336–51.

Amoore, Louise, and Alexandra Hall. "Taking People Apart: Digitised Dissection and the Body at the Border." *Environment and Planning D: Society and Space* 27, no. 3 (2009): 444–64.

Andreas, Peter. *Border Games: Policing the US-Mexico Divide*. 2nd ed. Ithaca, NY: Cornell University Press, 2009. First published 2000.

Anzaldúa, Gloria. *Borderlands/La Frontera: The New Mestiza*. San Francisco: Spinsters/Aunt Lute, 1987.

Aplin, John C., Jr., and Peter P. Schoderbek. "A Cybernetic Model of the MBO Process." *Journal of Cybernetics* 10, no. 1–3 (1980): 19–28.

Atanasoski, Neda, and Kalindi Vora. *Surrogate Humanity: Race, Robots, and the Politics of Technological Futures*. Durham, NC: Duke University Press, 2019.

Aune, Stefan. "Euthanasia Politics and the Indian Wars." *American Quarterly* 71, no. 3 (2019): 789–811.

Aune, Stefan. *Indian Wars Everywhere: Colonial Violence and the Shadow Doctrines of Empire*. Oakland: University of California Press, 2023.

Barnett, Lisa D. "Policing Peyote Country in the Early Twentieth Century." In *Border Policing: A History of Enforcement and Evasion in North America*, edited by Holly M. Karibo and George T. Díaz, 147–62. Austin: University of Texas Press, 2020.

Bateson, Gregory. *Steps to an Ecology of Mind: Collected Essays in Anthropology, Psychiatry, Evolution, and Epistemology*. New York: Jason Aronson, 1987. First published 1972.

Beller, Jonathan. *The World Computer: Derivative Conditions of Racial Capitalism*. Durham, NC: Duke University Press, 2021.

Beniger, James R. *The Control Revolution: Technological and Economic Origins of the Information Society*. Cambridge, MA: Harvard University Press, 1986.

Benjamin, Ruha. "Introduction: Discriminatory Design, Liberating Imagination." In *Captivating Technology: Race, Carceral Technoscience, and Liberatory Imagination in Everyday Life*, edited by Ruha Benjamin, 1–12. Durham, NC: Duke University Press, 2019.

Berelowitz, Jo-Anne. "Border Art since 1965." In *Postborder City: Cultural Spaces of Bajalta California*, edited by Michael Dear and Gustavo Leclerc, 143–81. New York: Routledge, 2003.

Blackhawk, Ned. *Violence over the Land: Indians and Empires in the Early American West*. Cambridge, MA: Harvard University Press, 2006.

Bokovoy, Matthew. *The San Diego World's Fairs and Southwestern Memory, 1880–1940*. Albuquerque: University of New Mexico Press, 2005.

Bousquet, Antoine. *The Eye of War: Military Perception from the Telescope to the Drone*. Minneapolis: University of Minnesota Press, 2018.

Bowker, Geoffrey C., Karen Baker, Florence Millerand, and David Ribes. "Toward Information Infrastructure Studies: Ways of Knowing in a Networked Environment." In *International Handbook of Internet Research*, edited by Jeremy Hunsinger, Lisbeth Klastrup, and Matthew Allen, 97–117. Dordrecht: Springer, 2010.

Bowker, Geoffrey C., and Susan Leigh Star. *Sorting Things Out: Classification and Its Consequences*. Cambridge, MA: MIT Press, 1999.

Boyce, Geoff. "The Rugged Border: Surveillance, Policing and the Dynamic Materiality of the US/Mexico Frontier." *Environment and Planning D: Society and Space* 34, no. 2 (2015): 245–62.

Boyce, Geoffrey Alan, and Samuel Norton Chambers. "The Corral Apparatus: Counterinsurgency and the Architecture of Death and Deterrence along the Mexico/United States Border." *Geoforum* 120 (2021): 1–13.

Boyer, Paul. *By the Bomb's Early Light: American Thought and Culture at the Dawn of the Atomic Age*. New York: Pantheon, 1985.

Bratton, Benjamin H. *The Stack: On Software and Sovereignty*. Cambridge, MA: MIT Press, 2015.

Braun, Sven, Michael Friedewald, and Govert Valkenburg. "Civilizing Drones: Military Discourses Going Civil?" *Science & Technology Studies* 28, no. 2 (2015): 73–87.

Brown, Nicholas A. "The Logic of Settler Colonialism in a Landscape of Perpetual Vanishing." *Settler Colonial Studies* 4, no. 1 (2014): 1–26.

Brown, Wendy. *Walled States, Waning Sovereignties*. New York: Zone Books, 2010.

Browne, Simone. *Dark Matters: On the Surveillance of Blackness*. Durham, NC: Duke University Press, 2015.

Browne, Simone. "Digital Epidermalization: Race, Identity, and Biometrics." *Critical Sociology* 36, no. 1 (2010): 131–50.

Brownell, Peter B. "Border Militarization and the Reproduction of Mexican Migrant Labor." *Social Justice* 28, no. 2 (2001): 69–92.

Brunton, Finn, and Helen Nissenbaum. *Obfuscation: A User's Guide for Privacy and Protest*. Cambridge, MA: MIT Press, 2015.

Byrd, Jodi A. *The Transit of Empire: Indigenous Critiques of Colonialism*. Minneapolis: University of Minnesota Press, 2011.

Cacho, Lisa Marie. *Social Death: Racialized Rightlessness and the Criminalization of the Unprotected*. New York: NYU Press, 2012.

Cadava, Geraldo. *The Hispanic Republican: The Shaping of an American Political Identity, from Nixon to Trump*. New York: HarperCollins, 2020.

Calavitta, Kitty. *Inside the State: The Bracero Program, Immigration, and the INS*. New York: Routledge, 1992.

Call, Steve. *Selling Air Power: Military Aviation and American Popular Culture after World War II*. College Station: Texas A&M University Press, 2009.

Campbell-Kelly, Martin, William Aspray, Nathan Ensmenger, and Jeffrey R. Yost. *Computer: A History of the Information Machine*. 3rd ed. New York: Routledge, 2016.

Canaday, Margot. *The Straight State: Sexuality and Citizenship in Twentieth-Century America*. Princeton, NJ: Princeton University Press, 2011.

Carpio, Genevieve. *Collisions at the Crossroads: How Place and Mobility Make Race*. Berkeley: University of California Press, 2020.

Carroll, Amy Sara. *REMEX: Toward an Art History of the NAFTA Era*. Austin: University of Texas Press, 2017.

Casanovas, Joan. *Bread or Bullets: Urban Labor and Spanish Colonialism in Cuba, 1850–1898*. Pittsburgh, PA: University of Pittsburgh Press, 1998.

Cebrowski, Arthur K., and John Garstka. "Network-Centric Warfare: Its Origins and Future." *United States Naval Institute Proceedings* 124, no. 1 (January 1998): 28–35.

Ceruzzi, Paul E. *Beyond the Limits: Flight Enters the Computer Age*. Cambridge, MA: MIT Press, 1989.

Ceruzzi, Paul E. *A History of Modern Computing*. Cambridge, MA: MIT Press, 1998.

Chaar López, Iván. "Alien Data: Immigration and Regimes of Connectivity in the United States." *Critical Ethnic Studies* 6, no. 2 (Fall 2020). https://doi.org/10.5749/ces.0602.lopez.

Chaar López, Iván. "Latina/o/e Technoscience: Labor, Race, and Gender in Cybernetics and Computing." *Social Studies of Science* 52, no. 6 (2022): 829–52. https://doi.org/10.1177/03063127221108515.

Chaar López, Iván. "Un-civil Technoscience: Anti-immigration and Citizen Science in Boundary Making." In *Technocreep and the Politics of Things Not Seen*, edited by Neda Atanasoski and Nassim Parvin. Durham, NC: Duke University Press, forthcoming.

Chacón, Jennifer M. "The Security Myth: Punishing Immigrants in the Name of National Security." In *Governing Immigration through Crime: A Reader*, edited by Julie A. Dowling and Jonathan Xavier Inda, 77–93. Stanford, CA: Stanford University Press, 2013.

Chamayou, Grégoire. *A Theory of the Drone*. Translated by Janet Lloyd. New York: New Press, 2015.

Chambers, Samuel Norton, Geoffrey Alan Boyce, Sarah Launius, and Alicia Dinsmore. "Mortality, Surveillance, and the Tertiary 'Funnel Effect' on the US-Mexico

Border: A Geospatial Modeling of the Geography of Deterrence." *Journal of Borderlands Studies* 36, no. 3 (2021). https://doi.org/10.1080/08865655.2019.1570861.

Chamblee, John F., Gary L. Christopherson, Mark Townley, Daniel DeBorde, and Rev. Robin Hoover. "Mapping Migrant Deaths in Southern Arizona: The Humane Borders GIS." Paper presented at the ESRI International User Conference, San Diego, CA, 2006.

Chandler, Katherine. "Apartheid Drones: Infrastructures of Militarism and the Hidden Genealogies of the South African Seeker." *Social Studies of Science* 52, no. 4 (2022): 512–35.

Chandler, Katherine. *Unmanning: How Humans, Machines and Media Perform Drone Warfare*. New Brunswick, NJ: Rutgers University Press, 2020.

Chavez, Leo R. *The Latino Threat: Constructing Immigrants, Citizens, and the Nation*. 2nd ed. Stanford, CA: Stanford University Press, 2013.

Chávez-García, Miroslava. *States of Delinquency: Race and Science in the Making of California's Juvenile Justice System*. Berkeley: University of California Press, 2012.

Cheney-Lippold, John. "*Jus algoritmi*: How the National Security Agency Remade Citizenship." *International Journal of Communication* 10 (2016): 1721–42.

Cheney-Lippold, John. *We Are Data: Algorithms and the Making of Our Digital Selves*. New York: NYU Press, 2016.

Chong, Sylvia. *The Oriental Obscene: Violence and Racial Fantasies in the Vietnam Era*. Durham, NC: Duke University Press, 2011.

Chun, Wendy Hui Kyong. *Control and Freedom: Power and Paranoia in the Age of Fiber Optics*. Cambridge, MA: MIT Press, 2006.

Chun, Wendy Hui Kyong. "Introduction: Race and/as Technology; or, How to Do Things to Race." *Camera Obscura: Feminism, Culture, and Media Studies* 24, no. 1 (2009): 7–34.

Churchland, Patricia S., V. S. Ramachandran, and Terrence J. Sejnowski. "A Critique of Pure Vision." In *Large-Scale Neuronal Theories of the Brain*, edited by Christof Koch and Joel L. Davis, 23–60. Cambridge, MA: MIT Press, 1994.

Cohen, Deborah. *Braceros: Migrant Citizens and Transnational Subjects in the Postwar United States and Mexico*. Chapel Hill: University of North Carolina Press, 2011.

Coleman, Beth. "Race as Technology." *Camera Obscura: Feminism, Culture, and Media Studies* 24, no. 1 (2009): 177–207.

Colomina, Beatriz. "Enclosed by Images: The Eameses' Multimedia Architecture." *Grey Room* 2 (Winter 2001): 6–29.

Coronil, Fernando. "Foreword." In *Close Encounters of Empire: Writing the Cultural History of U.S.-Latin American Relations*, edited by Gilbert M. Joseph, Catherine LeGrand, and Ricardo Donato Salvatore, ix–xii. Durham, NC: Duke University Press, 1998.

Crampton, Jeremy W. "Assemblage of the Vertical: Commercial Drones and Algorithmic Life." *Geographica Helvetica* 71 (2016): 137–46.

Critical Art Ensemble. *Electronic Civil Disobedience and Other Unpopular Ideas*. Brooklyn, NY: Autonomedia and Critical Art Ensemble, 1996.

Davis, Mike, Kelly Mayhew, and Jim Miller. *Under the Perfect Sun: The San Diego Tourists Never See*. New York: New Press, 2003.

Day, Iyko. *Alien Capital: Asian Racialization and the Logic of Settler Colonial Capitalism*. Durham, NC: Duke University Press, 2016.

Day, Iyko. "Being or Nothingness: Indigeneity, Antiblackness, and Settler Colonial Critique." *Critical Ethnic Studies* 1, no. 2 (Fall 2015): 102–21.

De Genova, Nicholas. "The Legal Production of Mexican/Migrant 'Illegality.'" *Latino Studies* 2, no. 2 (July 2004): 160–85.

De Genova, Nicholas. "Migrant 'Illegality' and Deportability in Everyday Life." *Annual Review of Anthropology* 31 (2002): 419–47.

De Genova, Nicholas. *Working the Boundaries: Race, Space, and 'Illegality' in Mexican Chicago*. Durham, NC: Duke University Press, 2005.

De Landa, Manuel. *A New Philosophy of Society: Assemblage Theory and Social Complexity*. London: Continuum, 2007. First published 2006.

De Lara, Juan. "Race, Algorithms, and the Work of Border Enforcement." *Information & Culture* 57, no. 2 (2022): 150–68.

De León, Jason. *The Land of Open Graves: Living and Dying on the Migrant Trail*. Berkeley: University of California Press, 2015.

Deleuze, Gilles, and Félix Guattari. *A Thousand Plateaus: Capitalism and Schizophrenia*. Translated by Brian Massumi. Minneapolis: University of Minnesota Press, 2005. First published 1987.

Delmont, Matt. "Drone Encounters: Noor Behram, Omer Fast, and Visual Critiques of Drone Warfare." *American Quarterly* 65, no. 1 (March 2013): 193–202.

Deloria, Phil J. *Playing Indian*. New Haven, CT: Yale University Press, 1998.

Derrida, Jacques. *Specters of Marx: The State of the Debt, the Work of Mourning, and the New International*. Translated by Peggy Kamuf. New York: Routledge, 1994.

Díaz-Barriga, Miguel, and Margaret E. Dorsey. *Fencing in Democracy: Border Walls, Necrocitizenship, and the Security State*. Durham, NC: Duke University Press, 2020.

Dixon-Román, Ezequiel. "Toward a Hauntology on Data: On the Sociopolitical Forces of Data Assemblage." *Research in Education* 98, no. 1 (2017): 44–58.

Doty, Roxanne. "Bare Life: Border-Crossing Deaths and Spaces of Moral Alibi." *Environment and Planning D: Society and Space* 29 (2011): 599–612.

Doty, Roxanne. "Fronteras Compasivas and the Ethics of Unconditional Hospitality." *Millennium: Journal of International Studies* 35, no. 1 (2006): 53–74.

Douhet, Giulio. *The Command of the Air*. Translated by Dino Ferrari. Washington, DC: Air Force History and Museums Program, 1998. First published 1942.

Du Bois, W. E. B. *The Souls of Black Folks*. State College: Pennsylvania State University, 2006.

Dunn, Timothy. *The Militarization of the US-Mexico Border, 1978–1992: Low-Intensity Conflict Doctrine Comes Home*. Austin, TX: Center for Mexican American Studies, 1996.

Edgington, Ryan H. *Range Wars: The Environmental Contest for White Sands Missile Range*. Lincoln: University of Nebraska Press, 2014.

Edwards, Paul N. *The Closed World: Computers and the Politics of Discourse in Cold War America*. Cambridge, MA: MIT Press, 1996.

Erickson, Ruth E. "Assembling Social Forms: Sociological Art Practice in Post-1968 France." PhD diss., University of Pennsylvania, 2014.

Escobar, Martha. *Captivity beyond Prisons: Criminalization Experiences of Latina (Im) migrants*. Austin: University of Texas, 2016.

Estades Font, María Eugenia. *La presencia militar de Estados Unidos en Puerto Rico, 1898–1918: Intereses estratégicos y dominación colonial*. Río Piedras: Ediciones Huracán, 1988.

Ettinger, Patrick. *Imaginary Lines: Border Enforcement and the Origins of Undocumented Immigration, 1882–1930*. Austin: University of Texas Press, 2009.

Farocki, Harun. "Phantom Images." *Public* 29 (2004): 13–22.

Fisher, Anna Watkins. *The Play in the System: Parasitical Resistance*. Durham, NC: Duke University Press, 2020.

Fitzgerald, Michael Ray. "The White Savior and His Junior Partner: The Lone Ranger and Tonto on Cold War Television (1949–1957)." *Journal of Popular Culture* 46, no. 1 (2013): 79–108.

Fojas, Camilla. *Border Optics: Surveillance Cultures on the US-Mexico Frontier*. New York: NYU Press, 2021.

Foley, Neil. *The White Scourge: Mexicans, Blacks, and Poor Whites in Texas Cotton Culture*. Berkeley: University of California Press, 1997.

Foucault, Michel. *The Birth of Biopolitics: Lectures at the Collège de France, 1978–79*. Edited by Michel Senellart. Translated by Graham Burchell. New York: Palgrave Macmillan, 2008. First published 2004.

Foucault, Michel. "A Preface to Transgression." In *Language, Counter-Memory, Practice: Select Essays and Interviews*, edited by Donald F. Bouchard, translated by Donald F. Bouchard and Sherry Simon, 29–52. Ithaca, NY: Cornell University Press, 1977.

Fox, Claire. *The Fence and the River: Culture and Politics at the US-Mexico Border*. Minneapolis: University of Minnesota Press, 1999.

Fox, Claire. "The Fence and the River: Representations of the US-Mexico Border in Art and Video." *Discourse* 18, no. 1 & 2 (Fall 1995/Winter 1996): 54–83.

Franklin, Seb. *Control: Digitality as Cultural Logic*. Cambridge, MA: MIT Press, 2015.

Franks, Travis B. "Non-Natives and Nativists: The Settler Colonial Origins of Anti-immigrant Sentiment in Contemporary Literatures of the US and Australia." PhD diss., Arizona State University, 2019.

Freeman, Eva C., ed. *MIT Lincoln Laboratory: Technology in the National Interest*. Lexington, MA: MIT Lincoln Laboratory, 1995.

Galison, Peter. "The Ontology of the Enemy: Norbert Wiener and the Cybernetic Vision." *Critical Inquiry* 21, no. 1 (Autumn 1994): 228–66.

Galison, Peter. "Removing Knowledge." *Critical Inquiry* 31, no. 1 (Autumn 2004): 229–43.

Gaspar de Alba, Alicia, and Georgina Guzmán. *Making a Killing: Femicide, Free Trade, and la Frontera*. Austin: University of Texas, 2010.

Genay, Lucie. *Land of Nuclear Enchantment*. Albuquerque: University of New Mexico Press, 2019.

Gillespie, Tarleton. "The Politics of 'Platforms.'" *New Media & Society* 12, no. 3 (May 2010): 347–64.

Goldstein, Alyosha. "Where the Nation Takes Place: Proprietary Regimes, Anti-statism, and US Settler Colonialism." *South Atlantic Quarterly* 107, no. 4 (2008): 833–61.

Gootenberg, Paul. *Andean Cocaine: The Making of a Global Drug.* Chapel Hill: University of North Carolina Press, 2009.

Gordon, Avery. *Ghostly Matters: Haunting and the Sociological Imagination.* Minneapolis: University of Minnesota Press, 2008. First published 1997.

Gregory, Derek. "Drone Geographies." *Radical Philosophy* 183 (2014). http://www.radicalphilosophy.com/article/drone-geographies.

Guidotti-Hernández, Nicole. *Unspeakable Violence: Remapping US and Mexican National Imaginaries.* Durham, NC: Duke University Press, 2011.

Hacking, Ian. "Biopower and the Avalanche of Printed Numbers." *Humanities in Society* 5, no. 1–2 (Winter and Spring 1982): 279–95.

Hacking, Ian. "Making Up People." *London Review of Books* 28, no. 16 (August 2006). https://www.lrb.co.uk/the-paper/v28/n16/ian-hacking/making-up-people.

Haffner, Jeanne. *The View from Above: The Science of Social Space.* Cambridge, MA: MIT Press, 2013.

Haggerty, Kevin D., and Richard D. Ericson. "The Surveillant Assemblage." *British Journal of Sociology* 51, no. 4 (2000): 605–22.

Hall, Stuart. "Encoding and Decoding in the Television Discourse." In *Essential Essays, Volume 1: Foundations of Cultural Studies,* edited by David Morley, 257–76. Durham, NC: Duke University Press, 2018.

Halpern, Orit. *Beautiful Data: A History of Vision and Reason since 1945.* Durham, NC: Duke University Press, 2014.

Hämäläinen, Pekka, and Samuel Truett. "On Borderlands." *Journal of American History* 98, no. 2 (September 2011): 338–61.

Haraway, Donna. *Simians, Cyborgs, and Women: The Reinvention of Nature.* New York: Routledge, 1991.

Harney, Stefano, and Fred Moten. *The Undercommons: Fugitive Planning and Black Study.* New York: Minor Compositions, 2013.

Hayles, N. Katherine. *How We Became Posthuman: Virtual Bodies in Cybernetics, Literature, and Informatics.* Chicago: University of Chicago Press, 1999.

Hecht, Gabrielle. *The Radiance of France: Nuclear Power and National Identity after World War II.* Cambridge, MA: MIT Press, 2009. First published 1998.

Hecht, Gabrielle, and Paul N. Edwards. *The Technopolitics of Cold War: Toward a Transregional Perspective.* Essays on Global and Comparative History. Washington, DC: American Historical Association, 2007.

Heims, Steve J. *Constructing a Social Science for Postwar America: The Cybernetics Group, 1946–1953.* Cambridge, MA: MIT Press, 1993.

Hernández, Kelly Lytle. *City of Inmates: Conquest, Rebellion, and the Rise of Human Caging in Los Angeles, 1771–1965.* Chapel Hill: University of North Carolina Press, 2017.

Hernández, Kelly Lytle. "The Crimes and Consequences of Illegal Immigration: A Cross-Border Examination of Operation Wetback, 1943 to 1954." *Western Historical Quarterly* 37, no. 4 (Winter 2006): 421–44.

Hernández, Kelly Lytle. *Migra!: A History of the US Border Patrol*. Berkeley: University of California Press, 2010.

Heyman, Josiah. "Capitalism and US Policy at the Mexican Border." *Dialectical Anthropology* 36, no. 3–4 (December 2012): 263–77.

Heyman, Josiah. "Constructing a Virtual Wall: Race and Citizenship in US-Mexico Border Policing." *Journal of the Southwest* 50, no. 3 (Autumn 2008): 305–33.

Heyman, Josiah. "Putting Power in the Anthropology of Bureaucracy: The Immigration and Naturalization Service at the Mexico-US Border." *Current Anthropology* 36 (1995): 261–87.

Heyman, Josiah. "United States Surveillance over Mexican Lives at the Border: Snapshots of an Emerging Regime." *Human Organization* 58, no. 4 (Winter 1999): 430–38.

Heyman, Josiah. "US Ports of Entry on the Mexican Border." *Journal of the Southwest* 43, no. 4 (2001): 681–700.

Hine, Thomas. *Populuxe*. New York: Knopf, 1986.

Hippler, Thomas. *Bombing the People: Giulio Douhet and the Foundations of Air-Power Strategy, 1884–1939*. Cambridge: Cambridge University Press, 2013.

Horton, Sarah B., and Josiah Heyman, eds. *Paper Trails: Migrants, Documents, and Legal Insecurity*. Durham, NC: Duke University Press, 2020.

Howie, Luke, and Perri Campbell. *Crisis and Terror in the Age of Anxiety: 9/11, the Global Financial Crisis and ISIS*. London: Palgrave Macmillan, 2017.

Hudspeth, Robert A. "Measuring the Effectiveness of Surveillance Technology at the US Southern Border." MA thesis, Naval Postgraduate School, 2019.

Huggins, Stephen. "Terrorism on the Great Plains." In *America's Use of Terror: From Colonial Times to the A-Bomb*, 124–44. Lawrence: University of Kansas Press, 2019.

Humane Borders. "Our Mission." Humane Borders website, n.d. Accessed February 22, 2108. https://humaneborders.org/our-mission/.

Huntington, Samuel P. "The Clash of Civilizations?" *Foreign Affairs* 72, no. 3 (1993): 22–49.

Inda, Jonathan Xavier. *Targeting Immigrants: Government, Technology, and Ethics*. Malden, MA: Blackwell Publishing, 2006.

Irwin, Matthew. "Suturing the Borderlands: Postcommodity and Indigenous Presence on the US-Mexico Border." *InVisible Culture* (May 2017): 25–26. https://ivc.lib.rochester.edu/suturing-the-borderlands-postcommodity-and-indigenous-presence-on-the-u-s-mexico-border/.

Jacoby, Karl. *Shadows at Dawn: A Borderlands Massacre and the Violence of History*. New York: Penguin Press, 2008.

Johnson, Benjamin Heber. *Revolution in Texas: How a Forgotten Rebellion and Its Bloody Suppression Turned Mexicans into Americans*. New Haven, CT: Yale University Press, 2003.

Johnson, Walter. *Soul by Soul: Life inside the Antebellum Slave Market*. Cambridge, MA: Harvard University Press, 1999.

Joseph, Gilbert M., Catherine LeGrand, and Ricardo Donato Salvatore, eds. *Close Encounters of Empire: Writing the Cultural History of US-Latin American Relations.* Durham, NC: Duke University Press, 1998.

Kang, S. Deborah *The INS on the Line: Making Immigration Law on the US-Mexico Border, 1917–1954.* New York: Oxford University Press, 2017.

Kaplan, Amy. *The Anarchy of Empire in the Making of US Culture.* Cambridge, MA: Harvard University Press, 2002.

Kaplan, Caren. *Aerial Aftermaths: Wartime from Above.* Durham, NC: Duke University Press, 2018.

Keehr, Karen M. "Air Power in Mexico during the Punitive Expedition of 1916." *Southern New Mexico Historical Review* VII, no. 1 (January 2000): 40–48.

Kelley, Robin D. G. "'We Are Not What We Seem': Rethinking Black Working-Class Opposition in the Jim Crow South." *Journal of American History* 80, no. 1 (June 1993): 75–112.

Kline, Ronald R. *The Cybernetics Moment or Why We Call Our Age the Information Age.* Baltimore: Johns Hopkins University Press, 2015.

Kolet, Kristin S. "Asymmetric Threats to the United States." *Comparative Strategy* 20 (2001): 277–92.

Kramer, Paul. *The Blood of Government: Race, Empire, the United States, and the Philippines.* Chapel Hill: University of North Carolina Press, 2006.

Kurutz, Gary. "The Only Safe and Sane Method: The Curtiss School of Aviation." *Journal of San Diego History* 25 (Winter 1979): 26–59.

LaFeber, Walter. *Inevitable Revolutions: The United States in Central America.* 2nd ed. New York: W. W. Norton, 1993.

Lassiter, Matthew D. "Impossible Criminals: The Suburban Imperatives of America's War on Drugs." *Journal of American History* (2015): 126–40.

Lassiter, Matthew D. "Pushers, Victims, and the Lost Innocence of White Suburbia: California's War on Narcotics during the 1950s." *Journal of Urban History* 41, no. 5 (2015): 787–807.

Latour, Bruno, and Jim Johnson. "Mixing Humans and Nonhumans Together: The Sociology of a Door-Closer." *Social Problems* 35 (1988): 298–310.

Law, John. *Aircraft Stories: Decentering the Object in Technoscience.* Durham, NC: Duke University Press, 2002.

Lazzarato, Maurizio. "Immaterial Labor." In *Radical Thought in Italy: A Potential Politics*, edited by Paolo Virno and Michael Hardt, translated by Paul Colilli and Ed Emory, 133–47. Minneapolis: University of Minnesota Press, 1996.

Lee, Erika. *At America's Gates: The Exclusion Era, 1882–1943.* Chapel Hill: University of North Carolina Press, 2003.

Lee, Erika. "Enforcing the Borders: Chinese Exclusion along the US Borders with Canada and Mexico, 1882–1924." *Journal of American History* 89, no. 1 (June 2002): 54–86.

Lefebvre, Henri. "Space and the State." In *State, Space, World: Selected Essays*, edited by Neil Brenner and Stuart Elden, translated by Gerald Moore, Neil Brenner, and Stuart Elden, 223–53. Minneapolis: University of Minnesota Press, 2009.

Lerner, Marc H. "William Tell's Atlantic Travels in the Revolutionary Era." *Studies in Eighteenth-Century Culture* 41 (2012): 85–114.

Leslie, Stuart W. *Cold War and American Science: The Military-Industrial-Academic Complex at MIT and Stanford.* New York: Columbia University Press, 1993.

Leslie, Stuart W. "Spaces for the Space Age: William Pereira's Aerospace Modernism." In *Blue Sky Metropolis: The Aerospace Century in Southern California,* edited by Peter J. Westwick, 127–58. Berkeley: Huntington-USC Institute on California and the West, 2012.

Levario, Miguel. *Militarizing the Border: When Mexicans Became the Enemy.* College Station: Texas A&M University Press, 2012.

Light, Jennifer. *From Warfare to Welfare: Defense Intellectuals and Urban Problems in Cold War America.* Baltimore: Johns Hopkins University Press, 2003.

Lin, Cindy Kaiying, and Steve J. Jackson. "From Bias to Repair: Error as a Site of Collaboration and Negotiation in Applied Data Science Work." *Proceedings of ACM Human-Computer Interaction* 7, CSCW1, article 131 (April 2023). https://doi.org/10.1145/3579607.

Lira, Natalie. *Laboratory of Deficiency: Sterilization and Confinement in California, 1900–1950s.* Berkeley: University of California Press, 2021.

López, Rick. *Crafting Mexico: Intellectuals, Artisans, and the State after the Revolution.* Durham, NC: Duke University Press, 2010.

Loza, Mireya. *Defiant Braceros: How Migrant Workers Fought for Racial, Sexual, & Political Freedom.* Chapel Hill: University of Carolina Press, 2016.

Lugo, Alejandro. *Fragmented Lives, Assembled Parts: Culture, Capitalism, and Conquest at the U.S.-Mexico Border.* Austin: University of Texas Press, 2008.

Magnet, Shoshana Amielle. *When Biometrics Fail: Gender, Race, and the Technology of Identity.* Durham, NC: Duke University Press, 2011.

Marez, Curtis. *Drug Wars: The Political Economy of Narcotics.* Minneapolis: University of Minnesota Press, 2004.

Martínez, Ignacio. "Settler Colonialism in New Spain and the Early Mexican Republic." In *The Routledge Handbook of the History of Settler Colonialism,* edited by Edward Cavanagh and Lorenzo Veracini, 109–24. London: Routledge, 2016.

Masco, Joseph. *The Nuclear Borderlands: The Manhattan Project in Post–Cold War New Mexico.* Princeton, NJ: Princeton University Press, 2020. First published 2006.

Masco, Joseph. "Nuclear Technoaesthetics: Sensory Politics from Trinity to the Virtual Bomb in Los Alamos." *American Ethnologist* 31, no. 3 (August 2004): 349–73.

Massey, Douglas S., Jorge Durand, and Karen A. Pren. "Why Border Enforcement Backfired." *American Journal of Sociology* 121, no. 5 (March 2016): 1557–1600.

Mbembe, Achille. *Critique of Black Reason.* Translated by Laurent Dubois. Durham, NC: Duke University Press, 2017.

Mbembe, Achille. "Necropolitics." Translated by Libby Meintjes. *Public Culture* 15, no. 1 (2003): 11–40.

Mbembe, Achille. "The Society of Enmity." *Radical Philosophy* 200 (November/December 2016).

McLucas, John L. *Reflections of a Technocrat: Managing Defense, Air, and Space Programs during the Cold War*, with contribution by Kenneth J. Alnwick and Lawrence R. Benson. Maxwell AFB, AL: Air University Press, 2006.

McLuhan, Marshall. *Understanding Media: The Extensions of Man*. Cambridge, MA: MIT Press, 1994. First published 1964.

McNeil, Joanne, and Ingrid Burrington. "Droneism." *Dissent* 61, no. 2 (Spring 2014): 57–60.

Medina, Eden. *Cybernetic Revolutionaries: Technology and Politics in Allende's Chile*. Cambridge, MA: MIT Press, 2014. First published 2011.

Mets, David R. *The Air Campaign: John Warden and the Classical Airpower Theorists*. Maxwell AFB, AL: Air University Press, 1998.

Mezzadra, Sandro, and Brett Neilson. *Border as Method, or the Multiplication of Labor*. Durham, NC: Duke University Press, 2013.

Miller, Todd. *More than a Wall: Corporate Profiteering and the Militarization of US Borders*. Amsterdam: Transnational Institute, 2019.

Mindell, David. *Digital Apollo: Human and Machine in Spaceflight*. Cambridge, MA: MIT Press, 2008.

Mindell, David A. *Between Human and Machine: Feedback, Control, and Computing before Cybernetics*. Baltimore: Johns Hopkins University Press, 2004.

Mitchell, William. *Winged Defense: The Development and Possibilities of Modern Air Power—Economic and Military*. New York: G. P. Putnam's Sons, 1926.

Molina, Natalia. "Constructing Mexicans as Deportable Immigrants: Race, Disease, and the Meaning of 'Public Charge.'" *Identities* 17, no. 6 (2010): 641–66.

Molina, Natalia. *Fit to Be Citizens?: Public Health and Race in Los Angeles, 1879–1939*. Berkeley: University of California Press, 2006.

Molina, Natalia. *How Race Is Made in America: Immigration, Citizenship, and Historical Power of Racial Scripts*. Berkeley: University of California Press, 2014.

Montejano, David. *Anglos and Mexicans in the Making of Texas, 1836–1986*. Austin: University of Texas Press, 1987.

Moses, Joshua. *Anxious Experts: Disaster Response and Spiritual Care from 9/11 to the Climate Crisis*. Philadelphia: University of Pennsylvania Press, 2022.

Muhammad, Khalil Gibran. *The Condemnation of Blackness: Race, Crime, and the Making of Modern Urban America*. Cambridge, MA: Harvard University Press, 2010.

Museo Universitario Arte Contemporáneo. *Juan Acha: Despertar revolucionario*. Ciudad de México: MUAC, 2017.

Myers, Lee. "Military Establishments in Southwestern New Mexico: Stepping Stones to Settlement." *New Mexico Historical Quarterly* 43, no. 1 (1968): 5–48.

Nakamura, Lisa. *Digitizing Race: Visual Cultures of the Internet*. Minneapolis: University of Minnesota Press, 2008.

Neocleous, Mark. *A Critical Theory of Police Power: The Fabrication of Social Order*. London: Verso, 2021. First published 2000.

Nevins, Joseph. *Operation Gatekeeper and Beyond: The War on "Illegals" and the Remaking of the US-Mexico Boundary*. 2nd ed. New York: Routledge, 2010. First published 2000.

Newcome, Laurence R. *Unmanned Aviation: A Brief History of Unmanned Aerial Vehicles*. Reston, VA: American Institute of Aeronautics and Astronautics, 2004.

Ngai, Mae. *Impossible Subjects: Illegal Aliens and the Making of Modern America*. Princeton, NJ: Princeton University Press, 2005.

Ngai, Mae. "The Strange Career of the Illegal Alien: Immigration Restriction and Deportation Policy in the United States, 1921–1965." *Law and History Review* 21, no. 1 (Spring 2003): 69–107.

Nurick, Lester. "The Distinction between Combatant and Noncombatant in the Law of War." *American Journal of International Law* 39, no. 4 (October 1945): 680–97.

Omi, Michael, and Howard Winant. *Racial Formation in the United States*. 3rd ed. New York: Routledge, 2014.

Ordaz, Jessica. *The Shadow of* El Centro: *A History of Migrant Incarceration and Solidarity*. Chapel Hill: University of North Carolina Press, 2021.

Paglen, Trevor. "Seeing Machines—Still Searching." *Fotomuseum Winterthur*, March 13, 2014. Accessed February 22, 2018. https://www.fotomuseum.ch/en/2014/03/13/seeing-machines/.

Pandya, Mihir. "The Vanishing Act: Stealth Airplanes and Cold War Southern California." In *Blue Sky Metropolis: The Aerospace Century in Southern California*, edited by Peter J. Westwick, 105–23. Berkeley: Huntington-USC Institute on California and the West, 2012.

Paredes, Américo. *"With His Pistol in His Hand": A Border Ballad and Its Hero*. Austin: University of Texas Press, 1958.

Plascencia, Luis F. B. "The 'Undocumented' Mexican Migrant Question: Re-Examining the Framing of Law and Illegalization in the United States." *Urban Anthropology and Studies of Cultural Systems and World Economic Development* 28, no. 2/3/4 (Summer, Fall, Winter 2009): 375–434.

Plotnick, Rachel. "Predicting Push-Button Warfare: US Print Media and Conflict from a Distance, 1945–2010." *Media, Culture & Society* 34, no. 6 (2012): 655–72.

Puar, Jasbir K. *Terrorist Assemblages: Homonationalism in Queer Times*. Durham, NC: Duke University Press, 2007.

Pugliese, Joseph. *State Violence and the Execution of Law: Torture, Black Sites, Drones*. London: Routledge, 2013.

Purcell, Mark, and Joe Nevins. "Pushing the Boundary: State Restructuring, State Theory, and the Case of US–Mexico Border Enforcement in the 1990s." *Political Geography* 24, no. 2 (2005): 211–35.

Rainger, Ronald. "Constructing a Landscape for Postwar Science: Roger Revelle, the Scripps Institution and the University of California, San Diego." *Minerva* 39, no. 3 (September 2001): 327–52.

Raley, Rita. *Tactical Media*. Minneapolis: University of Minnesota Press, 2009.

Ramírez, Marla Andrea. "The Making of Mexican Illegality: Immigration Exclusions Based on Race, Class Status, and Gender." *Journal of New Political Science* 40, no. 2 (2018): 317–35. https://doi.org/10.1080/07393148.2018.1449067.

Rana, Junaid. "The Language of Terror: Panic, Peril, Racism." In *State of White Supremacy: Racism, Governance, and the United States*, edited by Moon-Kie Jung,

João H. Costa Vargas, and Eduardo Bonilla-Silva, 211–28. Stanford, CA: Stanford University Press, 2011.

Rana, Junaid. "The 9/11 of Our Imaginations: Islam, the Figure of the Muslim, and the Failed Liberalism of the Racial Present." In *The Cambridge History of Asian American Literature*, edited by Rajini Srikanth and Min Hyoung Song, 503–18. Cambridge: Cambridge University Press, 2015.

Rana, Junaid. "The Racial Infrastructure of the Terror-Industrial Complex." *Social Text* 34, no. 4 (December 2016): 111–38.

Risen, James. *Pay Any Price: Greed, Power, and Endless War*. Boston: Houghton Mifflin Harcourt, 2014.

Robinson, Cedric J. *Black Marxism: The Making of the Black Radical Tradition*. Chapel Hill: University of North Carolina Press, 2000. First published 1983.

Rosas, Ana Elizabeth. *Abrazando el espíritu: Bracero Families Confront the US-Mexico Border*. Oakland: University of California Press, 2014.

Rosas, Gilberto. *Barrio Libre: Criminalizing States and Delinquent Refusals of the New Frontier*. Durham, NC: Duke University Press, 2012.

Rosas, Gilberto. "The Managed Violences of the Borderlands: Treacherous Geographies, Policeability, and the Politics of Race." *Latino Studies* 4, no. 4 (2006): 401–19.

Rosas, Gilberto. "Necro-Subjection: On Borders, Asylum, and Making Dead to Let Live." *Theory & Event* 22, no. 2 (April 2019): 303–24.

Rose, Nikolas. *The Politics of Life Itself: Biomedicine, Power, and Subjectivity in the Twenty-First Century*. Princeton, NJ: Princeton University Press, 2007.

Rosenblueth, Arturo, Norbert Wiener, and Julian Bigelow. "Behavior, Purpose, Teleology." *Philosophy of Science* 10, no. 1 (1943): 18–24.

Rothstein, Adam. *Drone*. New York: Bloomsbury, 2015.

Sánchez, Rosaura, and Beatrice Pita. "Rethinking Settler Colonialism." *American Quarterly* 66, no. 4 (December 2014): 1039–55.

San Diego Chamber of Commerce, Aviation Department. *The Aviation Industry Looks to San Diego!* San Diego: San Diego Chamber of Commerce, 1940.

Schaeffer, Felicity Amaya. "Automated Border Control: Criminalizing 'Hidden Intent' of Migrant Embodiment." *Kalfou* 6, no. 2 (Fall 2019): 177–98.

Schaeffer, Felicity Amaya. *Unsettled Borders: The Militarized Science of Surveillance on Sacred Indigenous Land*. Durham: Duke University Press, 2022.

Scott, Allen J. "The Aerospace-Electronics Industrial Complex of Southern California: The Formative Years, 1940–1960." *Research Policy* 20, no. 5 (October 1991): 439–56.

Shah, Nayan. *Contagious Divides: Epidemics and Race in San Francisco's Chinatown*. Berkeley: University of California Press, 2001.

Shah, Nayan. *Stranger Intimacy: Contesting Race, Sexuality and the Law in the North American West*. Berkeley: University of California Press, 2012.

Shannon, Claude. "A Mathematical Theory of Communication." *Bell System Technical Journal* 27, no. 3 (July 1948): 379–423.

Sharma, Nandita. *Home Rule: National Sovereignty and the Separation of Natives and Migrants*. Durham, NC: Duke University Press, 2020.

Shaw, Ian G. R. *Predator Empire: Drone Warfare and Full Spectrum Dominance*. Minneapolis: University of Minnesota Press, 2016.

Sherry, Michael S. *The Rise of American Air Power: The Creation of Armageddon*. New Haven, CT: Yale University Press, 1987.

Shragge, Abraham. "'A New Federal City': San Diego during World War II." *Pacific Historical Review* 63, no. 3 (August 1994): 333–61.

Simpson, Audra. *Mohawk Interrupted: Political Life across Borders of Settler States*. Durham, NC: Duke University Press, 2014.

Smallwood, Stephanie. *Saltwater Slavery: Middle Passage from Africa to American Diaspora*. Cambridge, MA: Harvard University Press, 2009.

Smith, Cornelius C., Jr. *Fort Huachuca: The Story of a Frontier Post*. Washington, DC: US Government Printing Office, 1978.

Spener, David. *Clandestine Crossings: Migrants and Coyotes on the Texas-Mexico Border*. Ithaca, NY: Cornell University, 2009.

Star, Susan Leigh, and Karen Ruhleder. "Steps towards an Ecology of Infrastructure: Complex Problems in Design and Access for Large-Scale Collaborative Systems." In *Proceedings of the 1994 ACM Conference on Computer Supported Cooperative Work*, 253–64. New York: Association for Computing Machinery, 1994.

Steinbergs, A. Z., H. D. Friedman, and D. R. Rothschild. *Wide Area Remote Surveillance*. Report No. RADC-TR-69-328. Rome Air Development Center, December 1970. Accession No. AD513692, NTRL.

Stern, Alexandra Minna. "Buildings, Boundaries, and Blood: Medicalization and Nation-Building on the US-Mexico Border, 1910–1930." *Hispanic American Historical Review* 79, no. 1 (February 1999): 41–81.

Stern, Alexandra Minna. *Eugenic Nation: Faults and Frontiers of Better Breeding in Modern America*. Berkeley: University of California Press, 2005.

Steyerl, Hito. "A Sea of Data: Apophenia and Pattern (Mis-)Recognition." *e-flux* 72 (April 2016). http://www.e-flux.com/journal/72/60480/a-sea-of-data-apophenia-and-pattern-mis-recognition/.

St. John, Rachel. *Line in the Sand: A History of the Western US-Mexico Border*. Princeton, NJ: Princeton University Press, 2011.

Stodola, E. K. *Line Intrusion Detector*. Report No. LWL-CR-06P73. Aberdeen Proving Ground, MD: US Army Land Warfare Laboratory, 1974. Accession No. AD780719, NTRL.

Stoler, Ann Laura. *Along the Archival Grain: Epistemic Anxieties and Colonial Common Sense*. Princeton, NJ: Princeton University Press, 2010.

Stoler, Ann Laura. *Duress: Imperial Durabilities in Our Times*. Durham, NC: Duke University Press, 2016.

Stoler, Ann Laura. "On Degrees of Imperial Sovereignty." *Public Culture* 18, no. 1 (December 2006): 125–46.

Strasser, Bruno, and Paul N. Edwards. "Big Data Is the Answer . . . but What Is the Question?" *Osiris* 32, no. 1 (2017): 328–45.

Suchman, Lucy. *Human-Machine Reconfigurations: Plans and Situated Actions*. 2nd ed. Cambridge: Cambridge University Press, 2007.

Suchman, Lucy. "Imaginaries of Omniscience: Automating Intelligence in the US Department of Defense." *Social Studies of Science* (2022): 1–26.

Suchman, Lucy. "Situational Awareness: Deadly Bioconvergence at the Boundaries of Bodies and Machines." *Media Tropes* 5, no. 1 (2015): 1–24.

Suchman, Lucy, Randall Trigg, and Jeanette Blomberg. "Working Artefacts: Ethnomethods of the Prototype." *British Journal of Sociology* 53, no. 2 (June 2002): 163–79.

Sunstein, Cass R. "Why They Hate Us: The Role of Social Dynamics." *Harvard Journal of Law and Public Policy* 25, no. 2 (Spring 2002): 429–40.

Terranova, Tiziana. "Free Labor: Producing Culture for the Digital Economy." *Social Text* 18, no. 2 (Summer 2000): 33–58.

Tichenor, Daniel J. *Dividing Lines: The Politics of Immigration Control in America.* Princeton, NJ: Princeton University Press, 2002.

Timmons, Patrick. "Trump's Wall at Nixon's Border." *NACLA Report on the Americas* 49, no. 1 (2017): 15–24.

Tiqqun. *The Cybernetic Hypothesis.* Translated by Robert Hurley. South Pasadena, CA: Semiotext(e), 2020.

Towghi, Fouzieyha, and Kalindi Vora. "Bodies, Markets, and the Experimental in South Asia." *Ethnos* 79, no. 1 (2014): 1–18.

Treviño, ToniAnn. "Mexican Americans and the War on Narcotics: Racialized Policing Practices and Community Responses in the Postwar Texas Borderlands." PhD diss., University of Michigan, 2022. https://doi.org/10.7302/4637.

Turner, Fred. *From Counterculture to Cyberculture: Stewart Brand, the Whole Earth Network, and the Rise of Digital Utopianism.* Chicago: University of Chicago Press, 2008.

Vanderwood, Paul, and Frank N. Samponaro. *Border Fury: A Picture Postcard Record of Mexico's Revolution and US War Preparedness, 1910–1917.* Albuquerque: University of New Mexico Press, 1988.

Veltman, Chloe. "Genesis of a High-Tech Hub." *Nature* 476 (December 11, 2003): 700–704.

Vukov, Tamara, and Mimi Sheller. "Border Work: Surveillant Assemblages, Virtual Fences, and Tactical Counter-Media." *Social Semiotics* 23, no. 2 (2013): 225–41.

Wagner, William. *Lightning Bugs and Other Reconnaissance Drones.* Fallbrook, CA: Armed Forces Journal International, 1982.

Wall, Tyler, and Torin Monahan. "Surveillance and Violence from Afar: The Politics of Drones and Liminal Security-Scapes." *Theoretical Criminology* 15, no. 3 (August 2011): 239–54.

Wang, Jackie. *Carceral Capitalism.* South Pasadena, CA: Semiotext(e), 2018.

Ward, John W. "The Meaning of Lindbergh's Flight." *American Quarterly* 10, no. 1 (1958): 3–16.

Warner, E. "Douhet, Mitchell, Seversky: Theories of Air Warfare." In *Makers of Modern Strategy: Military Thought from Machiavelli to Hitler,* edited by Edward Mead Earle, 485–503. Princeton, NJ: Princeton University Press, 1971. First published 1943.

Weheliye, Alexander G. *Habeas Viscus: Racializing Assemblages, Biopolitics, and Black Feminist Theories of the Human.* Durham, NC: Duke University Press, 2014.

Welch, Michael. *Scapegoats of September 11th: Hate Crimes & State Crimes in the War on Terror*. New Brunswick, NJ: Rutgers University Press, 2006.

Welch, Michael. "Seeking a Safer Society: America's Anxiety in the War on Terror." *Security Journal* 19, no. 2 (2006): 93–109.

Welch, Michael. "The Role of the Immigration and Naturalization Service in the Prison-Industrial Complex." *Social Justice* 27, no. 3 (2000): 73–88.

Weld, Kirsten. *Paper Cadavers: The Archives of Dictatorship in Guatemala*. Durham, NC: Duke University Press, 2014.

Westwick, Peter J., ed. *Blue Sky Metropolis: The Aerospace Century in Southern California*. Berkeley: Huntington-USC Institute on California and the West, 2012.

Whittle, Richard. *Predator: The Secret Origins of the Drone Revolution*. New York: Henry Holt, 2014.

Wiener, Norbert. "Cybernetics." *Scientific American* 175, no. 5 (1948): 14–19.

Wiener, Norbert. *Cybernetics, or Control and Communication in the Animal and the Machine*. Cambridge, MA: MIT Press, 1961. First published 1948.

Wiener, Norbert. *The Human Use of Human Beings: Cybernetics and Society*. Boston: Houghton Mifflin, 1950.

Williams, Raymond. "Structures of Feeling." In *Marxism and Literature*, 128–35. Oxford: Oxford University Press, 1977.

Wolfe, Patrick. "Land, Labor, and Difference: Elementary Structures of Race." *American Historical Review* 106, no. 3 (June 2001): 866–905.

Woodruff, Lily. *Dis-Ordering the Establishment: Participatory Art and Institutional Critique in France, 1958–1981*. Durham, NC: Duke University Press, 2020.

Note: Italicized page numbers refer to figures.

Printed and bound by CPI Group (UK) Ltd, Croydon, CR0 4YY

16/04/2025

14658728-0001